IMAGES
of America

HAITIANS IN CHICAGO

On the Cover: Haitians bring hope, art, culture, history, heritage, and pride that make up the rich tapestry of the city of Chicago, which was founded by a Haitian man, Jean Baptiste Point DuSable. (Courtesy of Haitian American Museum of Chicago's Community Archive.)

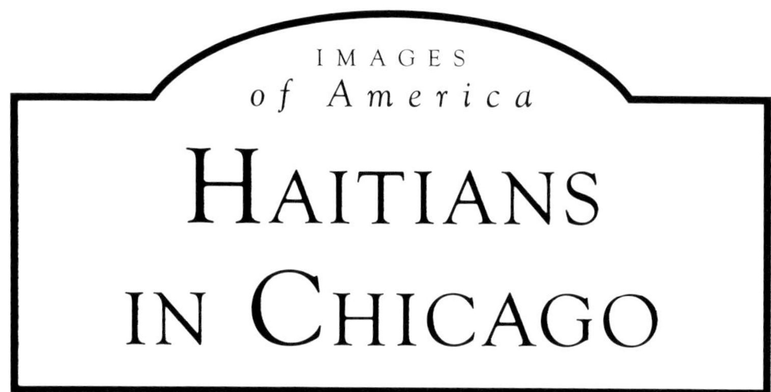

Haitian American Museum of Chicago

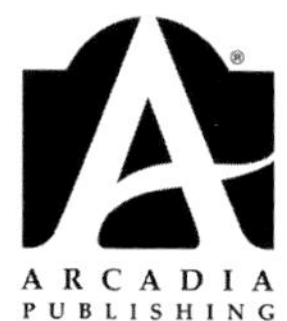

ISBN 978-1-4671-6200-5

Published by Arcadia Publishing
Charleston, South Carolina

Printed in the United States of America

Library of Congress Control Number: 2025932008

For all general information, please contact Arcadia Publishing:
Telephone 843-853-2070
Fax 843-853-0044
E-mail sales@arcadiapublishing.com

Visit us on the Internet at www.arcadiapublishing.com

This book is dedicated to the Haitian community. May it be a reminder of the significant contributions of the Haitian people in Chicago and beyond.

Contents

ACKNOWLEDGMENTS

Thank you to the individuals and organizations that helped and supported this project. This book is just the beginning in recognizing and recording the accomplishments of Haitians and Haitian Americans in Chicago. Most of the images seen in this book are courtesy of the Haitian American Museum of Chicago's Community Archive and Collections, unless otherwise noted.

INTRODUCTION

The Republic of Haiti, a country located in the Caribbean, has impacted the world through its art, history, and culture. Haiti gained its independence on January 1, 1804, from France after 13 years of slave revolution. Haiti became the only Black nation in the world that was born out of a successful slave revolt. It is important to mention that Haiti was the second independent country after the United States of America in 1779. Haiti has a complex, rich, and vibrant culture and history. From the day of Haiti's independence until the present, Haiti has experienced many natural disasters, political corruption, US occupation, and instability.

The majority of Haiti's population is of African origin. The two official languages spoken on the island are Haitian Kreyol and French. Haitian Kreyol is the spoken language of the people, and French is still used in more formal circumstances and is the main language of instruction in schools. In the question of religion, the Haitians practice primarily Christianity and Vodouism. It is understood by many experts that the main culture of Haiti today comes from centuries of slavery and colonialism. Haitians were able to create distinctive, robust, innovative art, music, dance, and literature from many years of slavery. As far as the economy, Haiti is known as the poorest country in the western hemisphere.

Due to a devastated economy, natural disasters, political corruption, and insecurity, Haitians attempt to improve their lives by migrating to other countries such as the United States, France, Canada, Cuba, the Dominican Republic, and others. Since the 1960s, during the Duvalier regime, to the most current migration in 2021, waves of Haitians have made their way to the United States.. Nowadays, a large number of Haitians have entered the United States from the Mexican border on a parole status, seeking asylum or seeking temporary protective status (TPS). Throughout the period of time, Haitians have migrated for political unrest or persecution or many have made their way to Chicago to find a better life. The book will cover the waves of Haitian migrations that started prior to and during the revolution, the US occupation, the Duvalier dictatorship regime, several periods of political instabilities, during and after the Duvalier regime, and recently, gang violence.

In Chicago, Haitians contributed and assimilated into the new environment and new home. They were able to find ways to come together through recreation by gathering in the parks, playing soccer, participating in street carnivals, and creating various organizations to help the assimilation of the home country and to have a voice in the new society. Various communication venues such as radio stations, television programs, and community and cultural centers were established to connect the community. An example is the Haitian American Museum of Chicago (HAMOC).

HAMOC's mission is to promote and preserve Haitian art, culture, history, and community in Chicago and beyond. In 2012, the museum became one of only two Haitian-specific museums in the United States (the other is located in Miami). HAMOC is the epicenter of Haitian culture and community in Chicago and throughout the Midwest. In order to contribute further and to expose the Chicago society, HAMOC has put together this book to shed light on the hardworking Haitians and vibrant Haitian community in Chicago.

Starting with the first non-indigenous migrant and resident of Chicago, Jean Baptiste Pointe DuSable, a Haitian man, and his wife, Kitiahawa, a Potawatomi woman, were the first family who began to build what is now Chicago. DuSable was born in St. Domingue (now Haiti) in St. Marc in 1745. He was an entrepreneur and had his trading post by the Chicago River. John Kinzie, a prominent Chicago politician, eventually purchased DuSable's home. Many establishments have been named after DuSable: DuSable Bridge, The DuSable Black History Museum and Education Center, Jean Baptiste Point DuSable Lake Shore Drive, and currently under development, DuSable Park. Chicago will enjoy the DuSable (Jean Baptiste Pointe) Park that will be located near the mouth of the Chicago River and the shore of Lake Michigan.

HAMOC, as the epicenter of the Chicago Haitian area, defines its community as a multicultural, diverse group of individuals, organizations, and artists who share in the museum's mission, DEIA (Diversity, Equity, Inclusion, and Accessibility) values, and goals and have an interest in Haitian, Black, and Afro-Diasporic art, culture, and history. To serve a diverse demographic base, HAMOC has an open-door policy and invites artists, scholars, students, and community members to the museum to explore more about Haitian art, culture, and history and intersecting themes such as race, class, and gender. Through collaboration, HAMOC acts as a cultural outlet for the community and a space for diverse voices and perspectives to be heard.

In recent years, desperate Haitians are leaving the country of Haiti to seek security and a better life. Gang violence and insecurity are the two main reasons for this current migration. This new wave adds to the migrants from the massive earthquake in 2010. The United States has been and continues to be the most popular destination for Haitians. Due to the current influx of Haitian migrants at the Texas-Mexico border since 2021, Chicago, as a sanctuary city, has allowed Haitians to find a new home. HAMOC, as an active organization, has a responsibility to help put Haitian migration in perspective by writing a book on the subject. This pictorial book is designed to reflect on the Chicago Haitian experience and their contributions to the city's tapestry while helping change and remove the negative stereotypes that harm Haitians. It serves a variety of communities across social, racial, cultural, economic, and generational and gender-diverse backgrounds. Throughout the chapters, the museum will educate the reader about the resiliency and vibrancy of Haiti and its people.

With this publication, HAMOC hopes to impact the greater Chicagoland community with a focus on the Haitian population in Chicago. The museum explores the intersectionality of Haitians, the Black diaspora, Indigenous groups, immigrant communities, and other underrepresented groups and topics that connect them. This book consists of several topics: Haitians in academia, Haitian churches, art and culture, Jean Baptiste Pointe DuSable, Haitian contributions to the Chicago World's Fair in 1893, waves of migration, and Chicago Haitian leaders. With the theme of "Haitians in Chicago," the reader will learn about the Chicago Haitians by indulging in the complexity of the first Black nation, consisting of its art, culture, history, and community and their connections with their homeland, Haiti.

HAMOC's intent in writing this book is to provide a sense of belonging by uplifting Haitians and diasporic communities in Chicago. Due to the geographic spread of the Haitian population in Chicago and the surrounding suburbs, this literary work provides a view of the existence of the Haitian community that seems at times invisible.

One

DuSable, Haitian Ties, and the Beginning of Chicago

When Jean-Baptiste Pointe DuSable established a fur-trading post at the mouth of the Eshikagou River and Lake Michigan around 1778, he was the first non-native settler in what later became Chicago. The trading post grew into a successful business, reflecting the importance of Chicago in transatlantic commerce and exchanges with major cities bordering the Mississippi River, which attracted other pioneers from the United States and Canada. This was the beginning of a vibrant world-class city.

Little is known about the life of DuSable before he reportedly left the town of St. Marc in central St. Domingue, now Haiti, and traveled to Louisiana and then up the Mississippi River to Illinois, where he purchased land in Peoria by 1773 and married a Potawatomi woman, Kitihawa, known as "Catherine." They migrated north to the confluence of the Chicago River and Lake Michigan, where they had a daughter, Suzanne, and a son, Jean-Baptiste Jr.

The first Chicago family lived there for the next 20 years, in harmony with various Native American groups who welcomed them. DuSable was described by those who met him as handsome, well-built, and a trustworthy Catholic. While being arrested for suspected sympathy for the American revolutionaries, he gained the trust of the British commander and went on to manage his estate after he was released. In 1800, before the implantation of Fort Dearborn on the southern bank of the Chicago River, heralding the westward expansion of the United States, DuSable sold his compound to Jean Lalime and returned to Peoria. After experiencing various legal and financial difficulties, he moved to St. Charles, Missouri, where he died in 1818.

The story of this Black man, born to a White Frenchman and a Black slave woman, who emigrated from the Caribbean married a Native American woman, became a successful entrepreneur, and lived in peace with his neighbors, has fascinated historians and the public alike. As the first Chicago Haitian immigrant, DuSable remains an inspiration to all Haitians who followed him, and he represents a triumph of the human spirit.

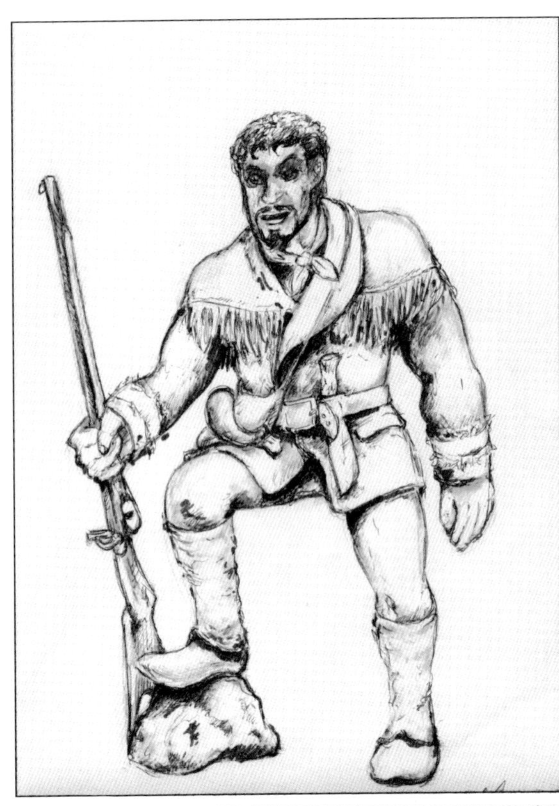

Jean Baptiste Point DuSable, born in 1745 in St. Domingue (now Haiti), set up at the very crucial trading post that facilitated commerce between the Great Lakes and Mississippi by situating at its mouth, where today stands Chicago, with close interactions through a mixed marriage to a local Indigenous Potawatomi woman named Kitihawa. Together, their local trading was the beginning of Chicago's economy. They remind one of those roles to which American history can also make great use.

DuSable, a sculpture by Useni Eugene Perkins, was installed in Useni Park in 2013. Perkins is a multimedia artist known to often focus on African American culture and history. This piece is part of a larger effort to enhance public spaces with art and build community through different artistic expressions. (Vivian G. Harsh Research Collection.)

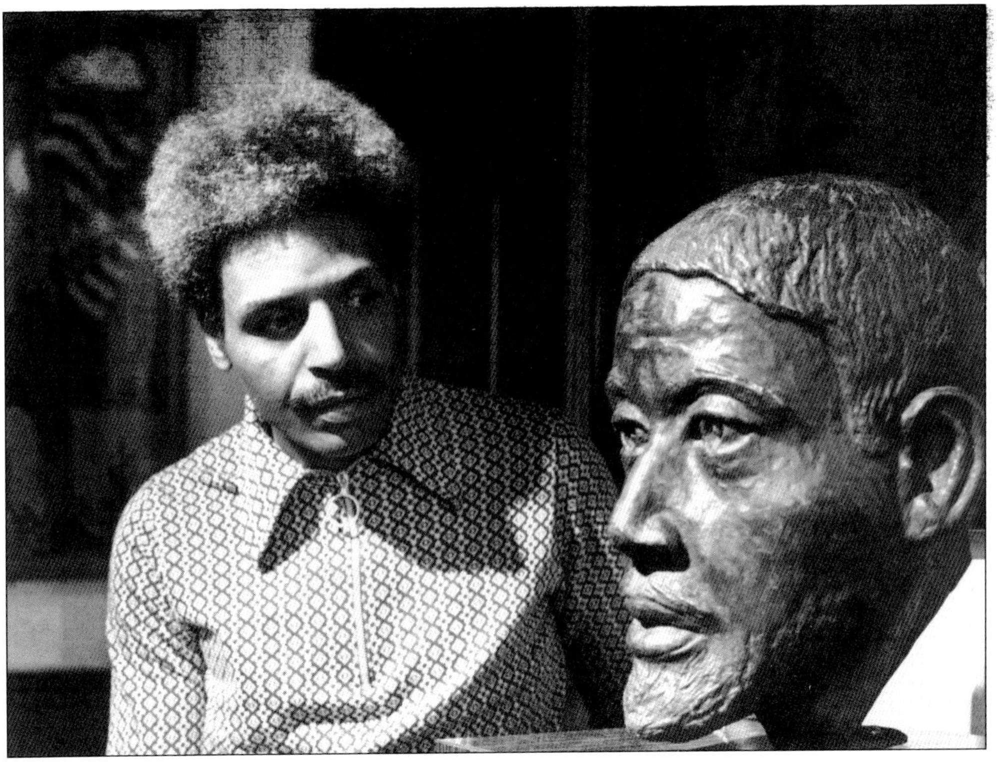

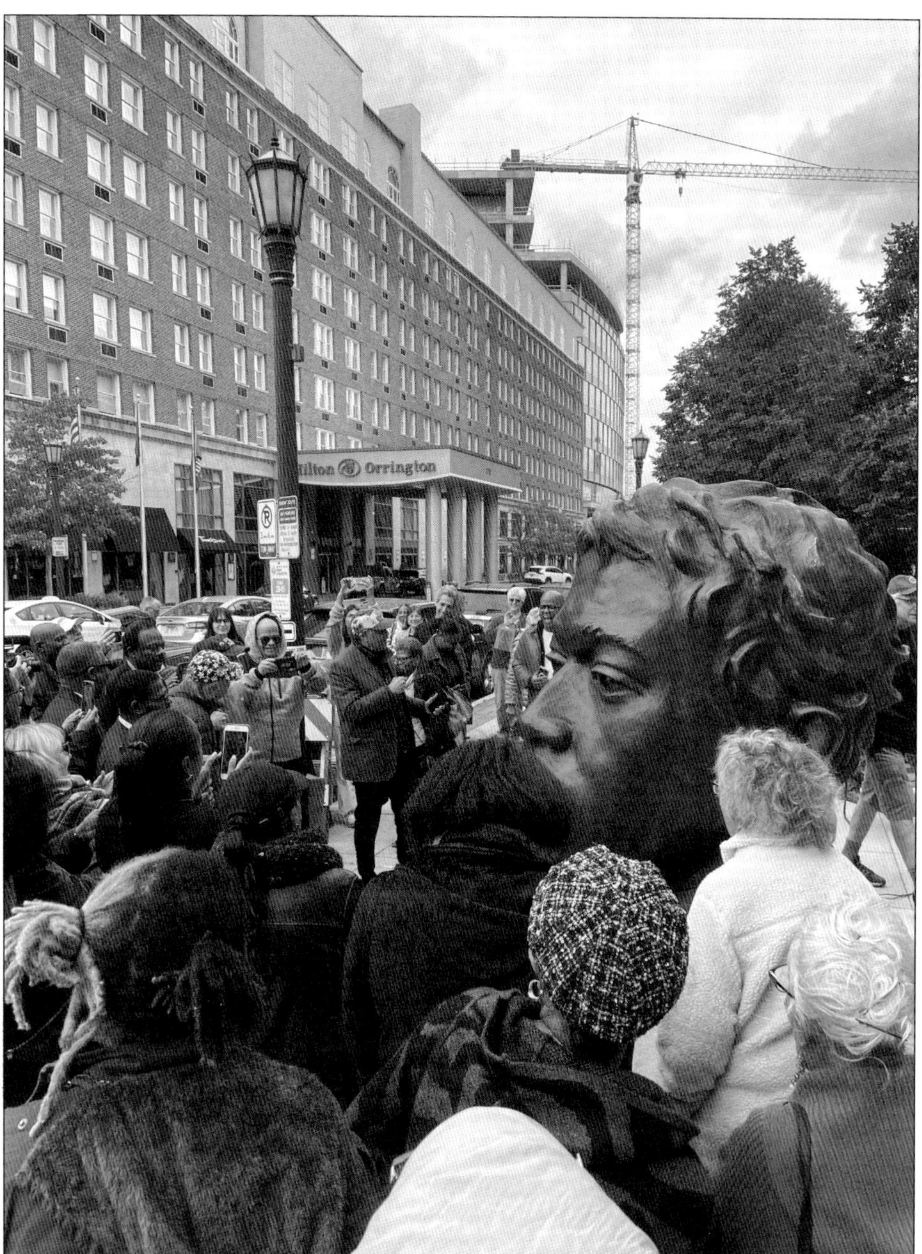

A bronze bust of Jean Baptiste Pointe DuSable stands tall, serving as a poignant reminder of Chicago's rich history. Installed in 2024 through the collaboration of the City of Chicago and a Haitian donor, this striking sculpture was crafted by Chicago-born artist Erik Blome. DuSable was born in St. Domingue, now Haiti, and is considered the first non-native settler of Chicago, arriving in the area sometime around 1779. DuSable is often referred to as the "Father of Chicago" because he built a successful business settlement that reached all over the Midwest. He developed a close relationship with some Indigenous peoples, including marrying a Potawatomi woman named Kitihawa. His legacy is carved not only with his entrepreneurship but also with his commitment towards cultural exchange and community building. The State of Illinois officially declared him the "Father of Chicago" in 1968, so his contribution will never be forgotten.

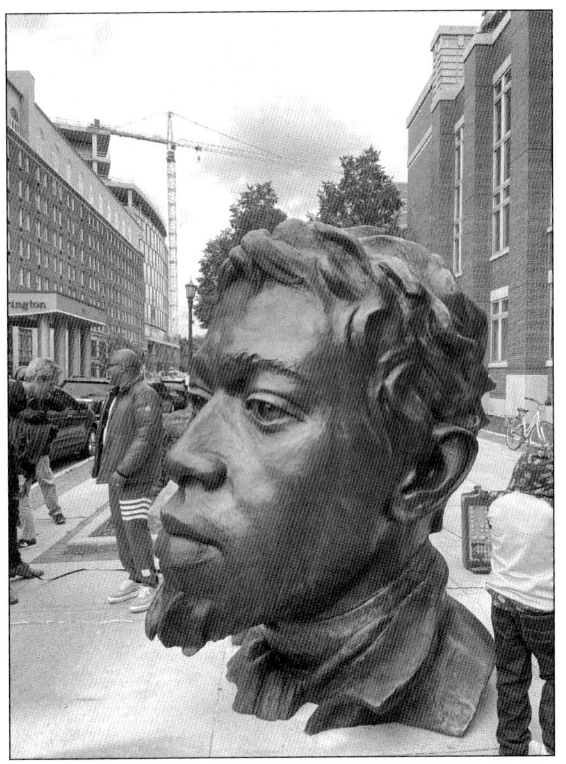

A bronze bust of Jean Baptiste Pointe DuSable, the "Father of Chicago," was unveiled in 2024 to recognize him as the very first non-native settler. Designed by Erik Blome, the sculpture honors the entrepreneurship and cultural exchange of DuSable, including his marriage to a Potawatomi, Kitihawa, which enriched the history of Chicago forever.

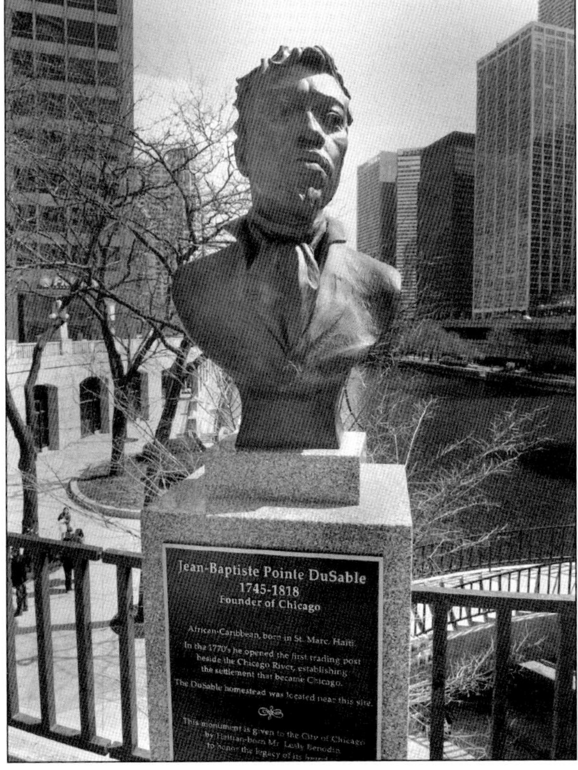

Lesly Belodin was a Haitian businessman who was well-liked for his philanthropy. He contributed much to the fields of Haitian culture and history. Among his largest donations was a bust of Jean Baptiste Point DuSable, which represented cultural diversity within Chicago. This bust provides a memorial to the life of DuSable and the important roles other migrant groups have played in American history.

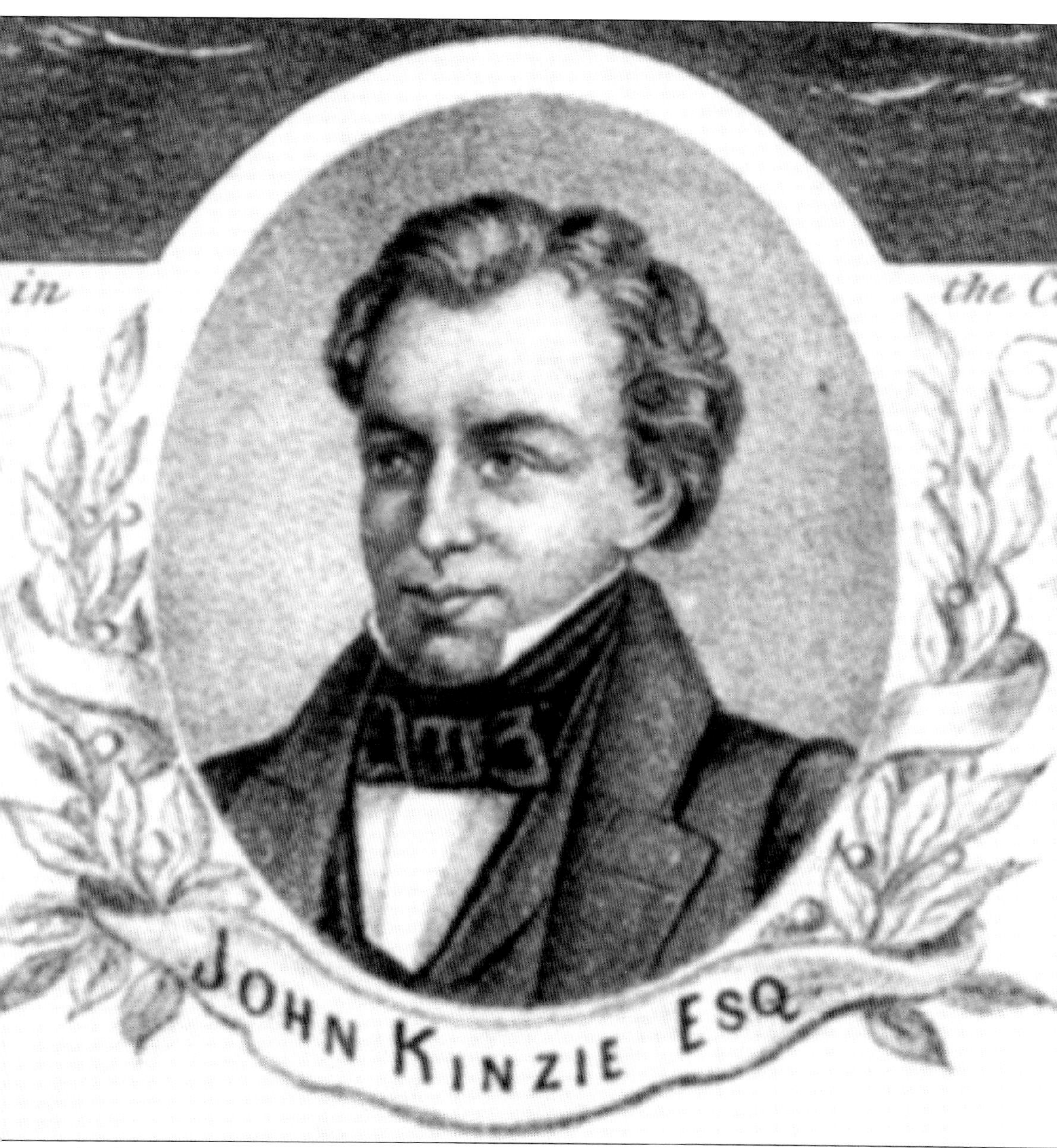

Both John Kinzie and Jean Baptiste Point DuSable played essential roles in Chicago's early years, shaping it to become one of the largest cities in the nation. DuSable was a voyager who came to the confluence of the Chicago River and Lake Michigan in the late 18th century and founded a trading post that turned out to be highly important for trade and contact between Native Americans and the settlers. The same trading post was used by Kinzie in the early 19th century, as Kinzie became a lucrative fur trader and one of the first residents and leaders that Chicago would have. Both men played major roles in shaping the economic landscape and cultural diversity of Chicago, and their legacies are intertwined in the narrative of the growth of the city from a trading post to a bustling urban center.

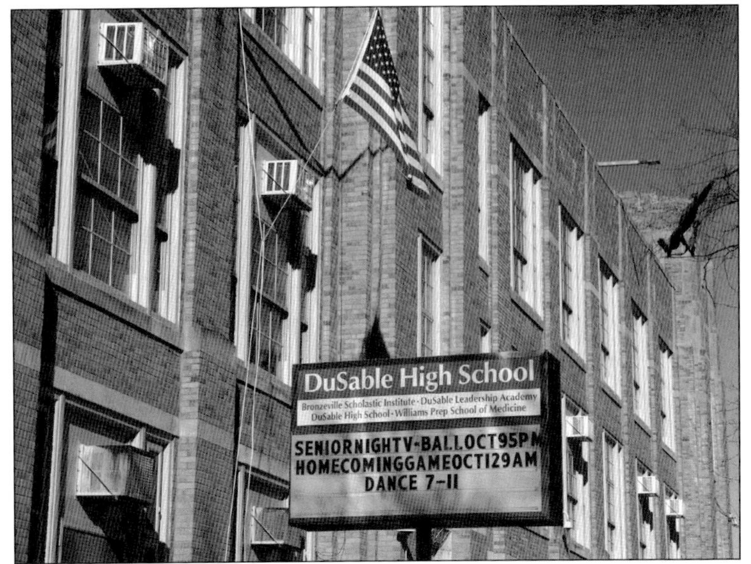

DuSable High School, located at 4934 South Wabash Avenue in Chicago, works on the objective of providing the best education under very supportive and enlightening circumstances, which helps in fostering student growth. For DuSable High School, its main focus has always been academics for excellence and individual growth in order to face challenges presented by their respective futures.

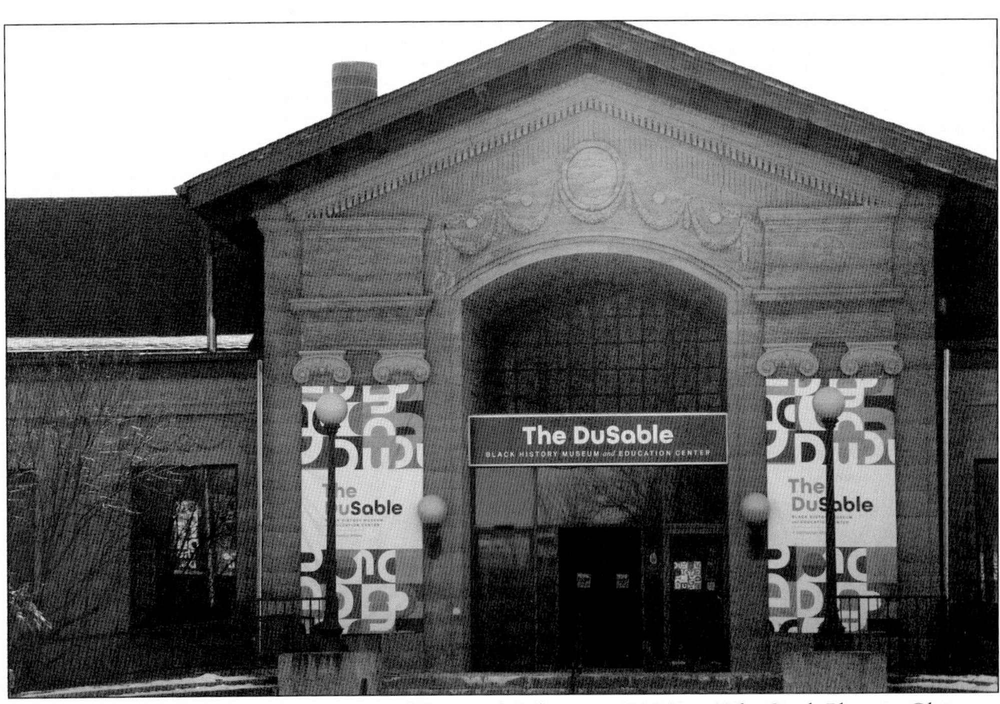

The DuSable Black History Museum and Research Library, at 740 East Fifty-Sixth Place in Chicago, is one of the leading cultural organizations responsible for the collection, preservation, and dissemination of information regarding the history and accomplishments of the African American population. There are several exhibits and programs available through the museum that make it an important stop for learning and contemplation regarding the African American experience.

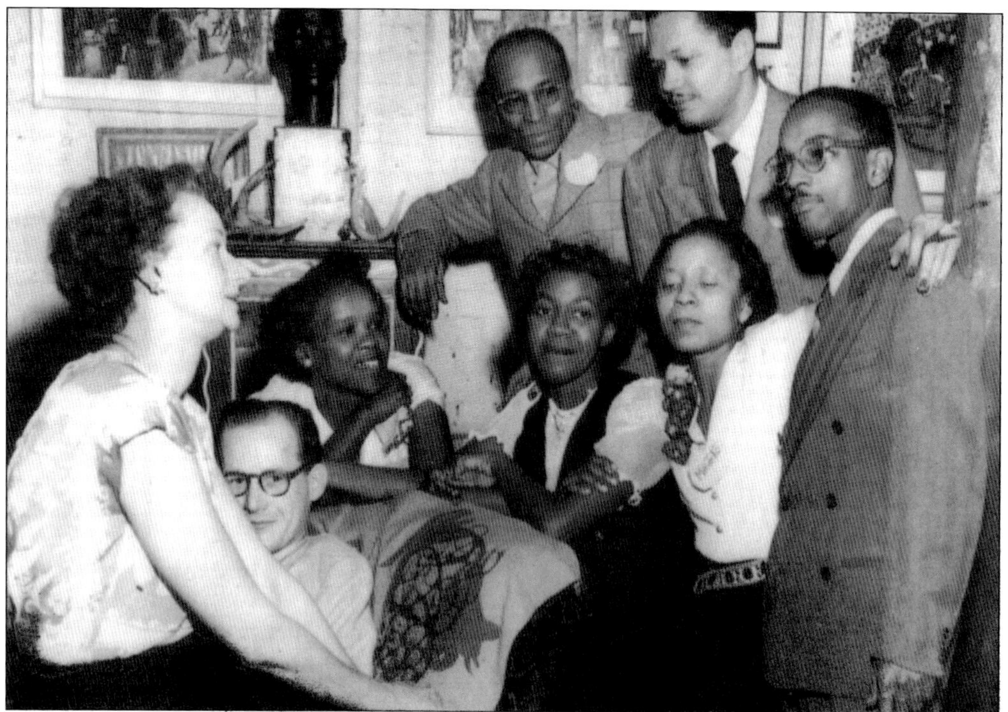

The very first Black museum, as named by its founder Dr. Margaret Taylor Burrough in 1961, the Ebony Museum of Negro History and Art was established to inform and educate the general public about Black history, culture and art. This museum has since been renamed several times to its current name, The DuSable Black History Museum and Education Center, in honor of Jean Baptiste Pointe DuSable. (Vivian G. Harsh Research Collection.)

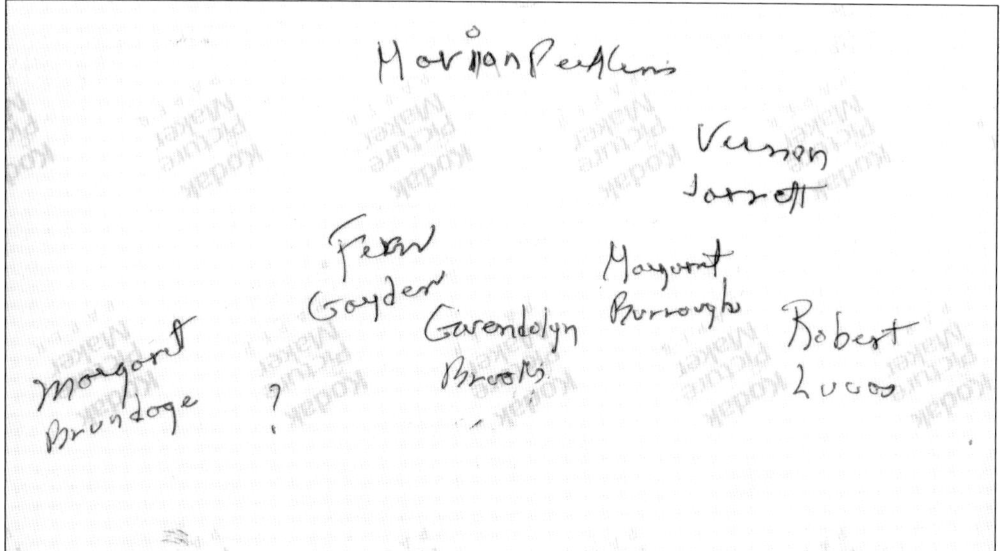

These handwritten signatures appear on the reverse side of the previous photograph. They belong to friends, peers, and colleagues of Dr. Margaret Taylor Burrough. Each name represents someone present at this significant gathering in Chicago, offering a personal record of the community surrounding Dr. Burrough at that special moment. (Vivian G. Harsh Research Collection.)

DuSable Was Indians' Friend; They Gave Him Wife

fact that its founder was a black man. Historian and Ebony Senior Editor Lerone Bennett Jr. calls the "DuSable gap" part of a general American pattern to repress any history which involves a black man as leader.

Dr. Etienne, who has a Ph.D. in geodetic engineering from the Geographic Institute in Paris, has heard stories of DuSable since he was a youth in his native Haiti. His ancestors from Haiti visited DuSable in the Chicago of the 1770s and brought back with them a portrait of DuSable and the first settlement which is now in Dr. Etienne's possession.

That settlement, which might properly be called a plantation, consisted of a log house 40 feet by 22, a bakehouse, dairy, smokehouse, poultry house, workshop, stable, barn and horse mill. DuSable established the first trading post and made friends with the Indians, who showed their faith in him by giving him one of their daughters to marry. For about 20 years DuSable lived in

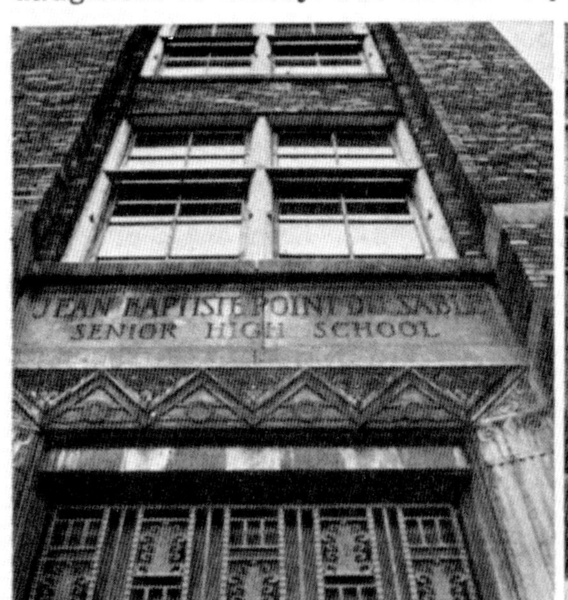

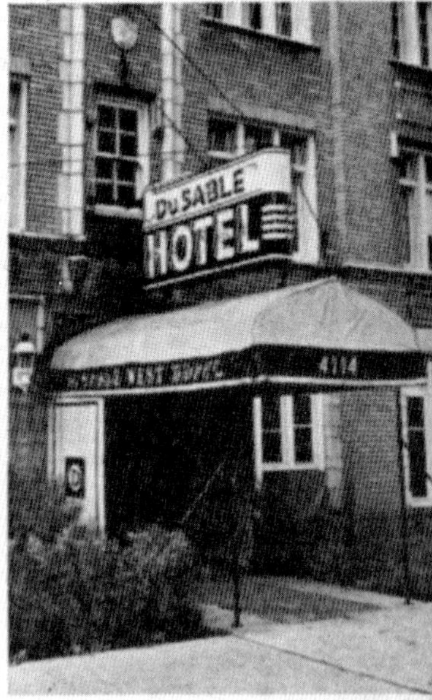

Only buildings honoring DuSable in Chicago are (l) DuSable High School and the DuSable Hotel.

24

The context of Jean Baptiste Point DuSable's legacy reflects broader sentiments on recognition and leadership for Black Americans. Despite being credited with founding Chicago, DuSable's legacy was long ignored—a process historian Lerone Bennett Jr. once called "the DuSable Gap." That reluctance to honor Black figures is reflected in the paucity of recognition DuSable received; at the time *Jet* magazine was published, he had only a high school and a hotel named after him.

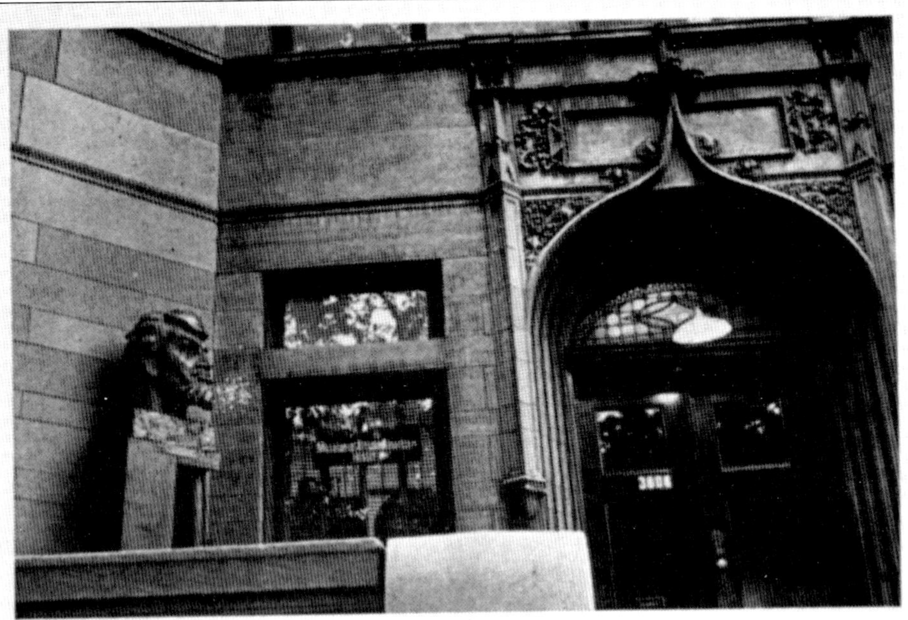

Bust of DuSable done by sculptor Robert Jones at Museum of African-American History; there is no permanent portrait of DuSable in Chicago Historical Society.

the wilderness that would become the second largest city in the United States.

When he left, he headed for Missouri with his good friend, Daniel Boone, and together they built the home that would become the mansion of the governor of Missouri, Dr. Etienne says.

Dr. Etienne is concerned with seeing that DuSable is given his proper place in Chicago's history. "I wish that period of history could be reopened and studied again," he says.

It was only by accident that Chicagoans recognized Dr. Etienne's existence in the city that his ancestor founded. Someone relayed his story to a member of the DuSable Heritage Committee, an organization of school administrators dedicated to seeing that DuSable is recognized by the city, who, in turn, told city officials of Dr. Etienne's presence. Recently Dr. Etienne and his wife Yolette were honored at an Illinois Sesquicentennial Celebration, and,

25

But attitudes evolved, and today, DuSable is considered to be the founder of Chicago, with several namesakes, including schools and organizations, as well as DuSable Lake Shore Drive. This change constitutes one more acknowledgment of Black leaders and their important positions in American history. (Vivian G. Harsh Research Collection.)

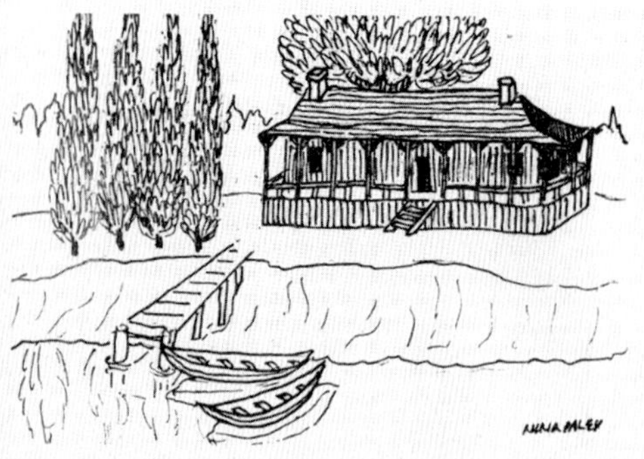

now, the second story

It begins at Chicago. The year is 1779. Jean Baptiste Point du Sable has built a trading post on the north side of the Chicago River, the first one there. He is Chicago's first settler. His place is the only one along the seven-hundred mile routh from Michilimackinac to St. Louis where a traveller can sleep under a roof, sit at a table, and eat a real meal. The people of the Potawattomi, his wife's people, have built a village on the other side of the river, and bring him the pelts from their winter hunting. He sells them, not to the British traders at Michilimackinac and Montreal, but down the Mississippi to a Spanish partner.

The British Commandant at Michilimackinac wrote of him, " . . . a handsome Negro, well educated and settled at Eschicagou."

"He was tall, and commanding in appearance. The Indians called him Me-cut-ta-we-os, or Black Meat." wrote General John Hunt, the first United States Commandant at Mackinac. "Six feet tall and well formed, of pleasing countenance" said others of his time.

He had come from Saint Dominigue, which is today called Haiti, travelling up the rivers from the Gulf of Mexico.

From the time the British took the north from the French they were troubled by settlers from the thirteen colonies picking up their possessions and crossing the wild Alleghenies to lands where no government reached and no taxes were collected. The King was dismayed at this. It was his right to allot lands, and not the right of these men to simply take it. It was his right to demand a share of any wealth they might amass, and they were beyond his reach.

The people to whose land the new settlers came were dismayed, for the farms drove off the wild animals on which they depended for meat, and the domestic animals, which they did not raise, got loose and destroyed their fields of corn and beans, squash and melons. They had, besides, a firm treaty with the British King that forbade settlement of his people west of the mountains.

But the men who dared to cross the mountains were so hungry for land that they were ready to fight the King and the Indians. They had come from centuries of serfdom on the fiefs of others, and spread before them was enough land to plow to feed their families like lords. They had come from centuries of hunger and poverty and west of the mountains was plenty. The bravest took their guns and their families and moved into forbidden lands.

It was the task of the Lieutenant Governor of Canada, Sir Henry Hamilton, to discourage these settlers. He had decided that nothing discourages a man so much as being dead, and he recruited the Miami and Ottawa who lived near his post at Detroit, and the Sac and Fox and Menominee and Winnebago of the Ouiscoinsing, for his work. He sent them south in raiding parties against the tiny settlements of farmers across the Ohio River, into the place called the Dark and Bloody Ground, Kentucky. They attacked the settlements, Boonesborough, Harrodsburg, and so on. They killed the people and took the booty. . . cloth, guns, steel and iron tools, knives, and now and then a child to adopt to replace one that had died. But mostly they killed and took the scalps, for Sir Henry Hamilton, the Hair Buyer, gave them fifty dollars for each one. They were evidence that the raids had really occurred. It was the Hair-Buyer's way of checking the accuracy of their reports. He liked the blond scalps. They were surely Kentuckians. The ones with black hair might be the scalps of Indians. The scalp of a baby brought as much as the scalp of a fighting man, and sometimes a skillful Indian could cut a big scalp in two. The King's Lieutenant Governor made a little extra money from sending the scalps along to England where they were sold in the Curiosity Shops of London.

The Menominee and Winnebago, the Sac and Fox, from the western edge of the Ouiscoinsing and the Miami and the Huron and Ottawa from the lands of Michigan and Ohio, sent their warriors to fight and die for the British in their war against their own people, but from the start the Potawattomi of Chicago had refused to fight, and for this the British blamed Jean Baptiste Point du Sable. The Indians of many nations who built their fires at Milwakie, the Green and Pleasant Land, and the Indians at the ford of the Rock River refused to join the British raiding parties against Kentucky. For this the British blamed du Sable, for they knew that the chiefs at those places, Siggenaak, Nakkewoin, Chourachon, were his friends.

And du Sable sent the furs from that whole rich area down the rivers to his Spanish partner, and the British exporters at Michilimackinac and Detroit thought that was bad for business.

Early in the year of 1778, George Rogers Clark, the Kentucky hunter, took a small band of men across the Ohio River to capture for the new nation the towns the British ruled along the Mississippi River. The people of the towns were French, and passionately on the side of

Jean Baptiste Point DuSable's house was a significant historical landmark. During the late 18th century, his house stood near the conjunction of the Chicago River and Lake Michigan and reflected a combination of Native American and French architectural influences, like his mixed heritage. This lowly one-and-one-half-story cabin was constructed from hand-hewn native logs and beams and covered with a thatched roof; the interior was very simple in design, scantily furnished, having only a great fireplace for cooking and heat. DuSable's home was at once his dwelling, a trading post, and a social focus for Natives, French explorers, and settlers alike. Although the cabin no longer exists, the site is remembered through a park and a replica as a commemoration of DuSable's perpetual legacy to his crucial role in the early history of Chicago, thus drawing the interest of visitors and historians alike. (Vivian G. Harsh Research Collection.)

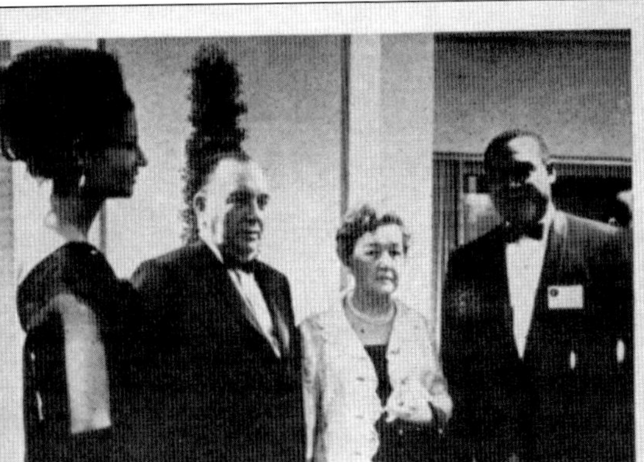

'hicago's Mayor Richard J. Daley and Mrs. Daley greet Dr. and Mrs. Etienne at the Sesquicentennial Celebration.

eek Support Of City For DuSable Statue

ince then, he has been invited to speak to organizations .bout DuSable.

Dr. Etienne is anxious to do more speaking in the hope hat this could bring the races closer together, and give ɪis people a positive identification with DuSable's ac-omplishments.

He is also concerned that white people learn of DuSable .nd Negro history. "White Society are modern slaves," he ays, explaining that they are slaves because of their ig-ɪorance of Negro history. "I do not know how many peo-ɪle, black and white, know that the vice president of the 'rench Cabinet (Gaston Monnerville) is a Negro, that be-'ause of the war Haiti waged against the troops of Na-ɪoleon, the U. S. was not invaded by the French Army as Napoleon had intended to do.

For now, he is working with the DuSable Heritage Com-ɪittee to have the city erect a statue to honor DuSable, ɪnd name a street or Lake Shore Drive after him.

:6

BUSINESS

Woodlawn Organization Faces U.S. Investigation

The Woodlawn Organization in Chicago, formed in 19 to unite Negro slum dwellers to gain a bigger voice what happens to them, is being investigated by the U. Senate to see if it should continue to get its $900,0 yearly grant from the government. Hearings are expect to be held soon by Sen. John McClellan's permane subcommittee on investigations. A recent report by co gressional auditors showed some accounting errors but deliberate fraud.

Negro Union Pres. Hopes To Restore Dignity

John T. Squire, 40, newly elected president of the Mu Carmen's Union in San Francisco, hopes to build a mo unified union and restore the dignity of the men who o erate San Francisco's street cars, buses and trolley coach Squire, who defeated the incumbent president Edward Coleman who had headed the union for eight years, wan better treatment from the public for the operators a greater protection to make their jobs safer.

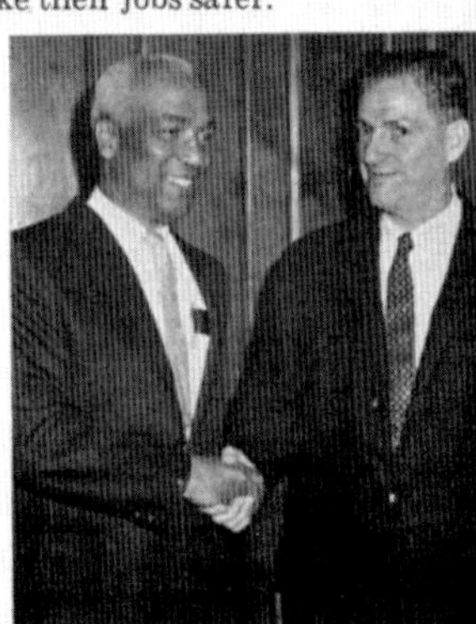

Promoted: Charles (Chuck) Watson (l) is congratulated in Chicago by Pres. Arnold Leavitt of Union Liquor Co. after being promoted to assistant to the board chairman. Union distributes Old Fitzgerald, Kentucky Tavern and House of Lords liquor.

A statue to honor Jean Baptiste Point DuSable has generated excitement, especially within the Haitian community, as one that would serve as a memorial and tribute to him while paying homage to the many pivotal contributions to American history made by people of African descent. The statue is a powerful symbol of cultural pride and a means of education for better awareness of the different stories that make up one's perception of history. The project now recognizes and celebrates the heritage of marginalized communities; it will range from paying homage to the foundational role people like DuSable have played in building the city of Chicago to epitomizing, in general, African Americans' contributions to the nation. This calls for a discussion of historical narratives often disregarded as one of inclusion and understanding. In the end, it will stand as a testament to resilience and the kaleidoscope of cultures that forged this city's identity, beckoning future generations to take heed and learn from their forefathers. (Vivian G. Harsh Research Collection.)

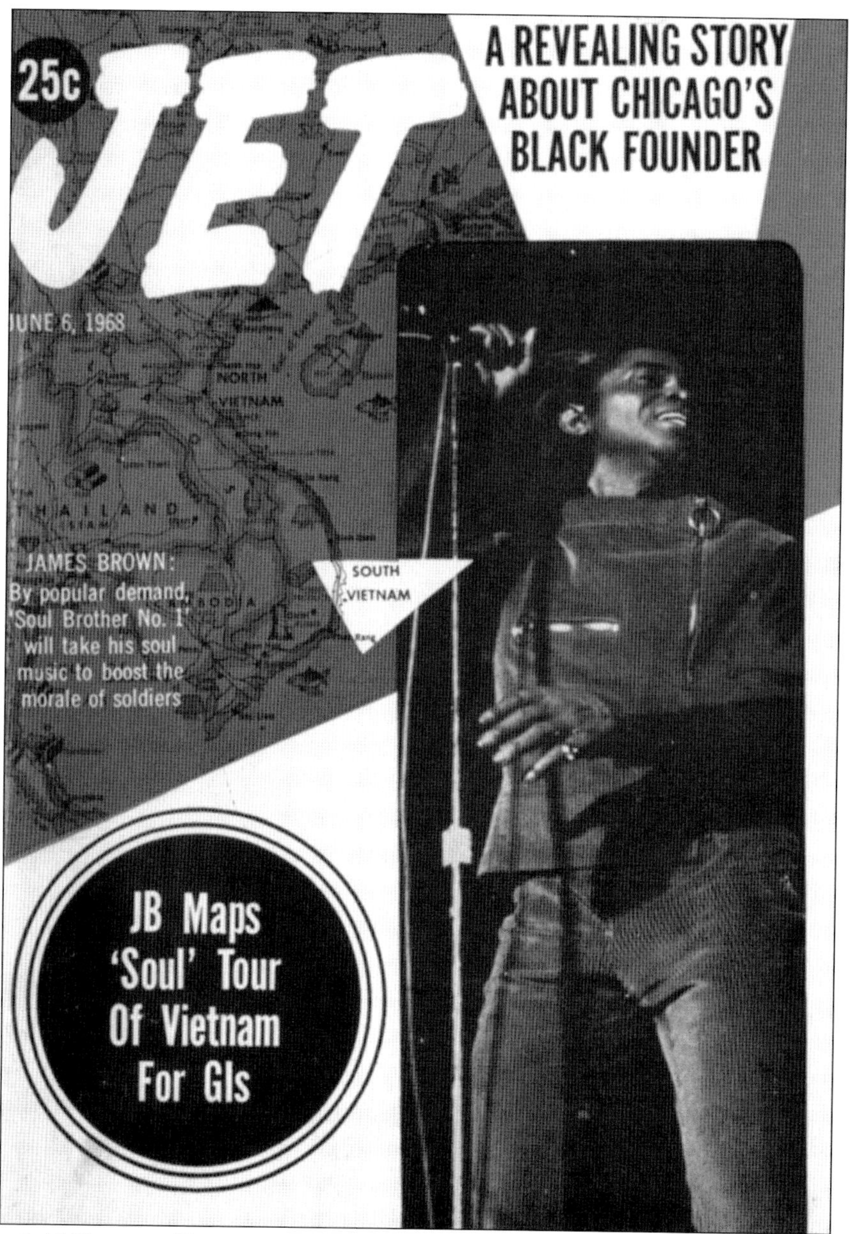

The June 6, 1968, issue of *Jet* magazine carried a story entitled "A Revealing Story About Chicago's Black Founder," regarding Jean Baptiste Point DuSable. This Haitian of African descent was a major trading post operator during the late 18th century, allowing trade and cultural interaction between groups. The article most likely gave information on DuSable's entrepreneurial spirit, issues being a Black man in an extremely White-dominated society, and how he affected the development of Chicago forever. *Jet* did this to highlight DuSable's contributions to center Black history as important within the American history umbrella. Stories like this form part of the general program for pride and knowledge to be developed about the community among African Americans themselves, persons, and their history, which the general history leaves behind. *Jet* reinforced in this way that Black history forms a component of American heritage necessary for identification and pride among its readers. (Vivian G. Harsh Research Collection.)

A REVEALING STORY ABOUT CHICAGO'S BLACK FOUNDER

DUSABLE'S KIN IN CHICAGO

By RUTHE B. STEIN

For ten years Dr. Fritz Etienne, 44, great-great-great-grandnephew of Chicago's founder and first settler, Jean Baptiste Point DuSable, has been a civil engineer for the city of Chicago. Nine of those ten years he lived in obscurity, unrecognized by the city or its citizens.

When he told people of his ancestral heritage, a heritage which included not only DuSable but six generations of men who fought in every major independence war in South, North and Central America, he was met with disbelief. Chicagoans would take him to the history books and show him the place where it said a white man, John Kinzie, was Chicago's first settler. So that, after a while of being laughed at, Dr. Etienne stopped telling people.

Most white Chicagoans had never heard of DuSable. Except for a high school, a hotel and a plaque which bear his name, the city has done nothing to advertise the

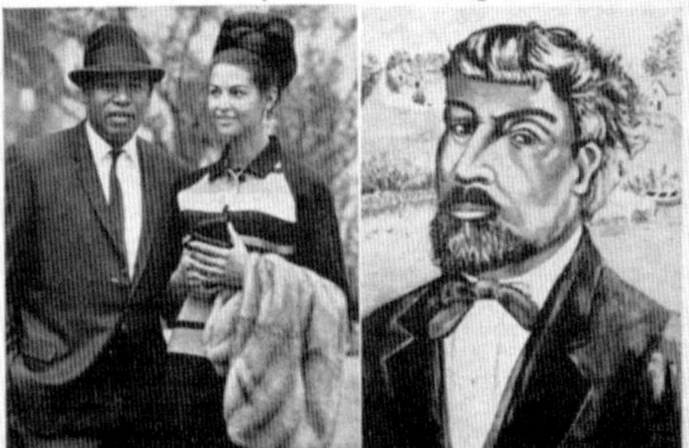

Dr. and Mrs. Etienne near the site where DuSable settled (l); portrait of DuSable in the foreground of his settlement.

22

TALKS ABOUT PIONEER SETTLER

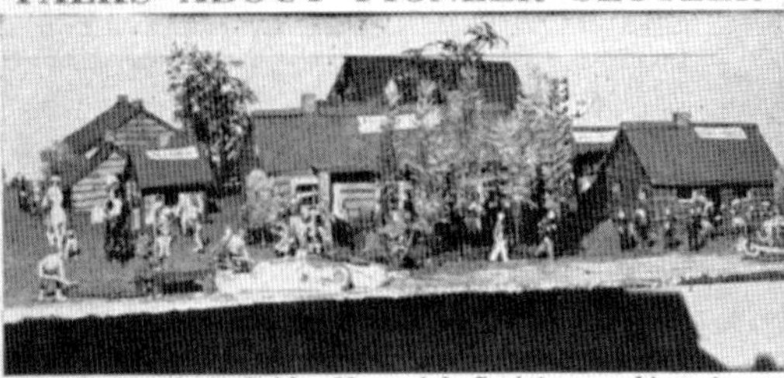

The National DuSable Memorial Society, working toward having DuSable properly recognized by the city, put together this replica of DuSable's estate.

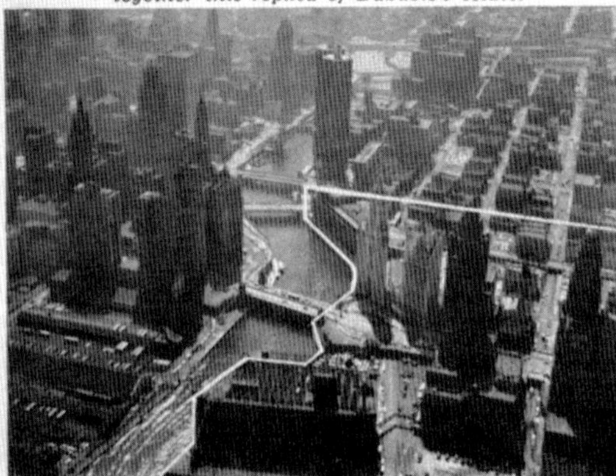

An aerial view of Chicago outlining what 200 years ago wa DuSable's estate.

2

Historically, Chicago has shown a reluctance to recognize Jean Baptiste Pointe DuSable as Chicago's founder, pointing to John Kinzie as Chicago's founding father instead. This can be seen in this image, as one of DuSable's descendants, Dr. Fritz Etienne, decided to forego telling other Chicagoans about his heritage due to the widespread lack of knowledge about DuSable's contribution to Chicago. There were still those who were fighting to have DuSable recognized throughout all of Chicago's history. Also pictured is an image of a replica of DuSable's estate, made by the National DuSable Memorial Society, as well as an aerial view and an outline of where DuSable's estate would have been in present-day Chicago at that time. Presently, some Chicagoans still do not know who Jean Baptiste Point DuSable is or that he was a Haitian man. Fortunately, academics, activists, and cultural organizations continue to make sure that his legacy is properly respected and recognized today. (Vivian G. Harsh Research Collection.)

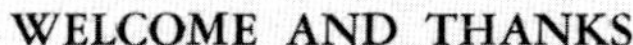

WELCOME AND THANKS

FROM THE OFFICERS AND THE MEMBERS OF THE CHICAGO DUSABLE SOCIETY WITH A CALL FOR TOGETHERNESS, CONSTRUCTIVE SPIRIT AND COOPERATIVE EFFORT TO PRESERVE AND ENRICH THE DUSABLE LEGACY, A PRECIOUS HISTORICAL HERITAGE AND AN INCENTIVE FOR PROGRESS FOR THE HAITIAN COMMUNITY.

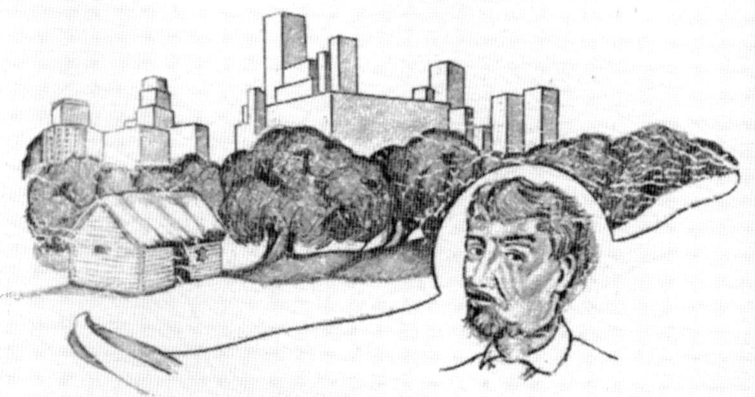

Chicago Dusable Society

First Anniversary

Dinner - Dance

and

Annual Humanities Lecture

Beverly Woods Restaurant

11532 South Western Avenue, Chicago

April 3, 1977

The Chicago DuSable Society was formed in dedication and commemoration of the meaningful contributions made by African Americans to Chicago's history and culture and took its rightful name from Jean Baptiste Point DuSable, commonly known as the founder of Chicago. It accomplished one of its first goals on April 3, 1977, when it hosted its first DuSable Day in honor and memory of DuSable himself and in recognition of African American history. It has different activities involved, education, events, and joint partnerships, all purposed to underline the crucial role of African Americans in Chicago. It has also worked to create monuments commemorating such vital contributions so that the rich heritage of African Americans is preserved and celebrated for generations to come. Society itself is quite vital in making sure that there is awareness and appreciation of this very important aspect of city identity. (Vivian G. Harsh Research Collection.)

Officers

DR. FRED CHAMPAGNE,
President

MRS. HUGUETTE AZOR,
Secretary

DR. MARC F. DAVID

DR. DAUGE BARTHELEMY

REV. LEFOND LAPOINTE

DR. CLAUSEL THEARD

Honorary Members

LOCHARD

DR. JANIN RAOUL

REV. CLEMENT L. PAPILLON

MR. ROGER ST. VICTOR HERARD

MR. ROBERT BENODIN

Advisory Members

DR. JANIN RAOUL

MR. ROBERT BENODIN

REV. CLEMENT L. PAPILLON

MR. ROGER ST. VICTOR

HERARD

MR. FRITZ MICHEL

MR. LESLIE BENODIN

Active Members in Good Standing

MR. LAFONTANT AUGUSTAVE

MR. JEAN-ROBERT ARMAND

MR. GERARD AZOR

MRS. GERARD AZOR

MR. EMILE ANDRE

REV. BERNARD BASTIEN

DR. DOUGE BARTHELEMY

MR. DANIEL BRISARD

DR. FRED CHAMPAGNE

MR. LOUIS D. CHARLES

DR. MAXINE FETHIER

MR. MARC-ANTOINE GAUTHIER

MR. MYRTHO JADOTTE

MR. EMMANUEL LEROY

REV. LAFOND LAPOINTE

DR. GERARD PIERRE-JEROME

MRS. DENISE SMITH

MRS. ROSE STARK

MR. DIEUDONNE STENIO

DR. CLAUSEL THEARD

DR. CLAUDE EMMANUEL

MR. SYLLA LECONTE

MR. SAUREL BERNARD

Associate Members

MR. MARC-AURELE JEANTY

MRS. COLETTE A. JEFFRIES

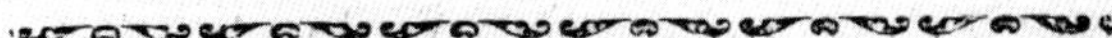

The Chicago DuSable Society is also very actively engaged in education, cultural events, and outreach programs, raising awareness about the DuSable legacy and the larger African American history of Chicago. These efforts include lectures, tours, and milestone commemorations that highlight this heritage. This list, from the first anniversary of the Chicago DuSable Society in 1977, shows the officers and members of the group during this time. Events like this raise awareness not only of the valuable contributions DuSable provided the city but also contribute more to knowledge regarding the lifespan of African Americans residing therein. The society's commitment has worked to shed light on the community, make known cultural achievements, and guarantee that the legacies live on into the future so the people of Chicago can be proud of them. (Vivian G. Harsh Research Collection.)

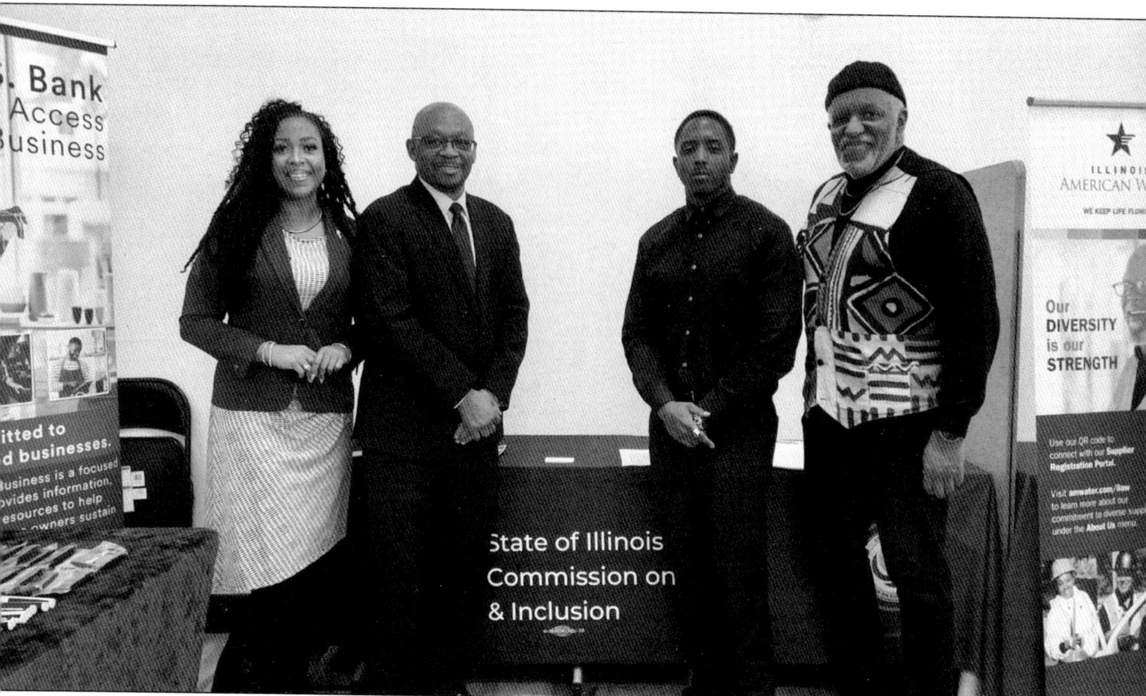

It is about unity, inclusiveness, and strength from within diversity. That is the reason for celebration in the Chicago community; the DuSable Summit launched in 2023 with the theme "Together, We Rise Stronger," really reflecting unity. It is so named after Jean Baptiste Point DuSable, recognized as the founder of Chicago. This event honors his memory while bringing forth community collaboration. The summit is for dialogue, education, and empowerment—a vehicle showcasing the rich tapestry of cultures to which the city owes its identity. By bringing individuals together with diverse backgrounds, the DuSable Summit aims to inspire collective progress while fostering the understanding of just how diversity further enriches community life. This celebration is one of remembrance of DuSable's historical impact and also encourages continuous efforts toward greater inclusivity and social harmony in Chicago. (Matthew Simpson and the Office of Economic Equity and Empowerment.)

Two

THE 1893 WORLD'S FAIR, FREDERICK DOUGLASS, AND THE HAITIAN PAVILION

By the opening of the World's Columbian Exposition, also known as the Chicago World's Fair, in 1893, Haiti had been an independent nation for almost 90 years. But its relationship with the United States was like that of an ant to an elephant. Although Haiti declared its independence in 1804, the US government did not recognize it until almost 60 years later, in 1862. The role of Jean Baptiste Pointe DuSable in the founding of the settlement that grew into today's Chicago is now—thanks to decades of advocacy on the part of African Americans—well established. But it was not at the time of the Chicago World's Fair. In fact, the fair took place after Reconstruction of the Confederate South had long been abandoned, during a particularly brutal period of White supremacy when the federal government had turned its back on the promises of "freedom, justice, and equality for all."

The presence of any representation of African American progress in the less than 30 years since the 13th Amendment ending legal slavery in the United States in 1865 was hard fought. That the single beacon of that progress was the Haitian Pavilion is even more telling and maybe simply because the one remaining symbol of the North's triumph over slavery was then ambassador to Haiti, Frederick Douglass.

Things got interesting when Ida B. Wells, by then a world-famous journalist and anti-lynching activist, recruited Douglass to join in protesting the dearth of any other Black presence at the fair. They both argued that the fair was particularly obligated to show how much their race had achieved in such a short period of time.

The Haitian Pavilion became the de facto representative of African American progress. After boycotting the fair and issuing a pamphlet, "The Reason Why the Colored American is Not in the World's Columbian Exposition," Ida B. Wells and other prominent African American leaders staged talks, meetings, and events throughout the run of the fair. After much wrangling and protests, the committee eventually forced the "White" powers to dedicate a single day to highlight the accomplishments of the African American community since slavery. It hosted and promoted a "Colored American Day" on August 25, 1893. Of course, most of the events were held at the Haitian Pavilion.

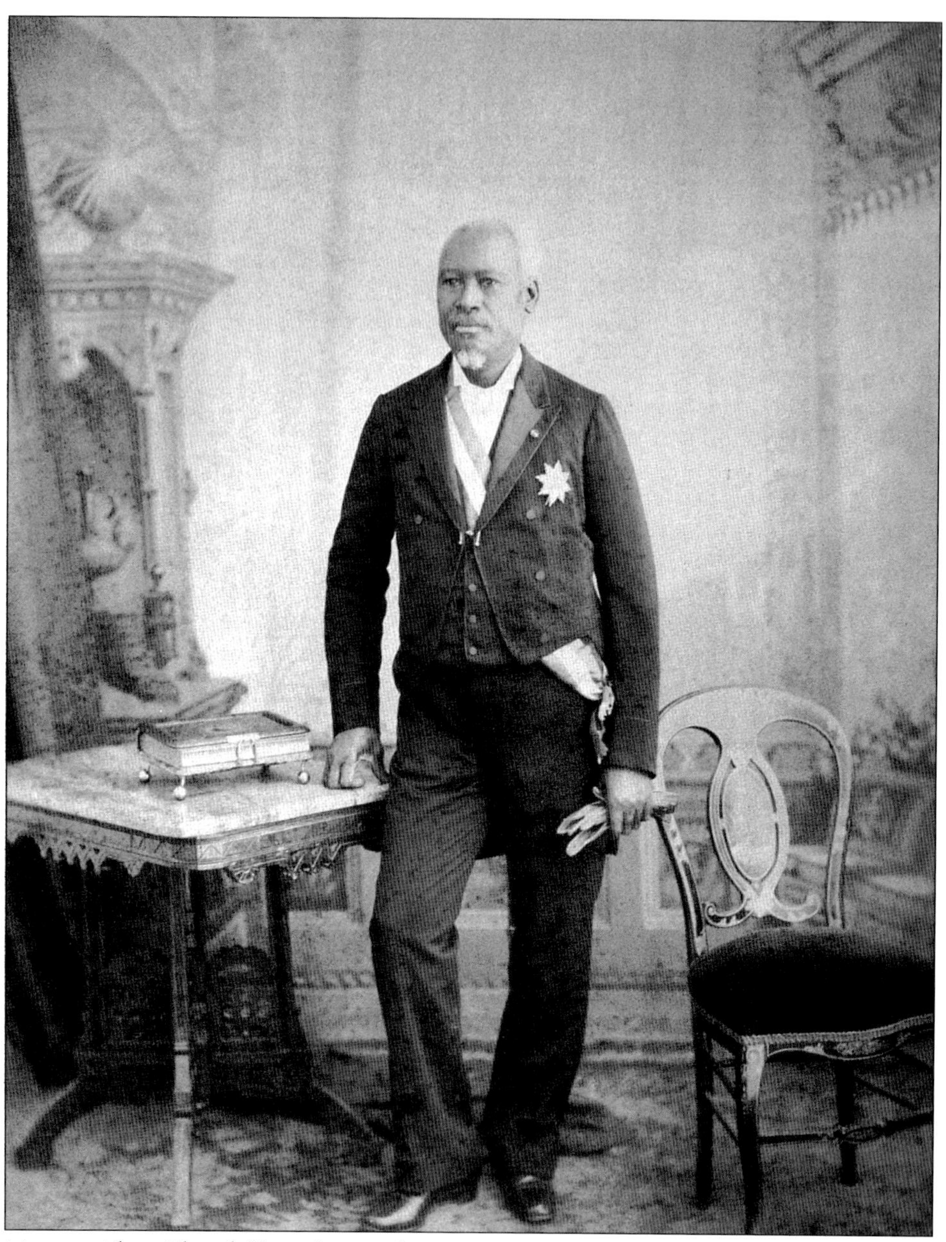

Haitian president Florvil Hyppolite made immense contributions toward representations for his country during the World's Columbian Exposition in Chicago, seeking its place on the international map with a view toward furthering the commerce and culture of the land. Fully recognizing what this exposition could do, he thus decreed that Haiti would join the grand parade of nations showcasing before the world all of its produce and achievements. To celebrate Haiti's presence, Hyppolite gave a self-portrait to Frederick Douglass, Haiti's diplomatic envoy to the fair. He acclaimed Hyppolite's intelligence, insight, and love for his country, showing that the presence of Haiti at such an important occasion was significant. It would not only raise the profile of Haiti on the international scene but also prove, as a nation, how committed it was toward maintaining friendly relations with other countries through cultural exchange and diplomacy. (National Park Service, US Department of the Interior.)

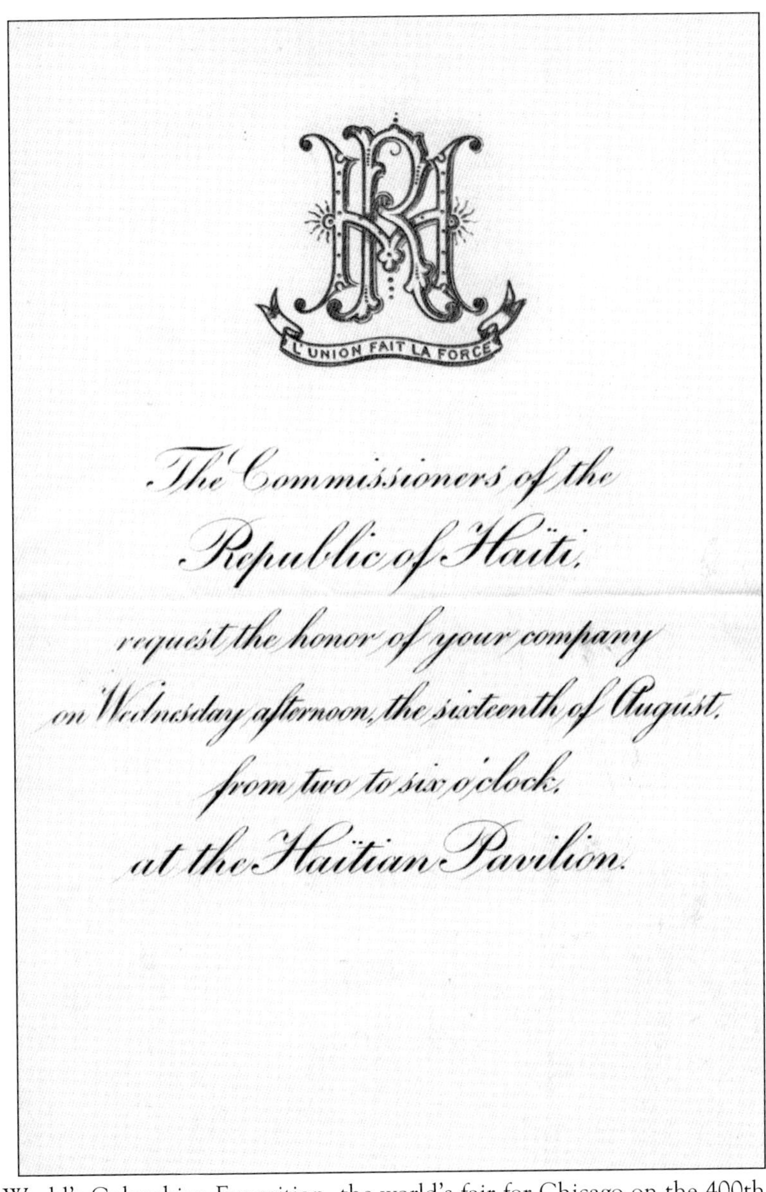
L'UNION FAIT LA FORCE

The Commissioners of the
Republic of Haïti,
request the honor of your company
on Wednesday afternoon, the sixteenth of August,
from two to six o'clock,
at the Haïtian Pavilion.

The 1893 World's Columbian Exposition, the world's fair for Chicago on the 400th anniversary of Christopher Columbus's arrival in the Americas, virtually excluded African American involvement in its public representations and festivities that were urbane in form yet fundamentally representative of the strong racism and segregation then. While it epitomized accomplishments that were done in American society, large quantities of the contributions and culture offered by African Americans were absolutely obscured or sidetracked. Innumerable proposals had been presented through different Black representatives for providing representation to a pavilion in their name based on African American achievement; however, this was even getting caught up in a line of many hindrances, starting with being unknown as human citizens and the deficiency of available funds. The result was reinforcement of racial stereotypes, sanitizing American history of many conflicts and achievements that reflected deeply entrenched systemic disparities. Despite the invitation sent by the Haitian government, the African Americans were not able to attend. (Vivian G. Harsh Research Collection.)

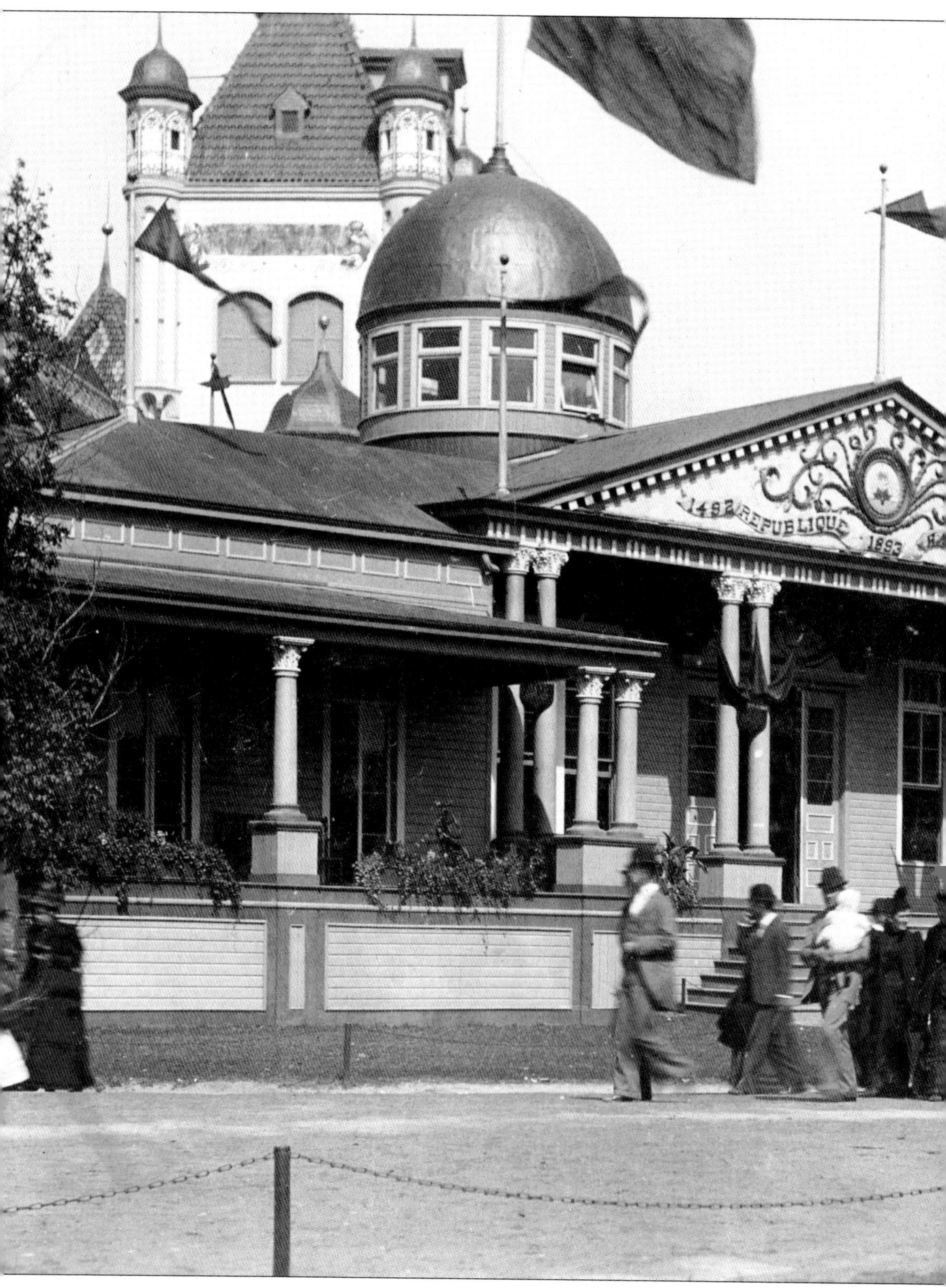
1492 REPUBLIQUE
1893

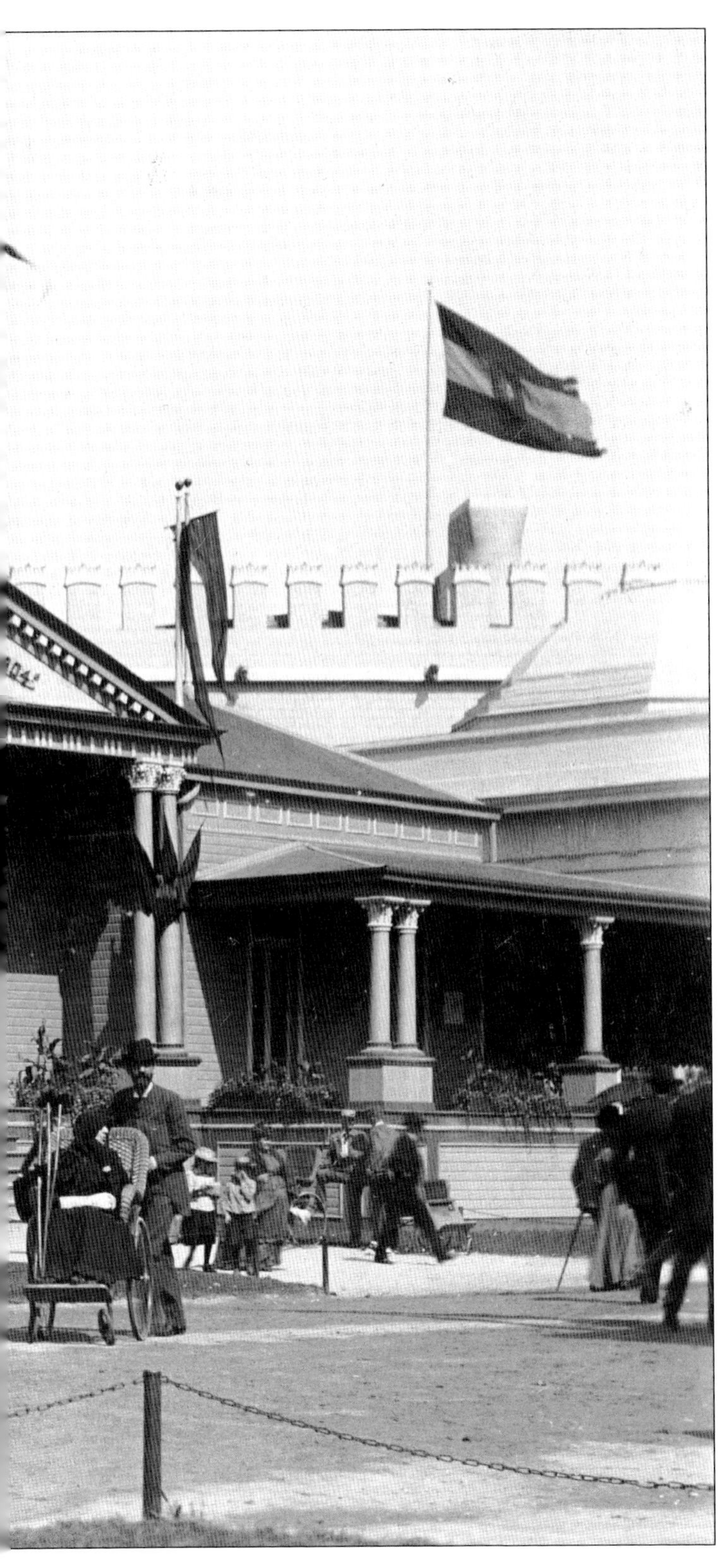

The Pavilion of the Republic of Haiti was proud to rise as the only one representing the Black population at the fair and, thus, a unique autonomous exhibition of African descent. This pavilion showcased the rich array of Haitian treasures, among which the sword of Toussaint Louverture was considered an important symbol of the nation's fight for freedom and independence. In addition to these historical artifacts, the pavilion had a dynamic display of Haitian paintings that represented this nation's great cultural heritage and artistic abilities. With each of these important contributions, the Haitian Pavilion represented not only its own history but also provided a powerful platform for representations of the greater African diaspora at the fair. (Chicago History Museum.)

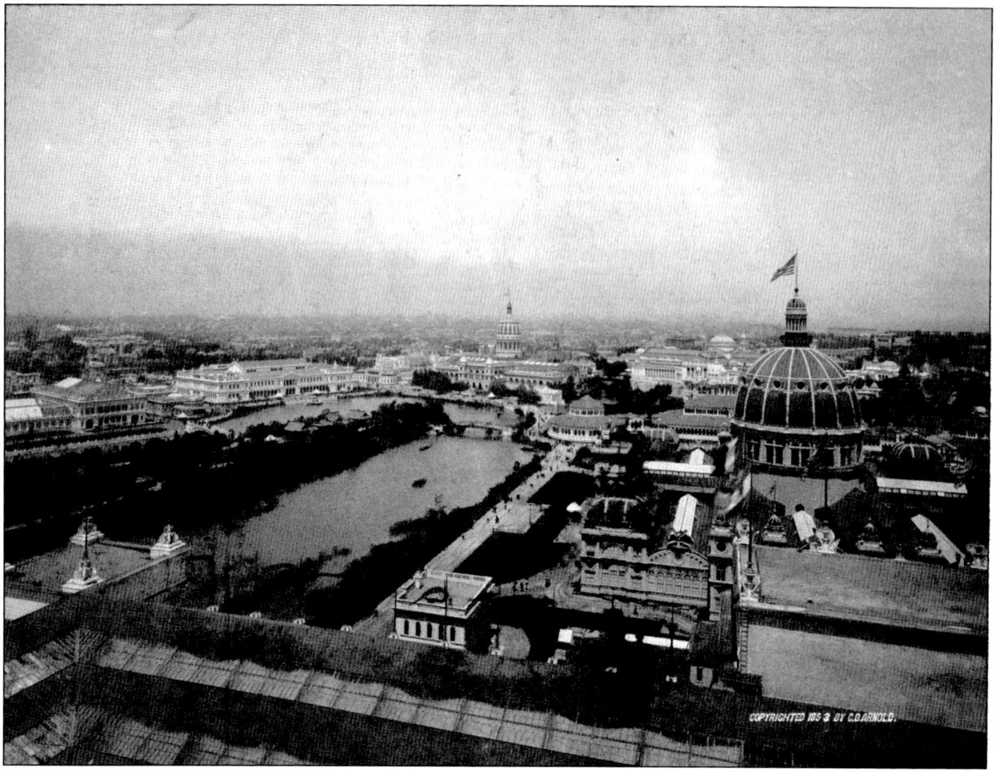

The explosion of gas in the Cold Storage Building fire at the 1893 Chicago World's Fair underlined how precarious early refrigeration might be. Luckily, no person was injured, but the pressing need for improved safety regulations was underlined as architecture and culture continued to surge forward at unprecedented rates. (Library of Congress.)

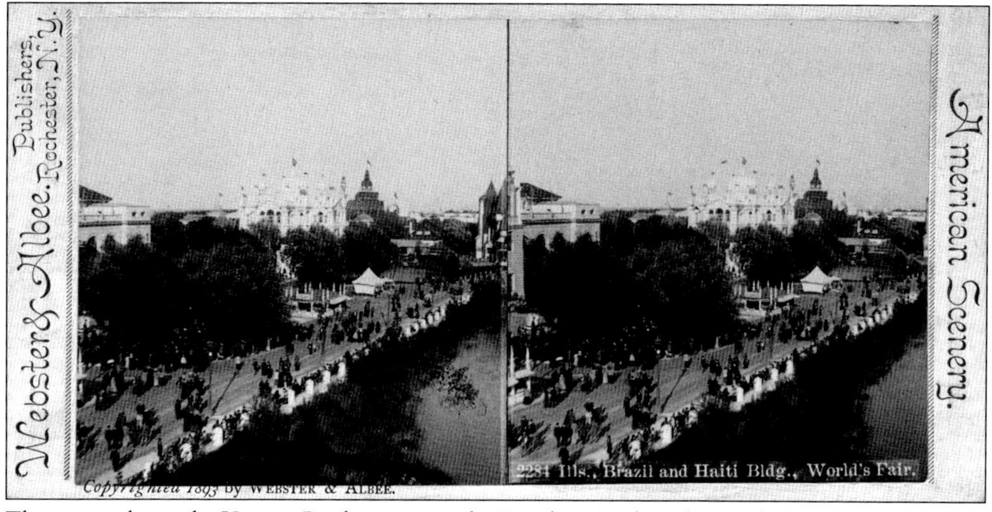

This image shows the Haitian Pavilion next to the Brazilian Pavilion during the World's Columbian Exhibition. It puts both into cultural context within the city of Chicago. The world's fair was a place where many cultures were displayed, and Haiti was no exception. It deeply affected the city, as Haitians were some of the first to make a path that many African Americans could follow to be heard and also shape the development and culture of the city. (Library of Congress.)

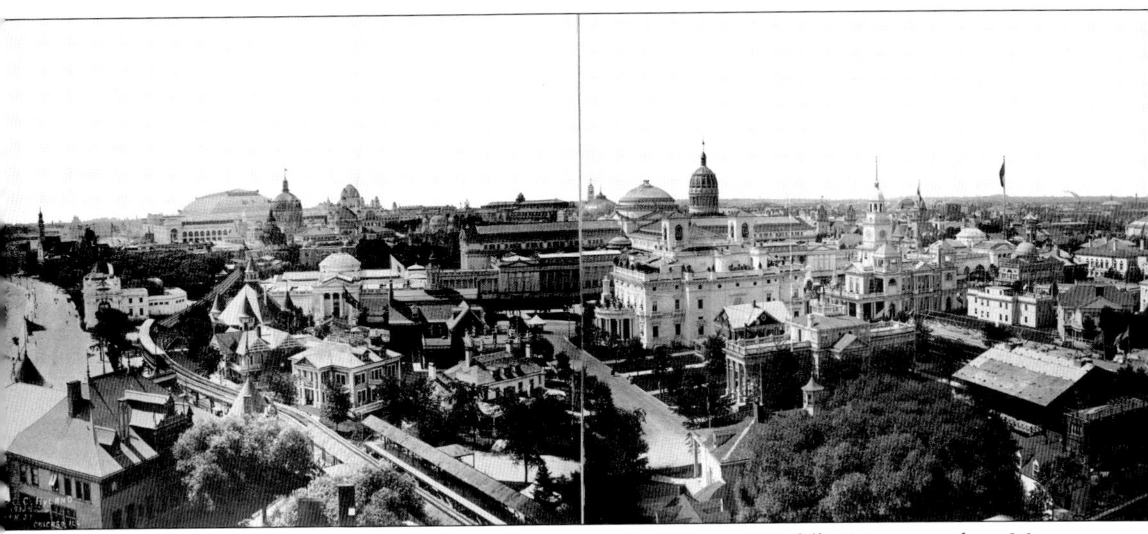

The World's Columbian Exposition, better known as the Chicago World's Fair, opened on May 1, 1893, in honor of the 400th anniversary of Christopher Columbus's arrival in the New World. During its six-month tenure, 26 million people came to see its displays on technology and culture, but African Americans were almost completely shut out of the fair, a situation emblematic of the racial hostilities of the day. One of the few exceptions was an exhibit prepared by Haiti, which contrasted with the discrimination and inequality so common during that period. The glaring omission was in huge contrast to the exposition's overall display of progress and unity, showing very clearly the ambiguity and contradiction in American culture. Hence, the exposition has become one of the milestones in American history—a sign of progress and failure regarding race relations and the inclusiveness of society in that transformative period of growth. It ultimately reminds people of the unfinished struggle for equality and the learning from the past that needs to take place. (Library of Congress.)

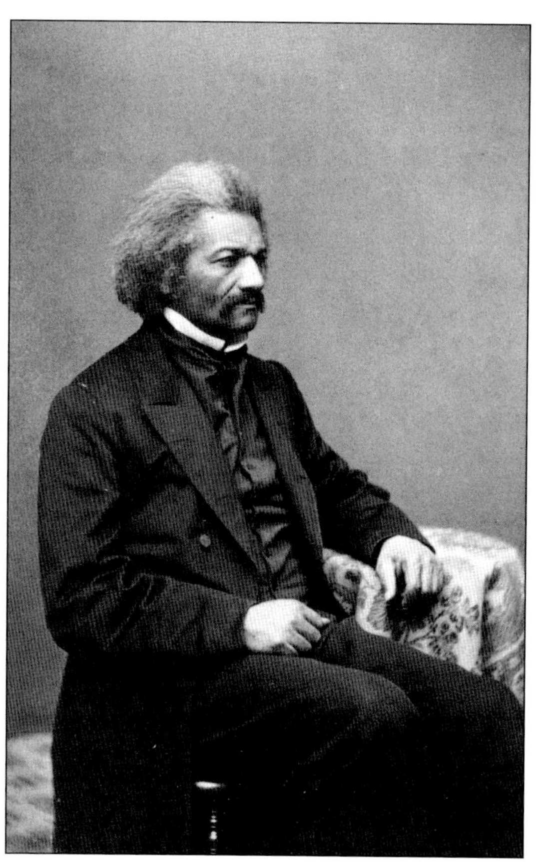

In his speech at the World's Columbian Exhibition in 1893, US minister to Haiti Frederick Douglass voiced a powerful, eloquent contradiction to racist stereotypes about Haiti, hailing it as a symbol of liberty and justice, while charging the United States to recognize its ideals. Douglass represented the African American community in this speech, as he emphasized Haiti's importance in the fight for freedom. (Library of Congress.)

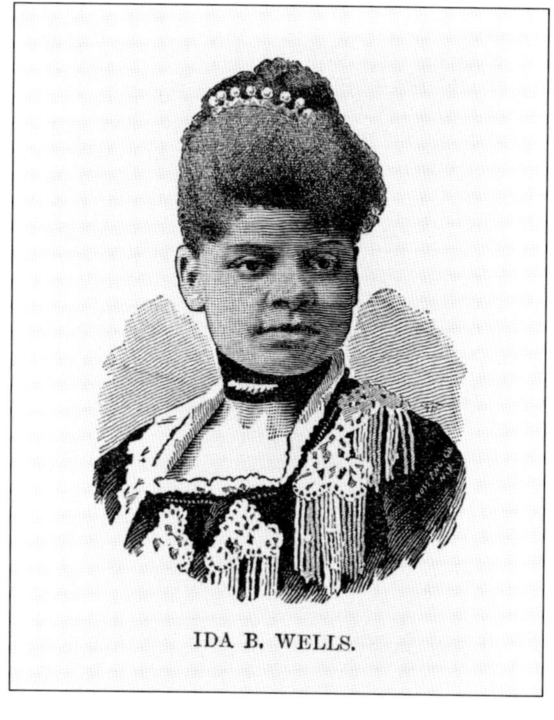

IDA B. WELLS.

Ida B. Wells was an independent journalist in the service of African American rights and made a huge contribution to the 1893 Chicago World's Fair. She joined hands with Frederick Douglass, without being invited to speak, to stand against lynching and to protest the exclusion of Black stories. From open-air speaking to tract distribution, her work was done to point out racial injustices and fight for equality. (Library of Congress.)

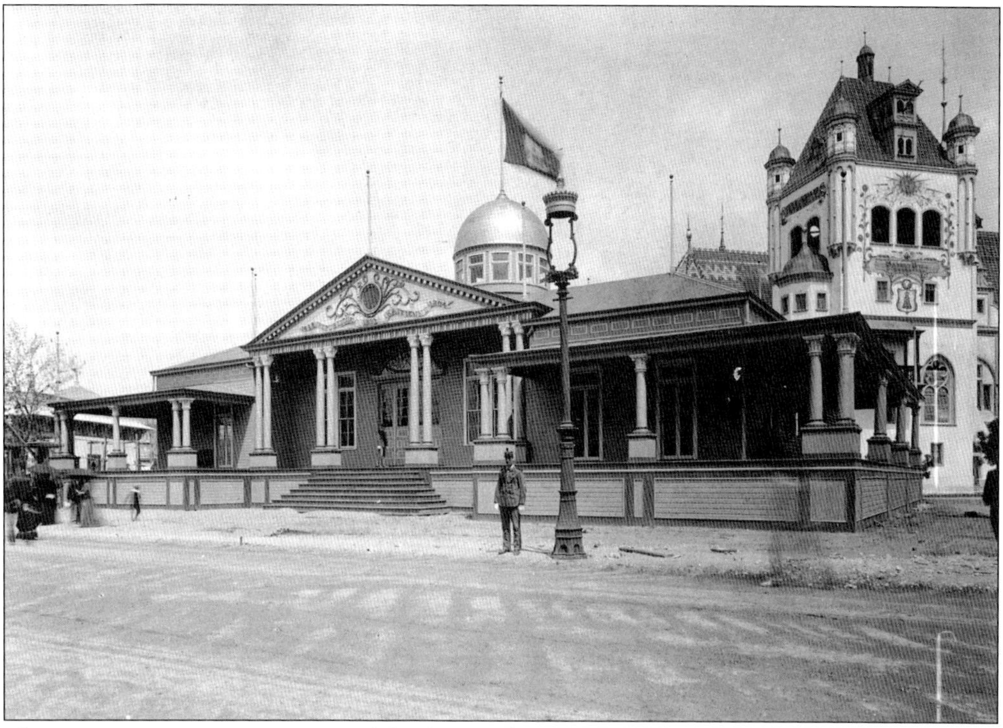

The Haitian government was one of the first to plan an exhibition space at the fair. The building was a one-and-a-half-story wooden structure with a central dome and veranda. It was located on a corner lot facing a major intersection in the foreign exhibits section. The building housed the offices of Haitian officials, including Frederick Douglass, and displayed the country's agricultural products. (Library of Congress.)

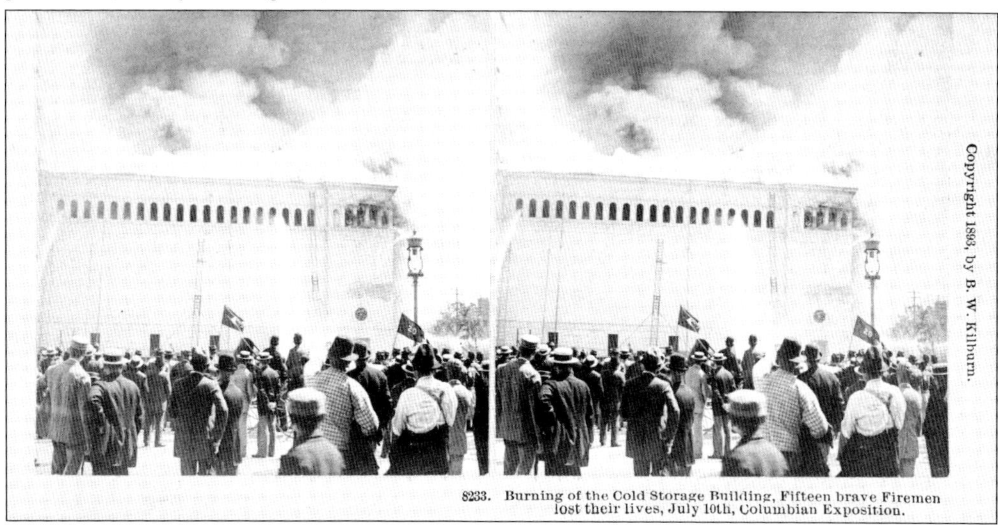

The Cold Storage Building fire at the Chicago World's Fair on July 10, 1893, pointed out a few dangers of early refrigeration technology; a gas explosion engulfed in flames a highly combustible wooden structure without destroying the main exposition buildings. Thankfully, no one was injured, which speaks volumes for increased safety regulation within public spaces touting innovative technologies. (Library of Congress.)

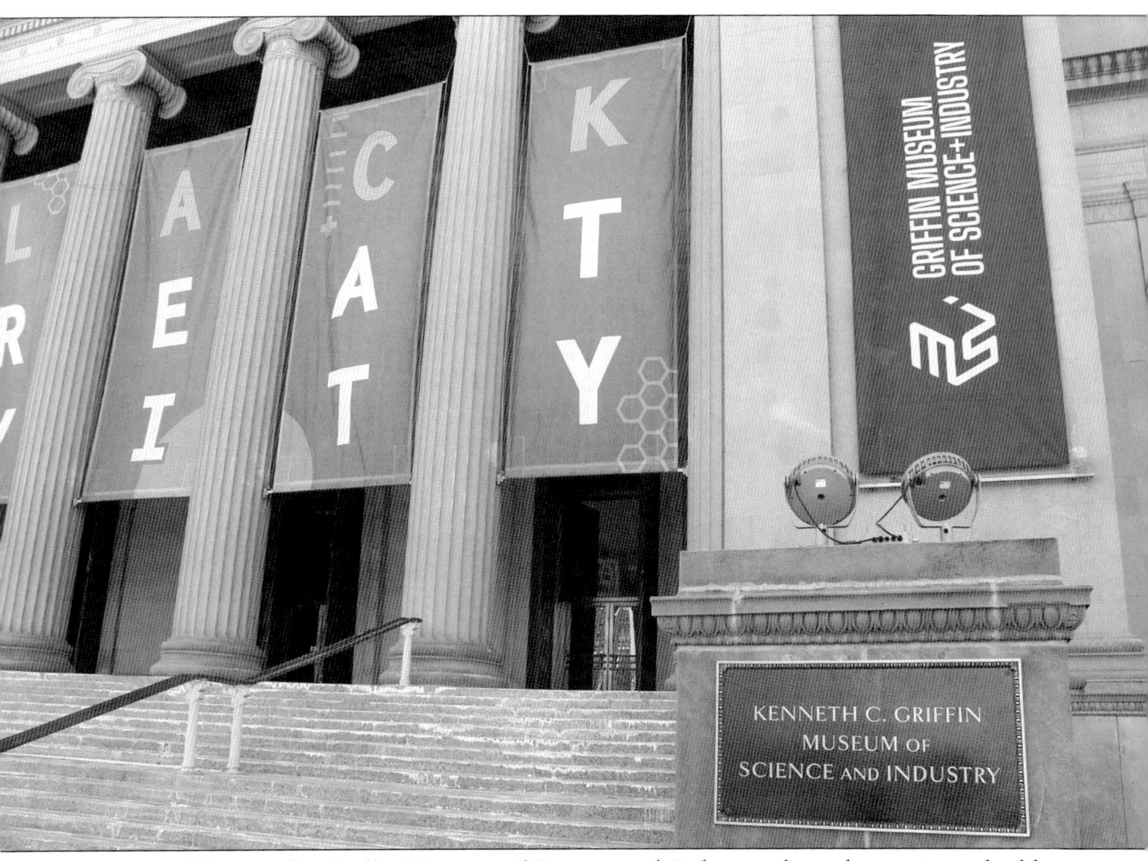

Pictured here is the Griffin Museum of Science and Industry, the only remaining building in sight from the 1893 world's fair. It had been known as the Palace of Fine Arts in 1893 and was reopened in the Windy City at the 1933 Century of Progress International Exposition. Today, it is not only a monument of architectural genius but has also been a dynamic center of education and exploration into the wonders of science and technology. Exhibitions have been on the development of various means of transport and methods of energy production, among others. The rich history and multifaceted mission of the museum make it a place that one must visit to learn about the past, while at the same time encouraging future generations in the quest for knowledge and further discovery.

Three

IMMIGRATION FROM THE 1950S ONWARD

The history of Haitian immigration to the United States began much earlier than with the so-called "boat people" of the late 20th century. During the Haitian Revolution (1791–1803), the French colony of Saint-Domingue saw a mass exodus of anti-liberty slave owners, along with their human cargo, immigrating to the United States, where slavery was still legal. As revolutionary Haiti continued to battle foreign attacks, civil war, and natural disasters, thousands more Haitians were compelled to emigrate. On January 1, 1804, Saint-Domingue ultimately evolved into the free, independent Republic of Haiti, and immigration to the United States subsided.

In 1915, the US government and US corporations that held business interests in the Caribbean were seeking to protect their regional hegemony from foreign powers (specifically Germany) and sent American troops to invade and occupy Haiti. Due to rapid industrialization, the US mainland was also experiencing an agricultural labor shortage. To replenish its dying farming industry, the American government imported workers from its protectorates, Cuba and Puerto Rico, and a large number of Haitian farmers were forced to immigrate and repopulate US-owned plantations on those islands as well as help fill the workforce at the Panama Canal.

During the occupation, corruption, forced labor practices, press censorship, racial segregation, and the wanton violence propagated by the US Marines sparked rebellions from Haitian guerrilla soldiers and nationwide political protests from students and journalists. By 1934, the American troops withdrew after installing a puppet government in order to retain control over Haiti's institutions, leaving behind an economically and politically devastated Haiti primed for dictatorship.

The Duvalier regime came to power in the 1950s and 1960s, causing a multitude of Haitian professionals to seek asylum elsewhere. At that time, the United States was attempting to rectify its labor shortage of professionally educated personnel, especially in the medical field, by facilitating the immigration of foreign nurses, doctors, and other professionals. Many middle-class Haitians of that generation used this opportunity to escape the political repression and economic failure of the Duvalier regime and immigrated to the United States.

This chapter offers a pictorial history of those immigrants who arrived in Chicago beginning in the early 1960s.

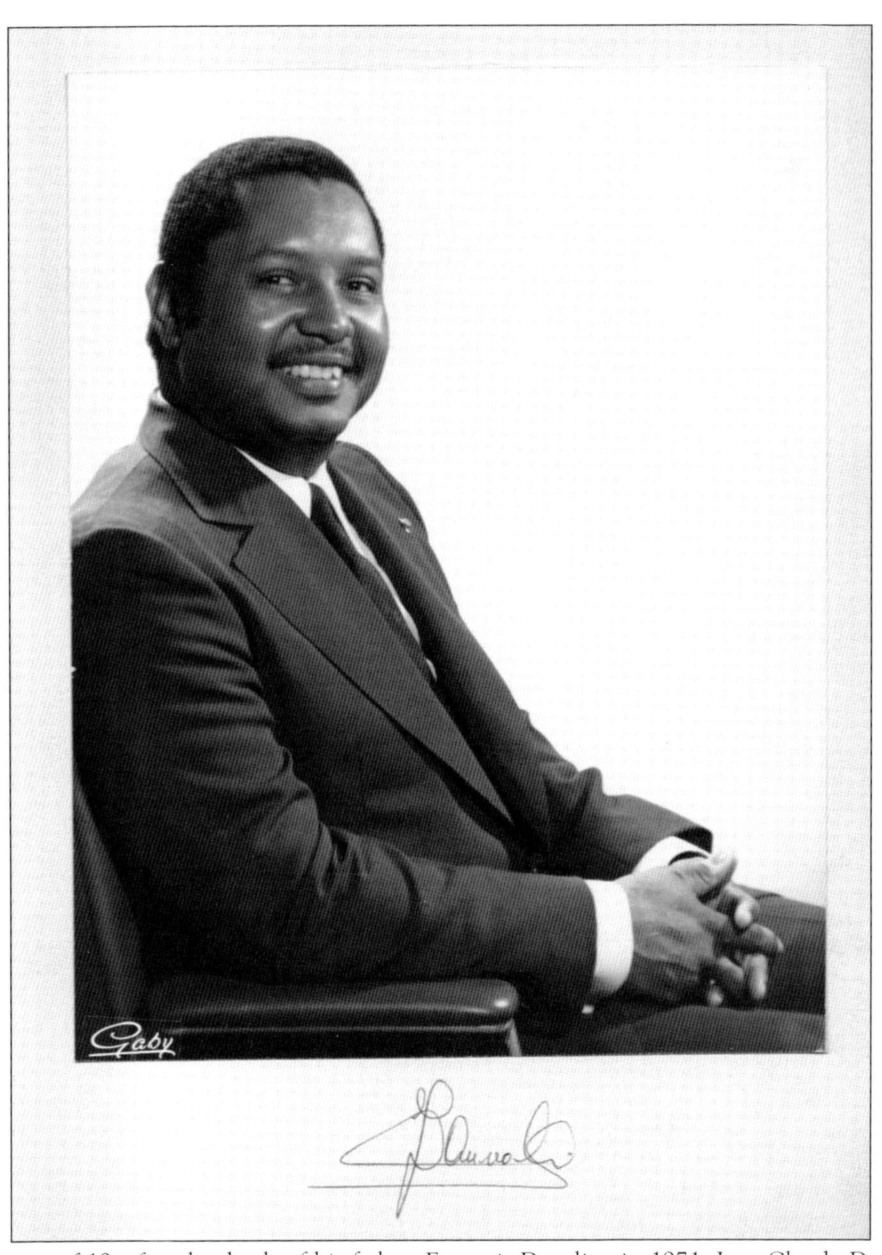

At the age of 19, after the death of his father, François Duvalier, in 1971, Jean-Claude Duvalier took over the presidency of Haiti until 1986. His regime was characterized by harsh political repression and general economic destitution, which forced many Haitians to immigrate abroad as they ran from the repressive regime. This period of instability and oppression, thus, became a part of Haitian social and political life to such an extent that it shaped generations of its citizens' experiences. The two combined, Duvalier's repressive rule and the deteriorating economic conditions, created an atmosphere of fear and desperation that stimulated a large exodus. While seeking greater opportunities and safety away from their homeland, these individuals added to a broader story of resilience and struggle that has continued to define Haiti to this day. The aftermath of this tumultuous period still echoes in the hearts as a grim reminder of what the Haitian people went through in their quest to be free and live a stable life.

In Haitian culture, the grandparents are very significant in the family for maintaining tradition, values, and history. They are also a source of wisdom, emotional support, and are very involved in child-rearing. They teach the importance of community through telling stories about their families and life experiences, which helps to strengthen their cultural identity and continuation of both family and cultural relationships.

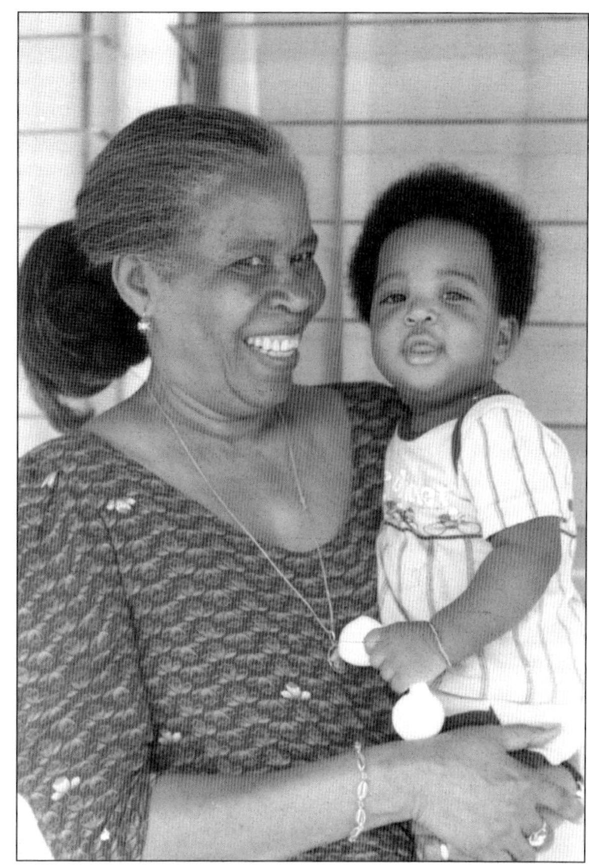

There are spirited social gatherings of friends and family over holidays and weekends. In Haiti, picnics are times when an array of foods is elaborately prepared, such as fried pork, spicy pickled vegetables, and refreshing drinks, and there is music and dancing. It is more than a meal—it is a picnic, symbolic of joy, bonding, and the sharing of cherished cultural traditions.

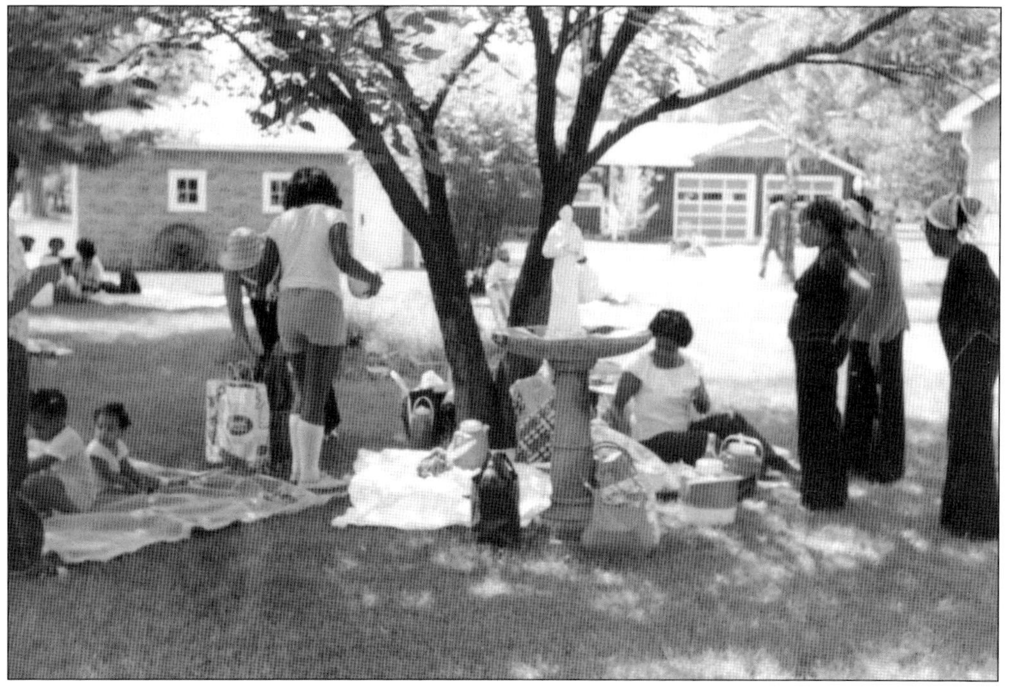

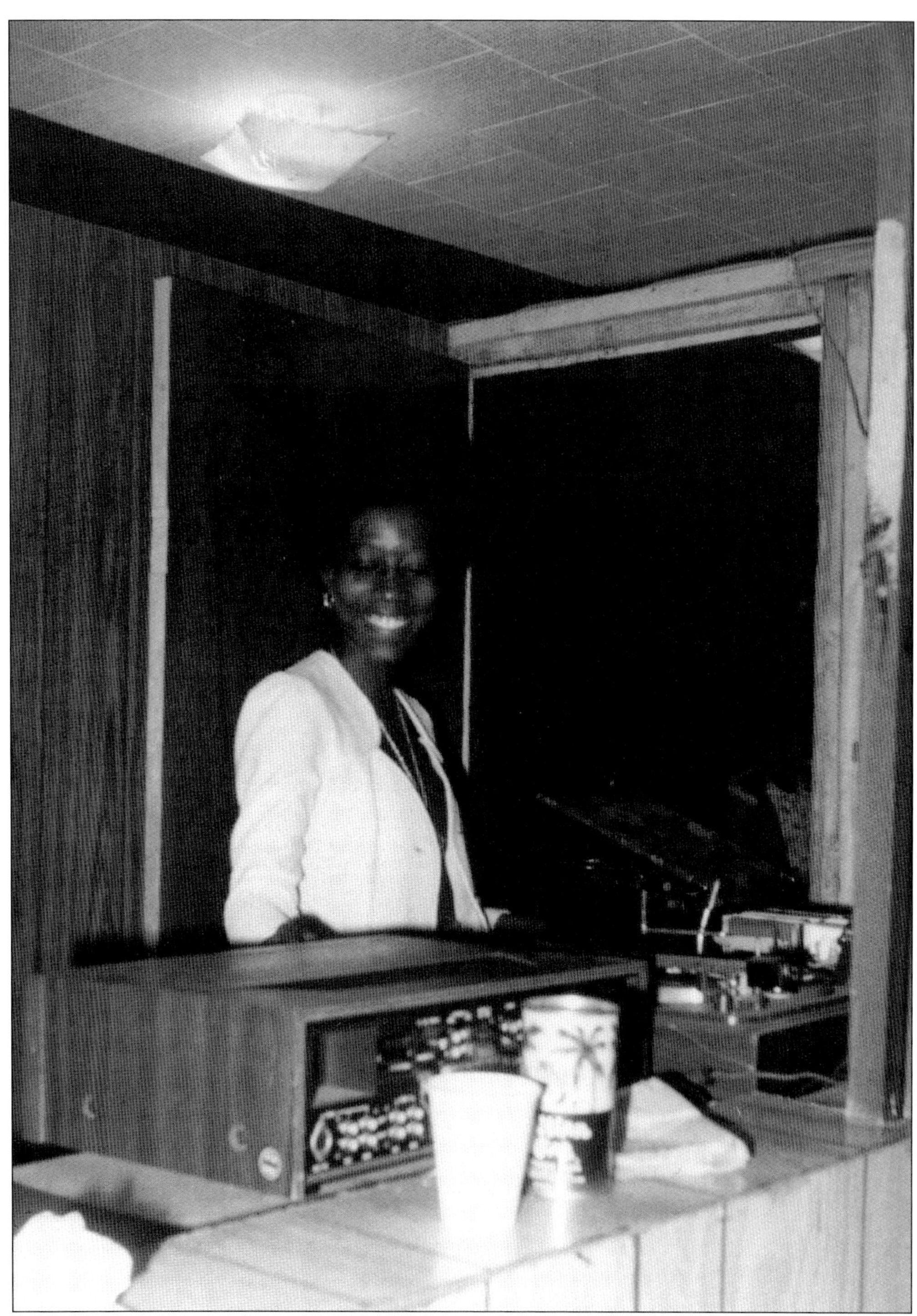

In the 1970s, Dupervil became an iconic vocalist and songwriter known for her swooning voice and electrifying live performances. Growing up in a musical family, she is fluid through its many genres, creating an indelible sound that resonates worldwide. With emotional songs about love and identity, he has inspired so many, thus finding her place in Haitian music history and beyond.

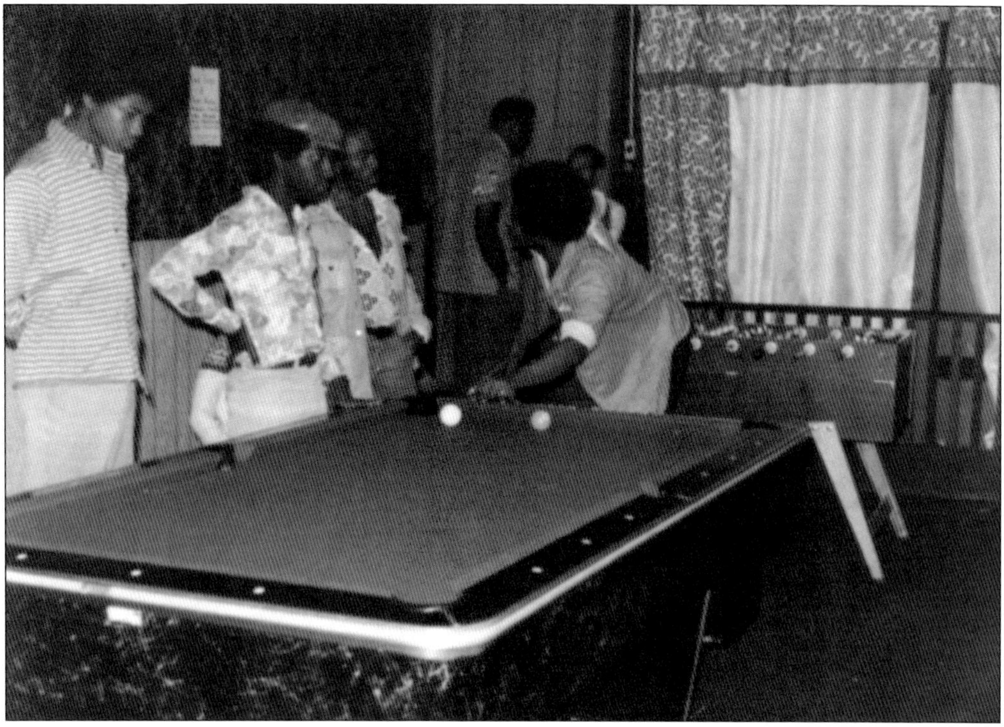

Young Haitians have fun playing pool among friends—some with a bit of competition. This would not only get them out but also nurture friendships and further build relationships within their community. The air is thick with loud, contagious laughter that makes for quite the scene. In a show of resiliency and spirit, young Haitians bond over simple, communal moments.

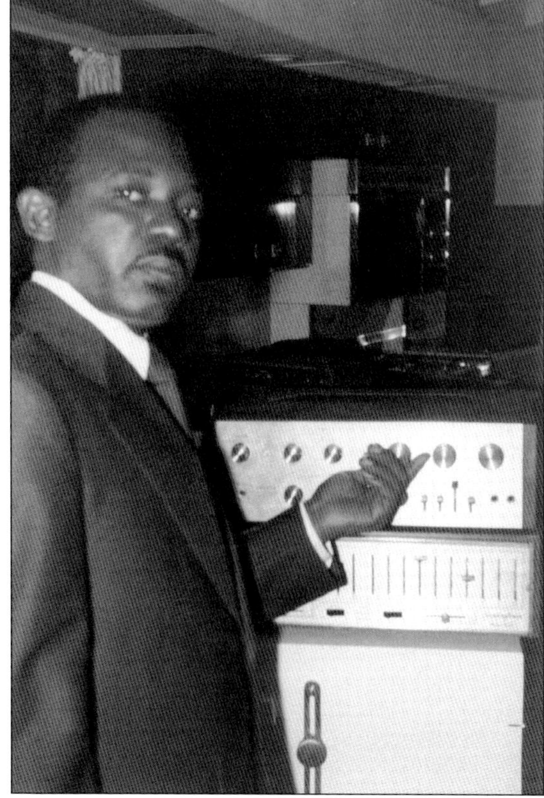

The music of Haiti reflects a very rich and varied culture, drawing its inspiration from the many influences at work. Popular genres include Konpa, an infectiously rhythmic genre, largely danceable, and Mizik Rasin, a style in which Vodou beats blend with rock and jazz. In Haitian culture, music is an important medium of social commentary and national expression.

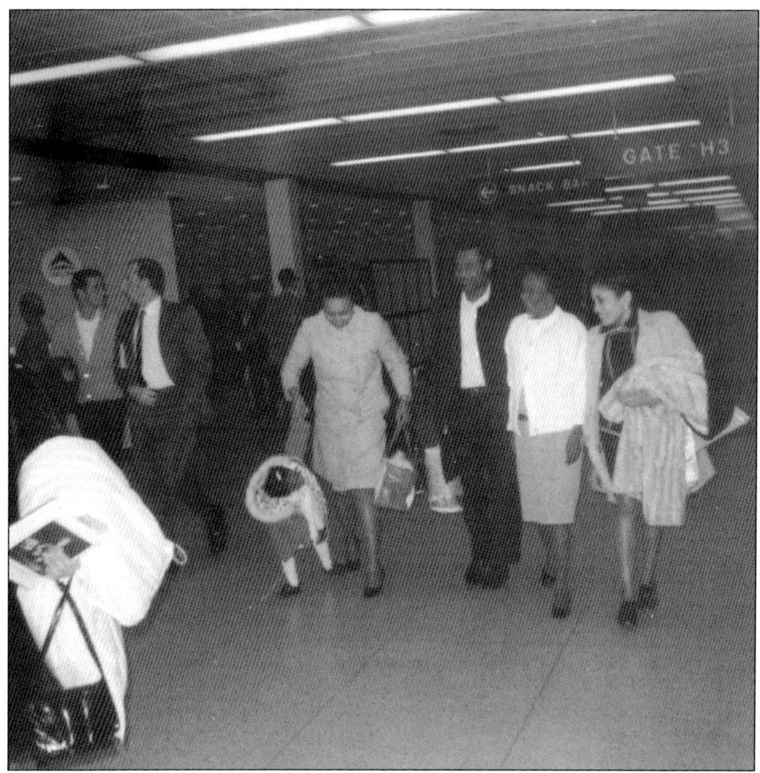

It was the early 1970s, and at the airport, in something of a balmy and anticipatory mood, this family waits for their grandmother's arrival. Her visit was not just a reunion but a meaningful change in their daily lives. Welcoming her as a caretaker, she filled the home with love, stories of yore, and cherished moments, making it a haven of laughter and security.

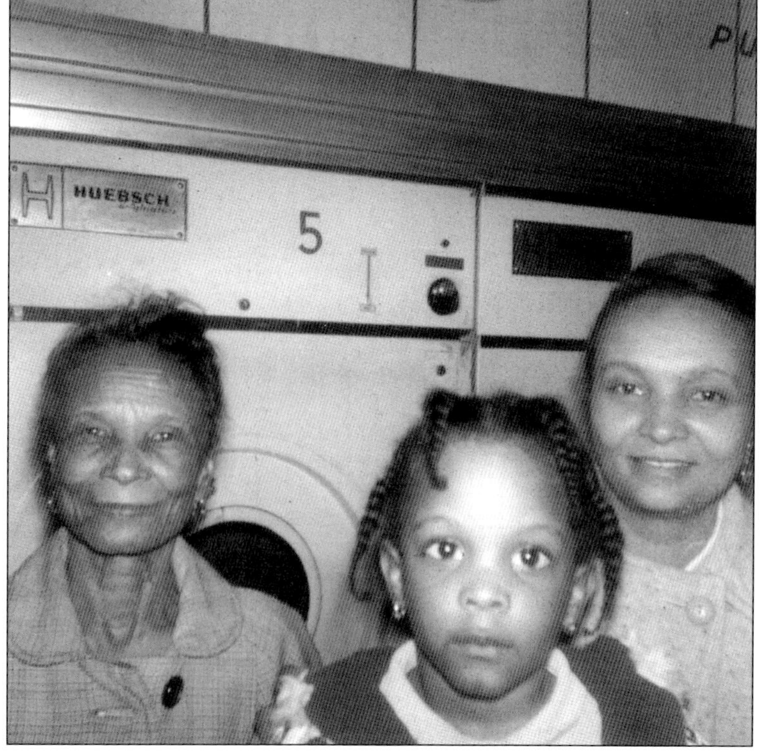

In a South Side, Chicago, laundromat filled with the hum of washing machines, three generations of a Haitian family come together in a burst of warmth. The chain of gold hoop earrings worn by the grandmother is traditional. The mother straddles the past and the present, teaching the daughter pride via her own pierced ears. As such, this ritual makes the laundromat a haven for culture and connection.

Outside in their new Chicago community, Haitian women gather to have a conversation. These moments reflect the strength of Haitian women supporting one another, carrying culture and determination across borders, and shaping new beginnings while holding fast to the traditions that root them in belonging.

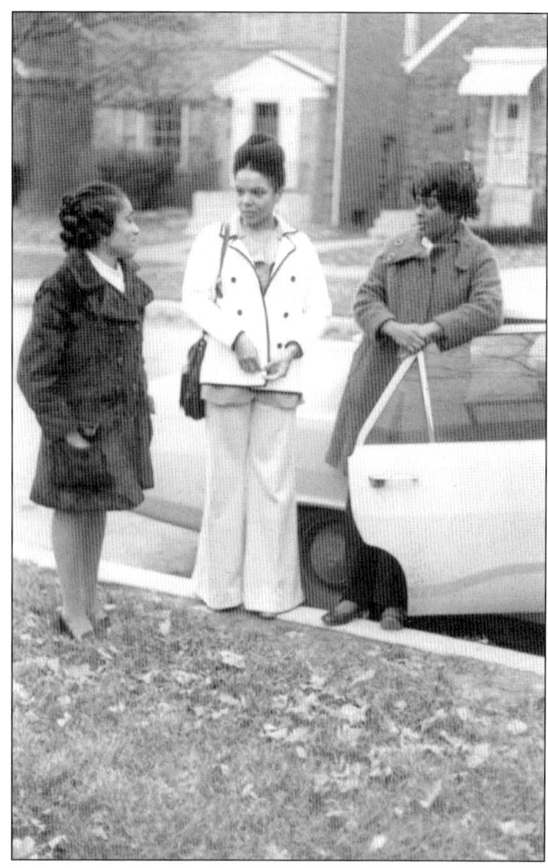

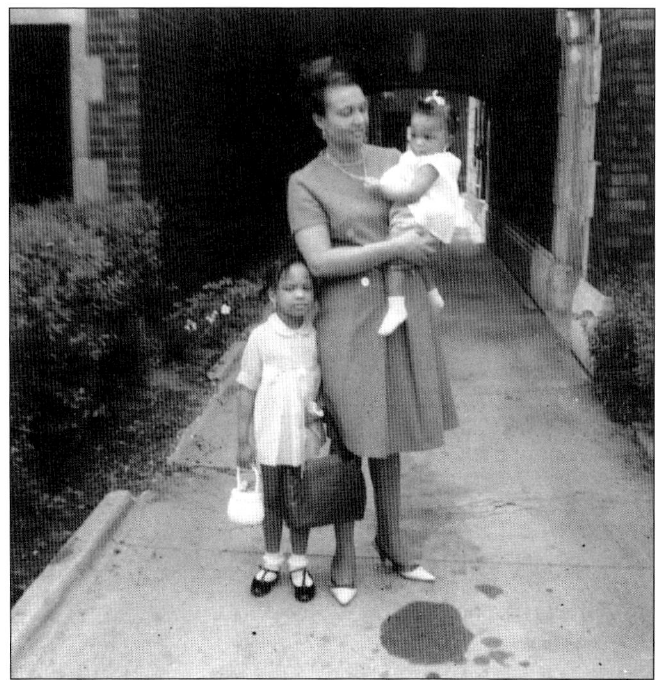

Clyde Street in South Side, Chicago, sketches a warm picture of a mother and two children embracing each other as an ideal example of family bonding. Most likely captured by their father, the photograph depicts his love for photography while capturing urban life's vibrant warmth. It speaks volumes about family bonding in the midst of the hustle and bustle of city life.

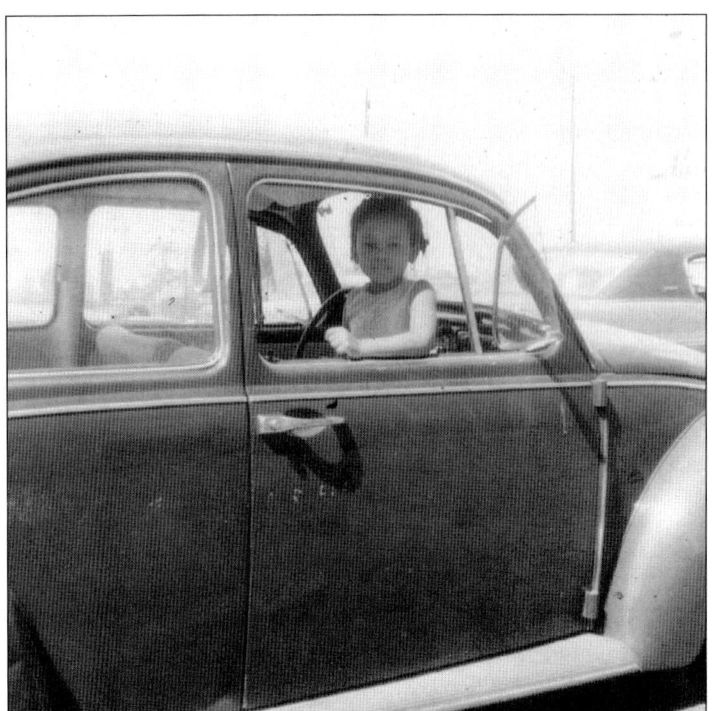

This photograph from the 1970s depicts a young Haitian girl in a Volkswagen. This car is emblematic of her family's pride and roots. A car is more than transport; it signifies commutes, family bonding, and cherished moments. This automobile, as a means of transportation, represents one family's collective experience, hopes, and dreams in the congested streets of Chicago and, most importantly, that of their family bonding.

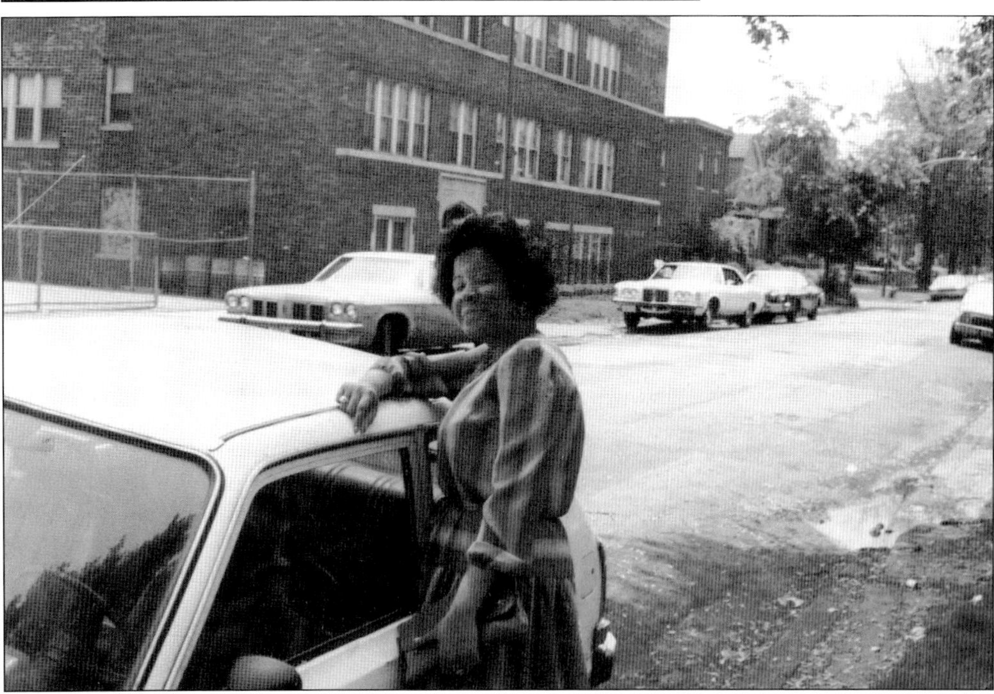

For immigrants, car ownership also represents a milestone that gives them an opportunity for personal freedom and increased mobility. It opens up the labor market, social relationships, and services—a way of engaging more deeply with the new surroundings and continuing their cultural heritage. The car ends up being more than just a means; it becomes part of their integration into society.

In the 1970s, many young Haitians found solace along the vibrant Chicago lakefront, where the beauty of Lake Michigan contrasted with their challenging lives. Amidst laughter and soothing waves, they drew strength from their cultural roots, thus representing hope and resilience in the direction of a brighter future for the bustling city.

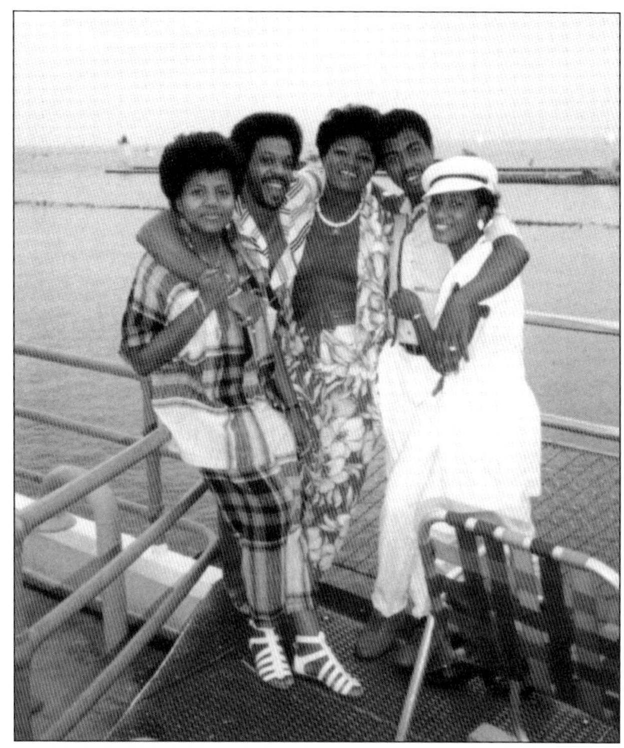

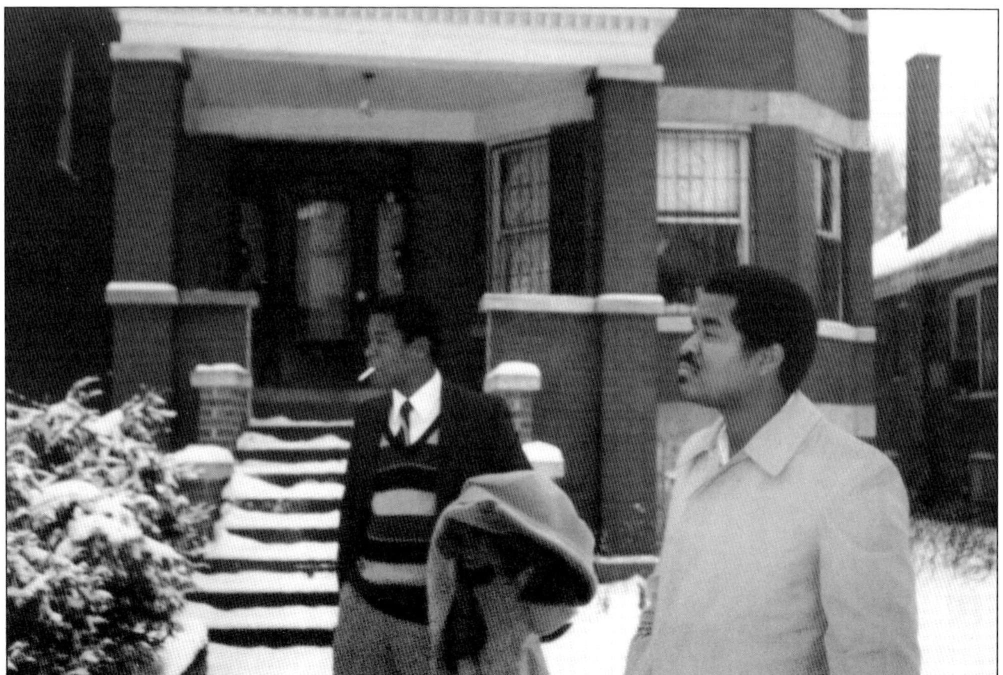

Haitians are accustomed to the warm Caribbean climate, and it is extremely difficult for them to get used to the harsh cold of Chicago winters. This adjustment is reflected in their reluctance to wear coats or their tendency to remove them despite frigid temperatures. Such habits point out the striking difference between their native environment and their new surroundings.

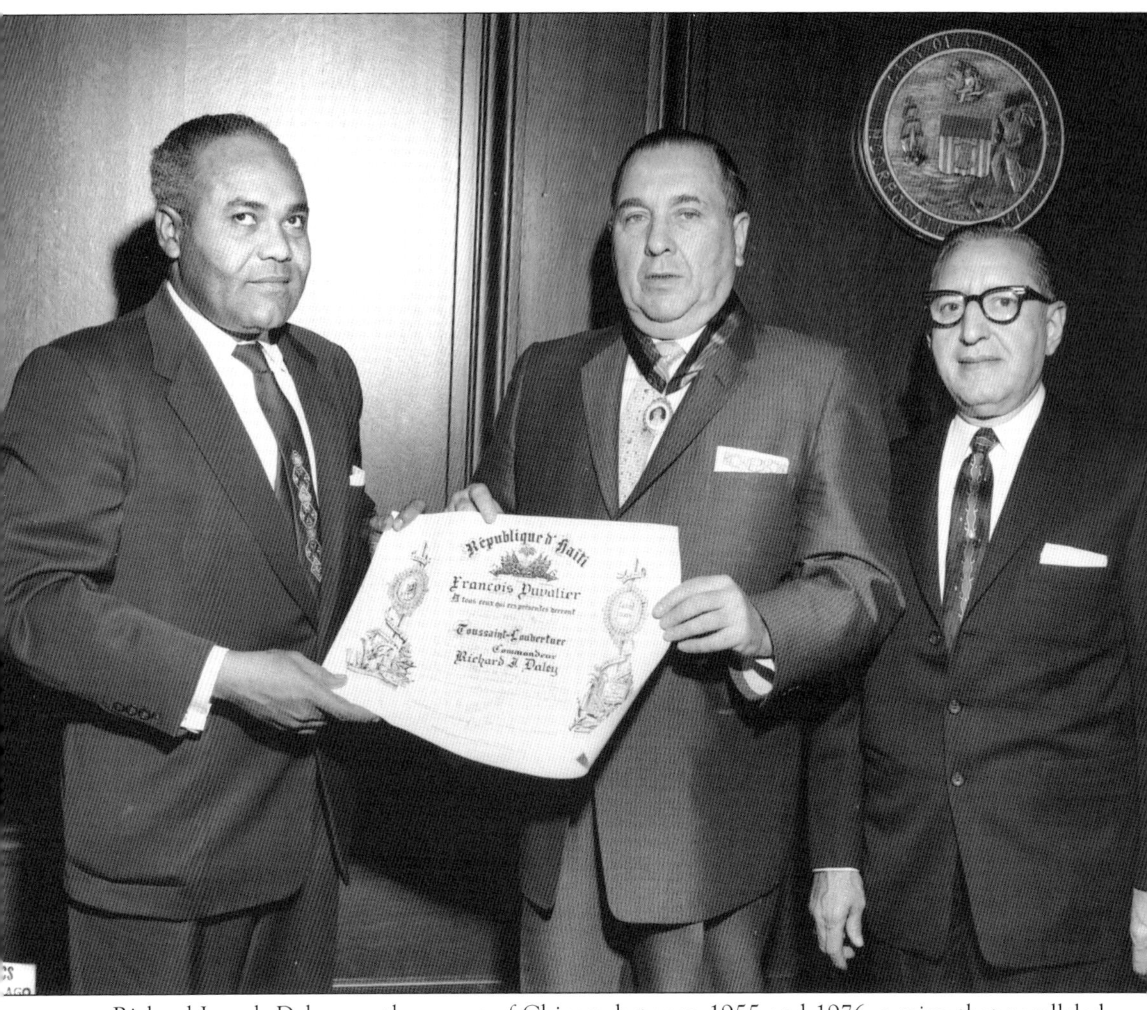

Richard Joseph Daley was the mayor of Chicago between 1955 and 1976, a reign that paralleled Haitian dictator François Duvalier's between 1957 and 1971. A delegate of Duvalier once went on a mission to Chicago and presented a certificate on behalf of his master in what was considered, until then, the most unique moment in the history of the city. This period also saw the first large wave of Haitian immigrants coming to Chicago, enticed by new opportunities and the repressive regime in their country. Haitian immigrants brought new life into the cultural fabric of the city with their traditions, food, and community life. Their stories of resilience and adaptation continue to shape the narrative of Chicago as a diverse urban landscape. The connection between Daley's administration and the Duvalier regime draws out the complex connections of local and global histories. It underlines how political events create migration and community-formation patterns. (Vivian G. Harsh Research Collection.)

It has now turned colorful for many Haitian immigrants who have found their neighborhoods friendly to live in. Full of rich culture and an excellent work ethic, they lighten the area, buying homes and setting up businesses. A thriving community boosts not only the economy of the locale but also adds a certain cultural essence to the South Side, filling it with unity in diversity.

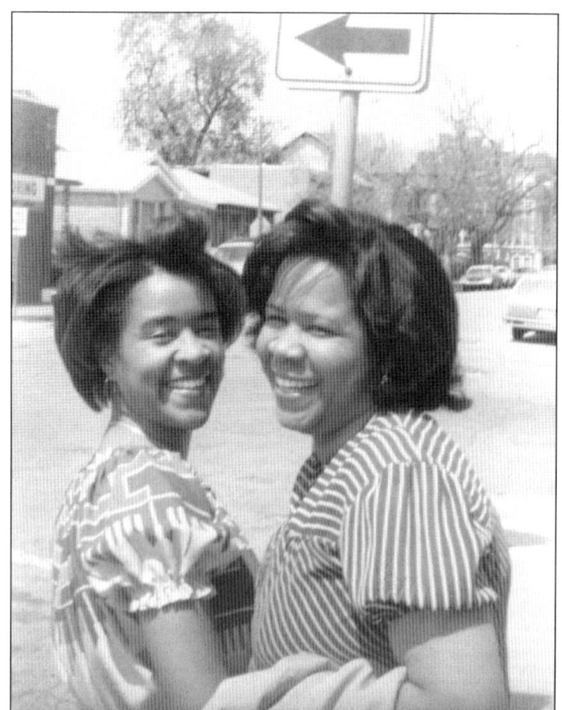

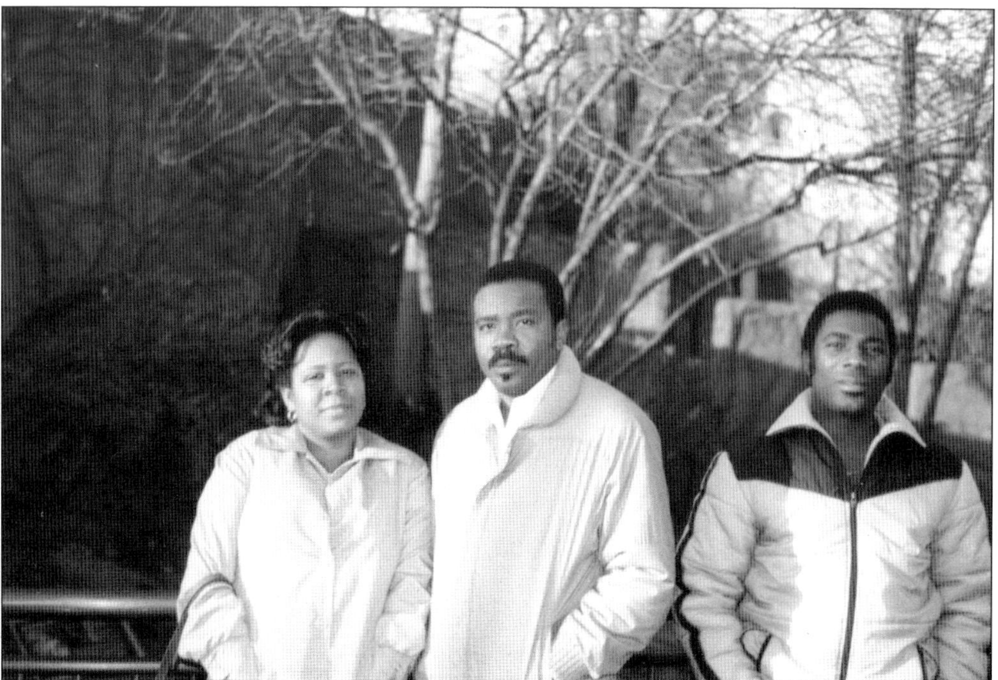

The Haitians have merged into their new home, Chicago, while keeping the beauty of their cultural heritage intact. Their customs are alive with music, food, and the sense of cultural balance that is both Haitian and American. Although they are now physically located somewhere different, the Haitian community continues to share personal tales of their homeland while expressing their excitement to newly opened doors of opportunity in Chicago.

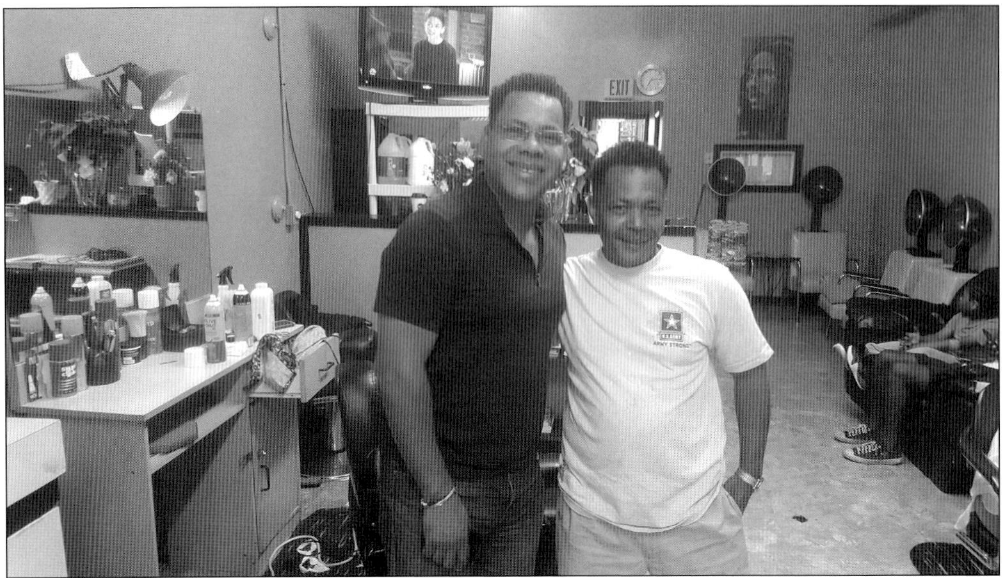

Thervil's Barber Shop, founded by Haitian owner Jean Thervil at Seventy-Fifth Street and Preston Avenue from the 1960s to the 1980s, served as a major gathering point for the Haitian community in Chicago. Here, in this photograph from the 1970s, a popular Haitian entertainer stops by the shop to meet with the local Haitian population. The barbershop is now located at 2249 East Eighty-Third Street.

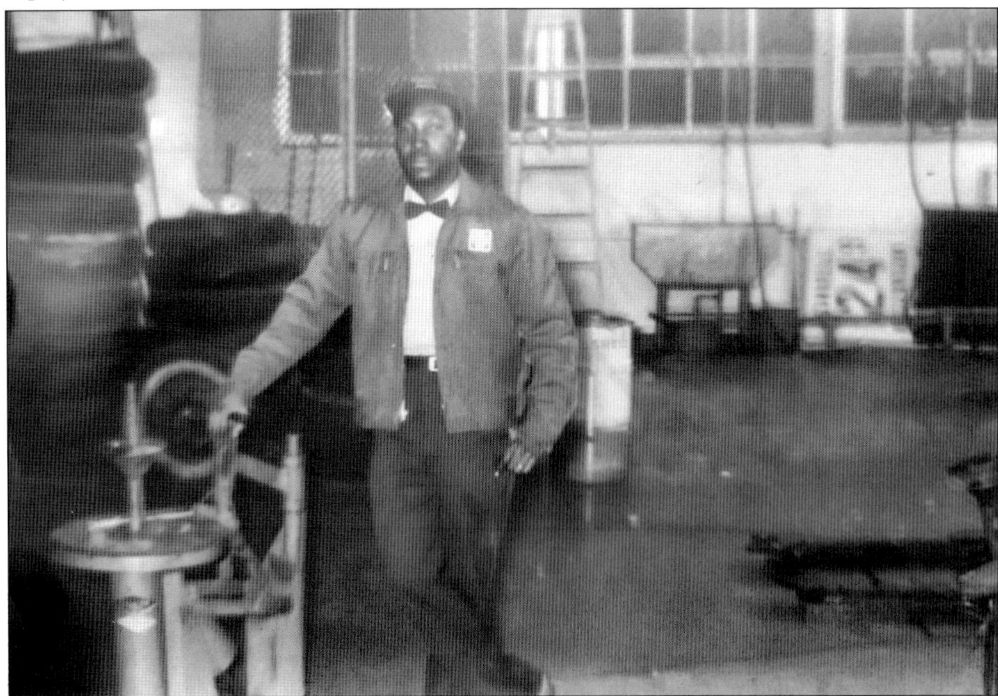

This is the photograph of a hardworking Haitian man who started working at this gas station in the United States. Not only a time for hard work, it was also the moment of a new beginning in life, and thus, determination and resilience going through each challenge of a new country, a man like him symbolizes the best example of hope and opportunities in a new way.

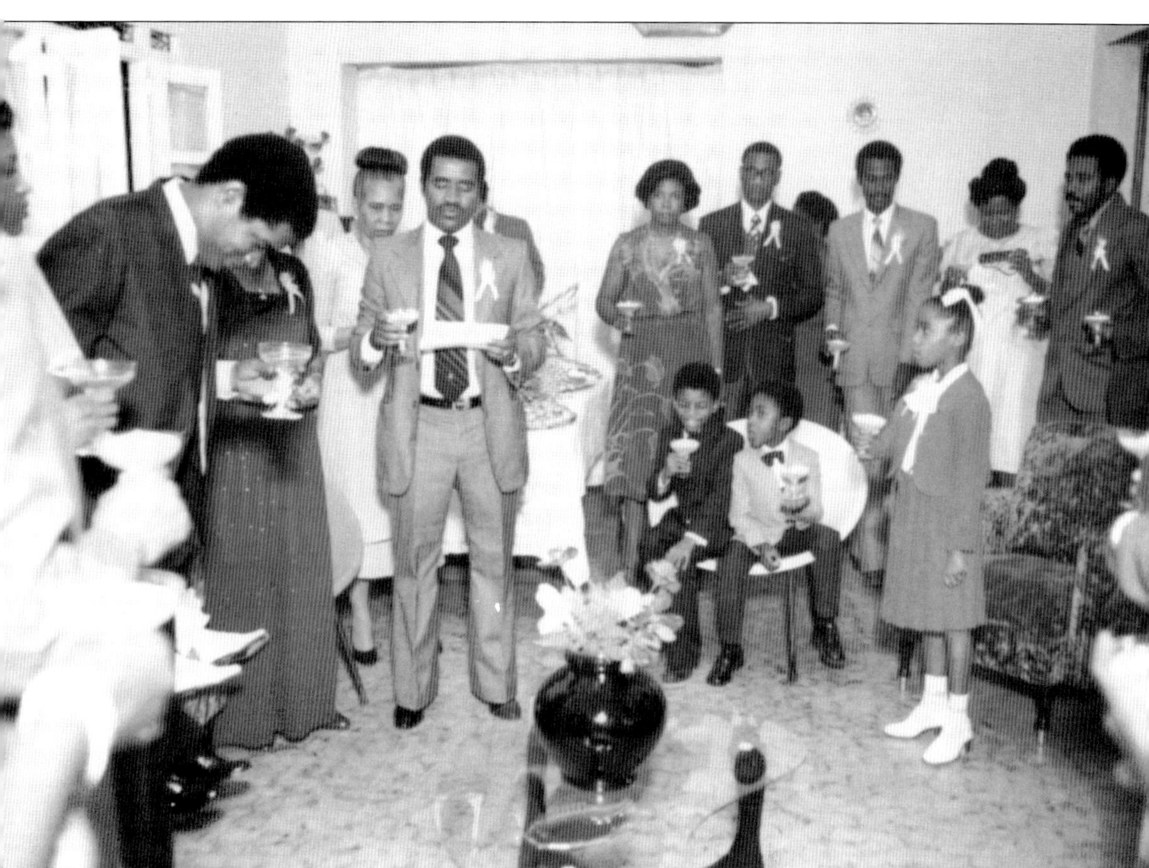

Migration often begins with profound sacrifice—leaving behind familiar landscapes, cherished languages, and close-knit communities in Haiti in pursuit of new possibilities. Yet even amid uncertainty, Haitian families provide continuity, strength, and guidance for the next generation in their new home. Gatherings such as this are more than celebrations; they are living testaments to resilience, shared memory, and the love that binds generations together. In every embrace, in every story retold, fragments of history are carried forward, preserved in hearts and homes. Family becomes both anchor and bridge: grounding the next generation in traditions that endure, while connecting them to new places where identity evolves but never disappears. Migration is not merely a journey of survival, but a journey of preservation. Through family, culture, and shared values, the collective story remains rooted in love, dignity, and belonging.

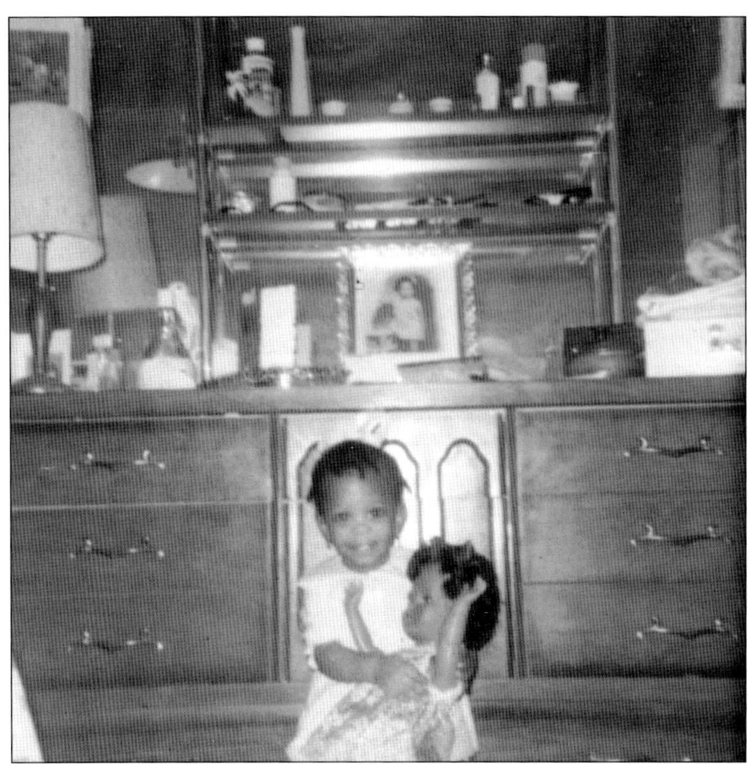

It is uncommon to see a Black child playing with a Black doll, yet Haitian families often prioritize instilling a strong sense of identity within the home. In this image, the Haitian girl embraces a Black doll, symbolizing comfort and security. This nurturing connection highlights the importance of representation and the emotional bonds that help shape a child's self-esteem and cultural identity.

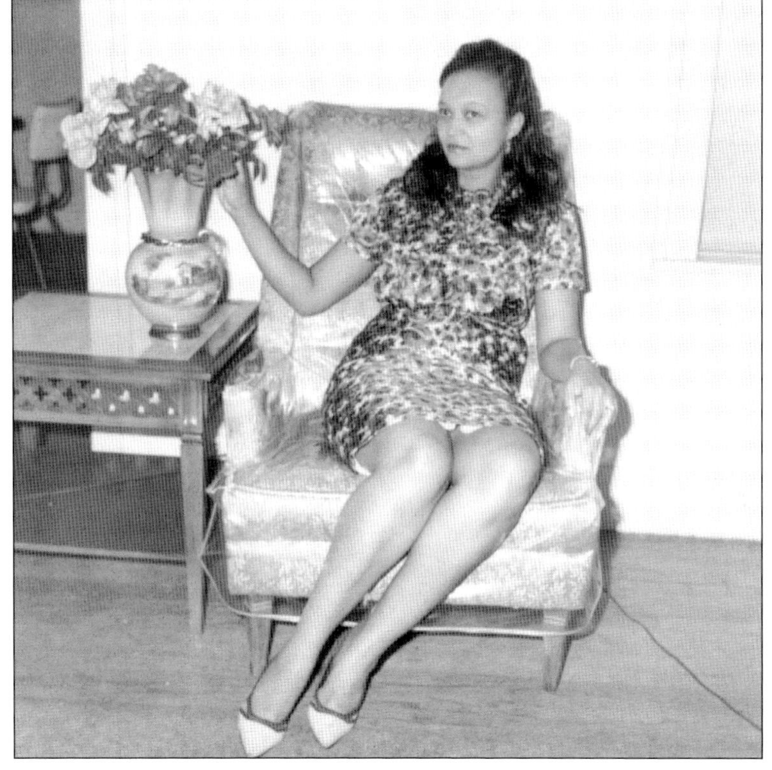

This image represents the resilience of the immigrant influx into the city of Chicago during the 1960s. Most of them were running away from the repressive Duvalier regime. The Haitian immigrants were mostly educated individuals who easily adapted to the new environment. They were less like immigrants, as their immigration was not induced on the basis of economic reasons; rather, they felt threatened by the political and social situations in Haiti.

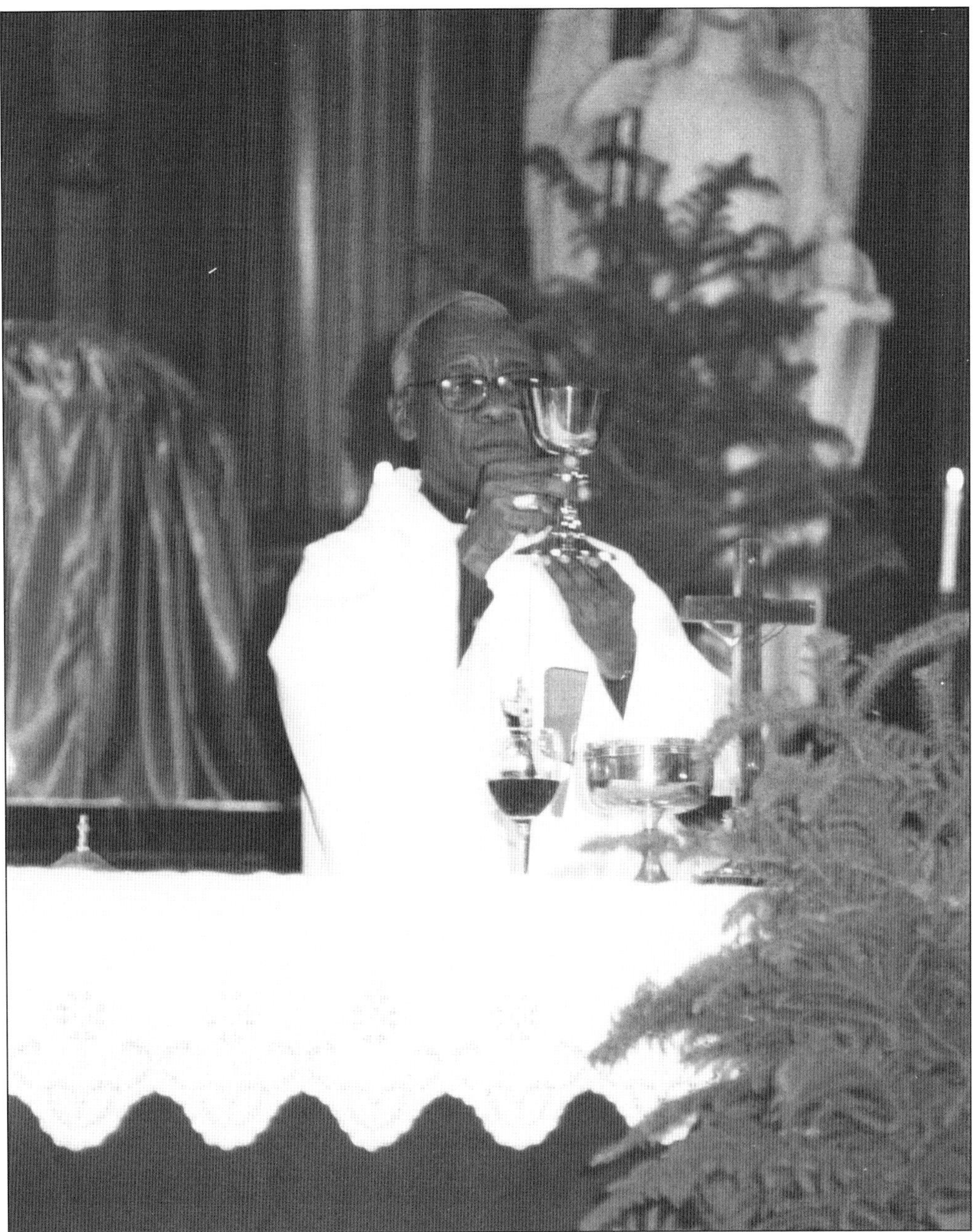

Religion is a critical aspect of daily living for most Haitians and gives many an important sense of stability and bonding. This fact has given impetus to Chicago to have its priests give a touch of home and perpetuate the bond through continuous culture. These same priests, during special masses, celebrate their faith but also reinforce bonds with members of the diaspora.

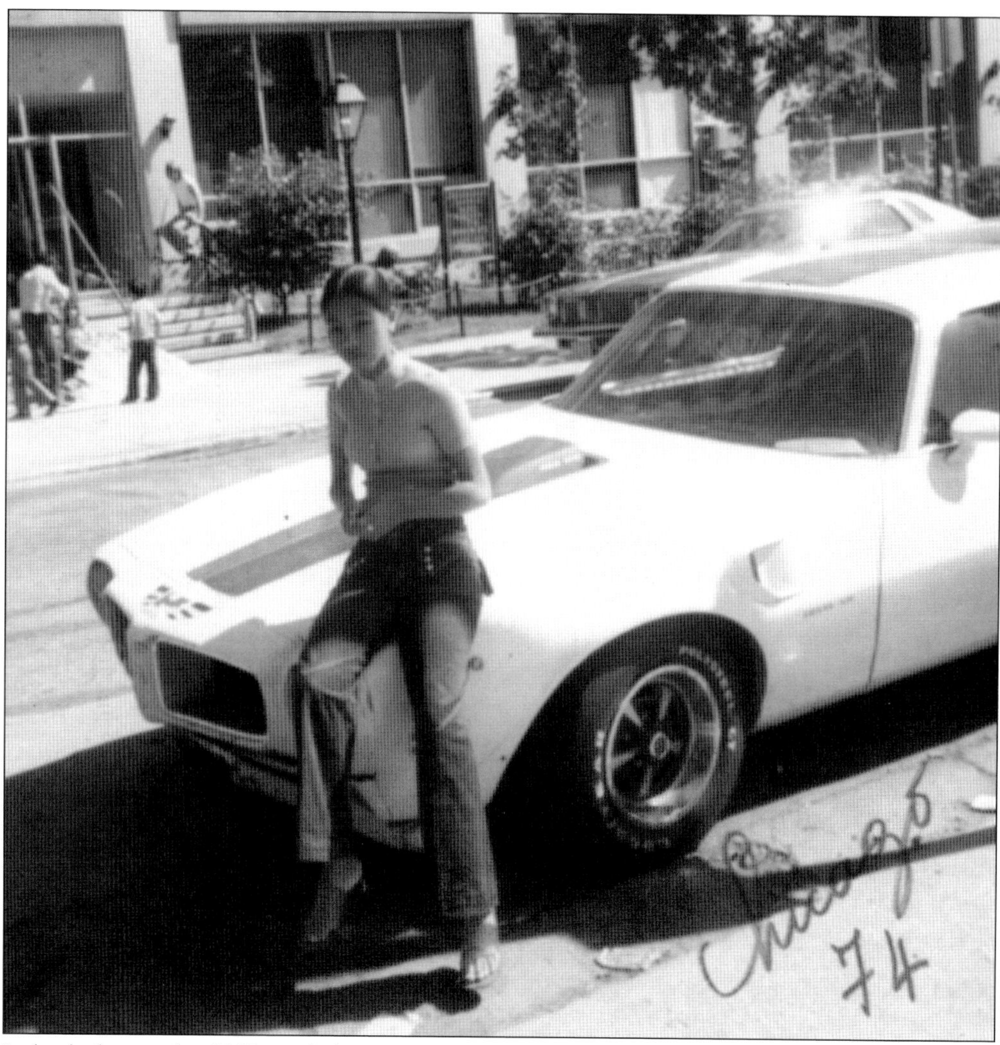

Indeed, during the 1960s and the 1970s, many young Haitians were sent to live with relatives in Haiti due to the hard times that were mostly associated with them while in Chicago. The kids would return during the summer break to the United States to reunite with their parents, a meeting of two worlds. One touching example is a young girl, who, in 1974, reflects upon her experience as an immigrant through the intricacies of maintaining a dual culture. She discusses the struggle to balance her Haitian heritage with the American way of life and the feelings of belonging and alienation that often plagued her. She enjoyed the warmth and family traditions in Haiti, but at the same time, she wanted to seek out opportunities and freedom in the United States. Her story is the embodiment of the hardship faced by many young immigrants while managing an intricate tapestry of identity, family, and cultural expectations in a world that feels divided between two homes.

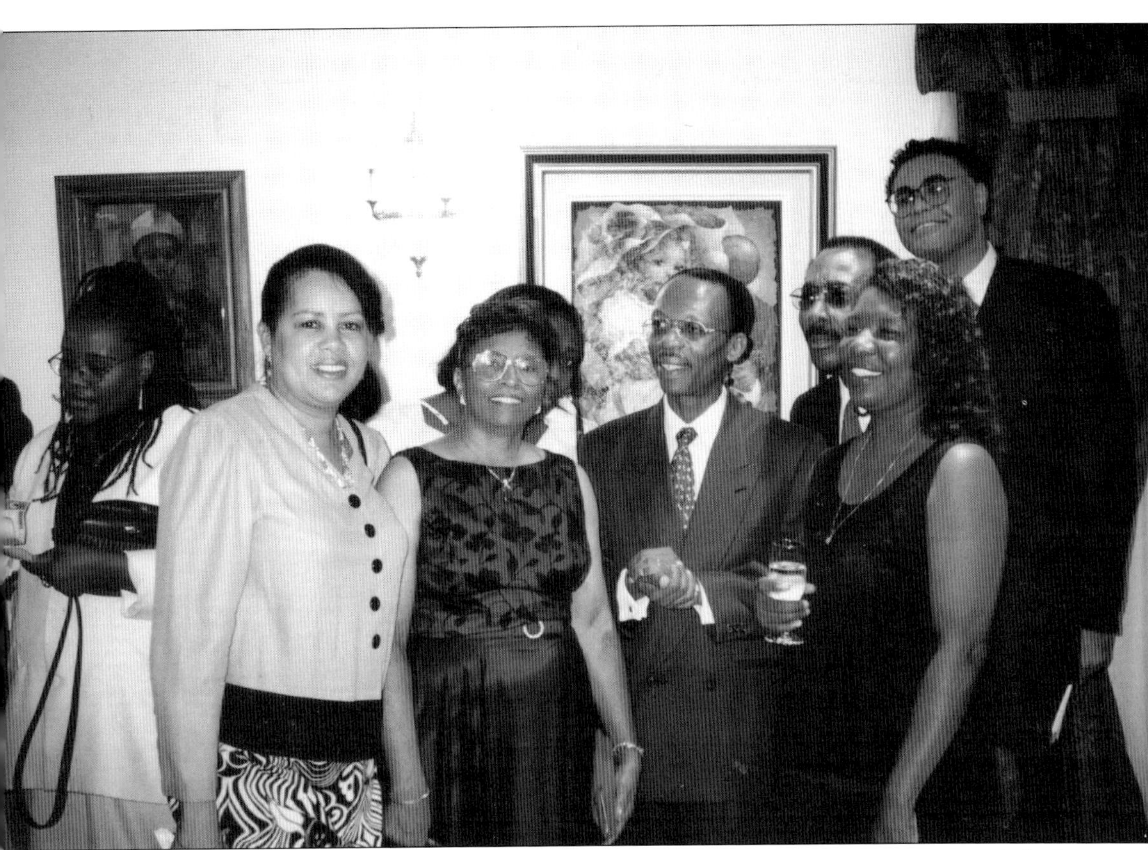

Jean-Bertrand Aristide entered the Haitian presidency from 1991 to 1994. During such high political unrest, he came to Chicago to speak with local Haitian community leaders about how connected Haiti's struggles were with those of its diaspora. This era also saw a great number of Haitian immigrants coming to the United States and, more particularly, to Chicago, adding great cultural richness to the city. These new arrivals brought not only diversity, but they also put a face on the difficulties faced by people trying to flee instability in their home country. Their stories reflect the greater immigration narrative, epitomizing people's resilience to make lives worth living amidst the complexities of displacement. The troubles around Aristide's presidency and interactions with the Haitian community in Chicago detail how political events can drive migration, along with expectations of misfortunes immigrants face. More importantly, these dynamics underscore profound global events occurring for immigrants with local communities and the immigrant experience.

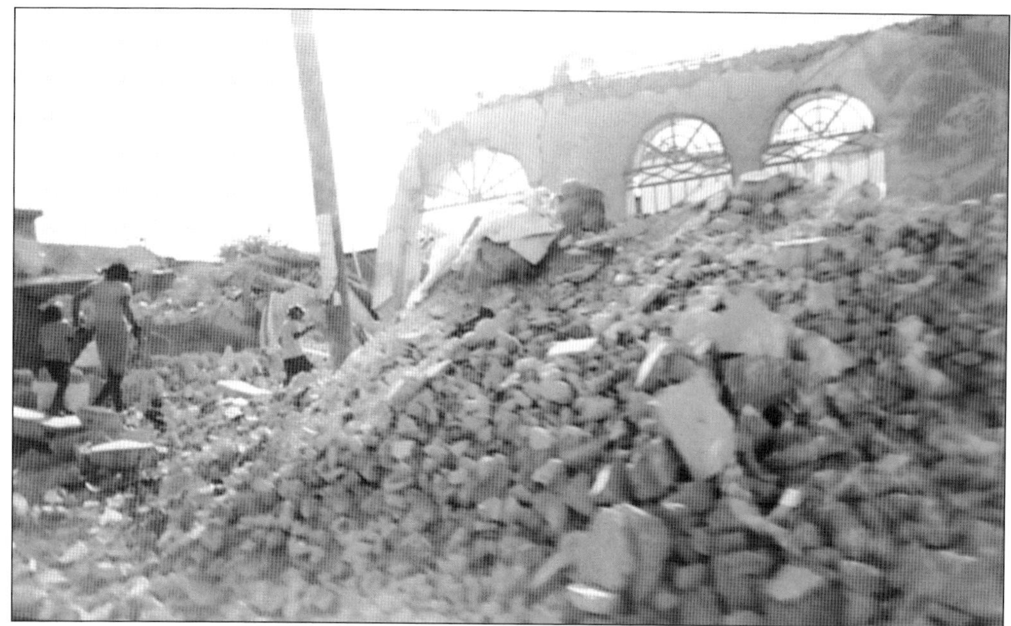

Temporary Protection Status (TPS) has been a key vehicle for Haitians in desperate need of escape from the harsh realities that immediately followed the earthquake in 2010. This allows them to find shelter and work, ensuring their families' survival in the United States. Applications have been continuously extended due to ongoing crises, but TPS remains uncertain amidst legal challenges, a call for international solidarity, and the many complexities of immigration policies.

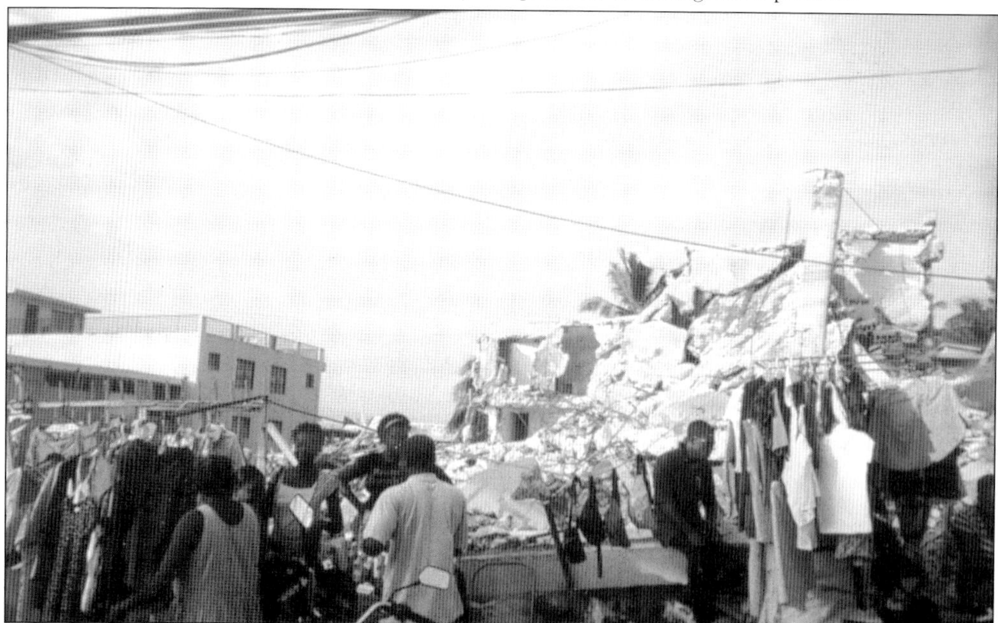

Fifteen years after the deadliest earthquake in 2010, survivors continue to show strength and resilience. Many struggled, piecing together their lives from within, building new businesses and finding support for the education of their children. Much difficulty is still being overcome today. Though the scars of their losses are so deep, these people are the embodiment of hope and determination.

Four

Haitians in Academia

Haitians in Chicago form a vibrant migrant community. Migrating mostly since the 1960s, they are part of a larger wave of immigrants. Haitians migrate mainly to the United States but also to Canada, France, and lately, due to gang violence, to the Dominican Republic. In the Chicago area, including the suburbs, they number from 30,000 to 35,000, according to leaders in the community. That number is increasing quickly because of a combination of factors, including Biden's administration policy—the Humanitarian Parole—providing temporary legal status to Cubans, Nicaraguans, Venezuelans, and Haitians.

This chapter focuses on Haitians who are part of academia and linked in one way or another to the city of Chicago. Some of them have studied, taught, or still teach there. Others have lived in the city before moving elsewhere. Still others have been integrated because of their commitment to the city of Chicago and the Haitian community. The educators or scholars are faculty at schools, colleges, and universities and provide conferences and seminars. They are or have been part of an academic community, either in Chicago or elsewhere, and are at all levels of the academic spectrum, from elementary schools to colleges and universities. They come from different fields, both in the social sciences and experimental sciences.

Their work constitutes an important contribution to the development of their respective discipline and/or to the growth of the Haitian community. Some of them, like Michel-Rolph Trouillot, have reached international recognition, and their intellectual contribution is acknowledged in colleges and universities. Others, like Jean-Claude Brizard, have occupied prominent positions in the administration of the City of Chicago or elsewhere.

Still, the limited selection of scholars in this book does not do justice to the set of Chicago-linked Haitians in academia. Therefore, the reader is invited to consider the Haitian scholars presented here as a sample rather than an exhaustive population.

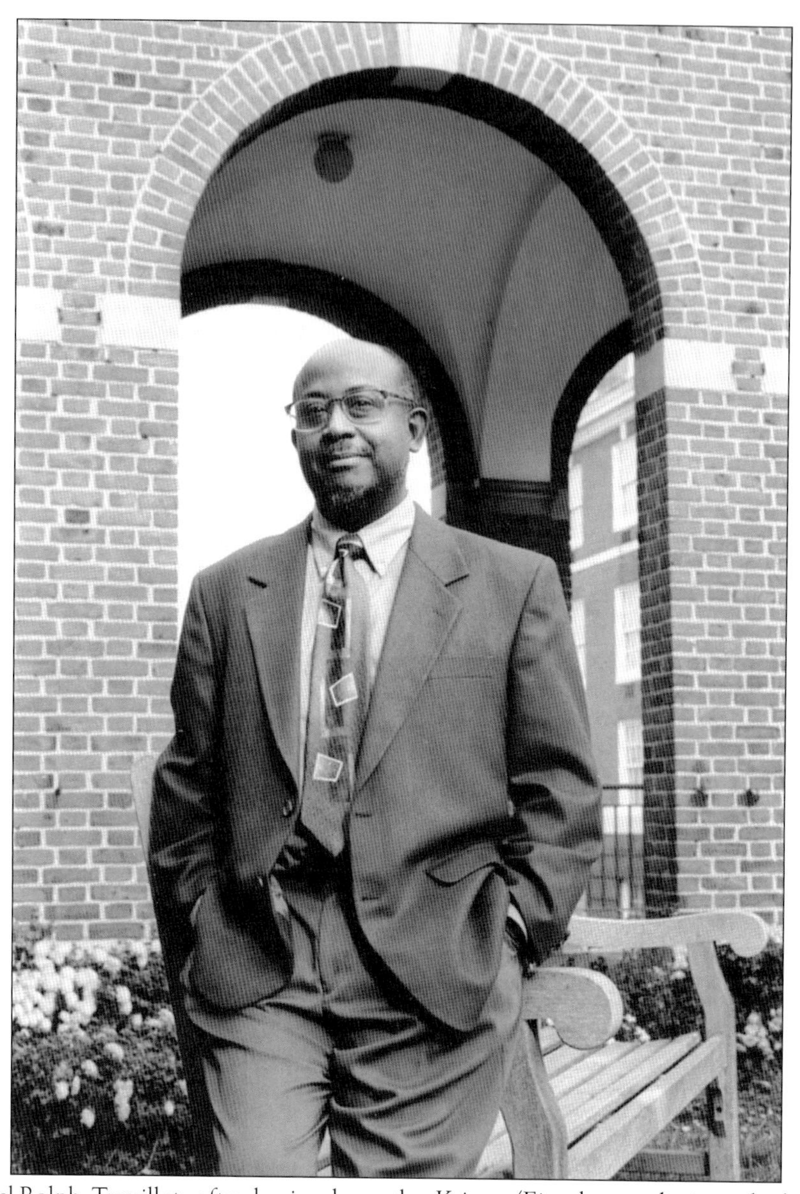

Dr. Michel-Rolph Trouillot, after having been the Krieger/Eisenhower distinguished professor of anthropology and director of the Institute for Global Studies in culture, power, and history at Johns Hopkins University, joined the University of Chicago as a professor of anthropology. He first became known in Haiti for the publication of the first book-length social science work written in Haitian Creole, *Ti dife boule sou Istwa Ayiti*, 1977 (second edition, 2012). (The English version is *Stirring the Pot of Haitian History*, 2021.) Another important book, *Les racines historiques de l'État duvaliérien*, 1986, was published soon after the Duvalier dictatorship ended. (The English version is *Haiti, State Against Nation, The Origins and Legacy of Duvalierism*, 1990). He became an internationally renowned scholar with the publication of *Silencing the Past: Power and the Production of History* in 1995. He also published *Global Transformations: Anthropology and the Modern World*, 2003. Trouillot's work influenced scholars worldwide and can be said to be the origin of the wave of seminal works published in the United States on Haitian history and, particularly, on the Haitian Revolution and its symbolism. (University of Chicago.)

Born in Haiti, Serge J.C. Pierre-Louis, MD, MPH, left his country after graduating from medical school. He then specialized in neurology, epilepsy, and public health. Dr. Pierre-Louis has been on faculty at Rush University for over 30 years as associate professor of neurology and on staff at Stroger Cook County Hospital, where he teaches neurology and epilepsy. He has also volunteered at several hospitals in Haiti over the years.

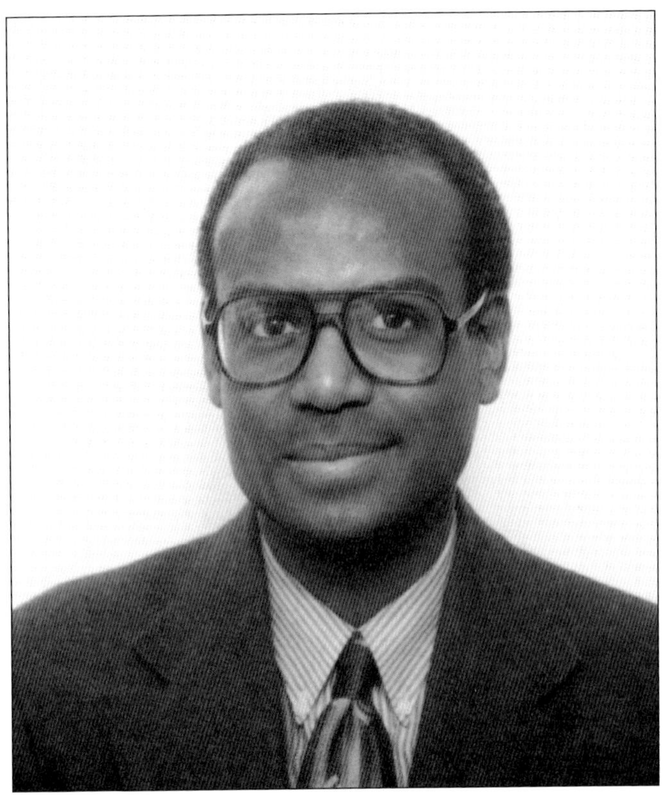

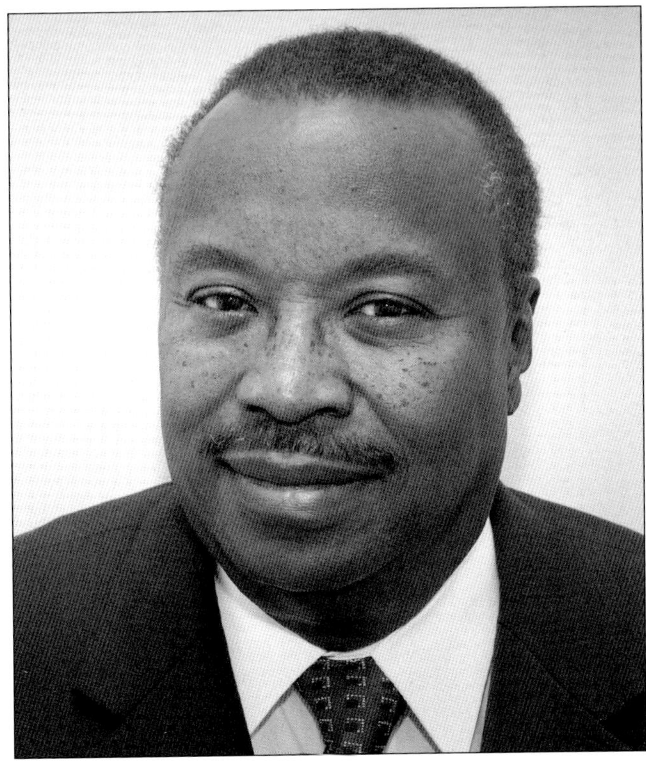

Jean C. Alexandre was born and raised in Haiti. He held a series of positions in academia, serving as a clinician and assistant professor at Loyola University Medical Center. He cared deeply about the Chicago Haitian community and his home country. Dr. Alexandre was nominated as Haitian ambassador to the United Nations and served from 2001 to 2003. He passed away in April 2023.

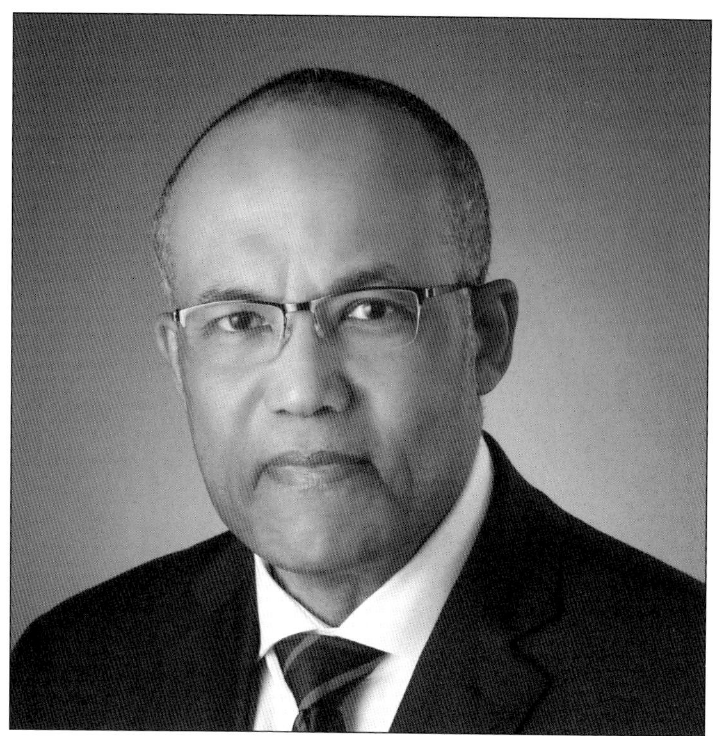

Dr. Ludovic Comeau Jr. is a Haitian-born graduate in business and law from the State University of Haiti, with a masters of business administration and a doctorate from universities in the United States. He is an associate professor at DePaul University and a recognized economist who has contributed to the development and civil society of Haiti through research and initiatives such as Groupe de Reflexion et D'Action pour une Haiti Nouvelle (GRAHN), which translates to "Think Tank and Action Group for a New Haiti."

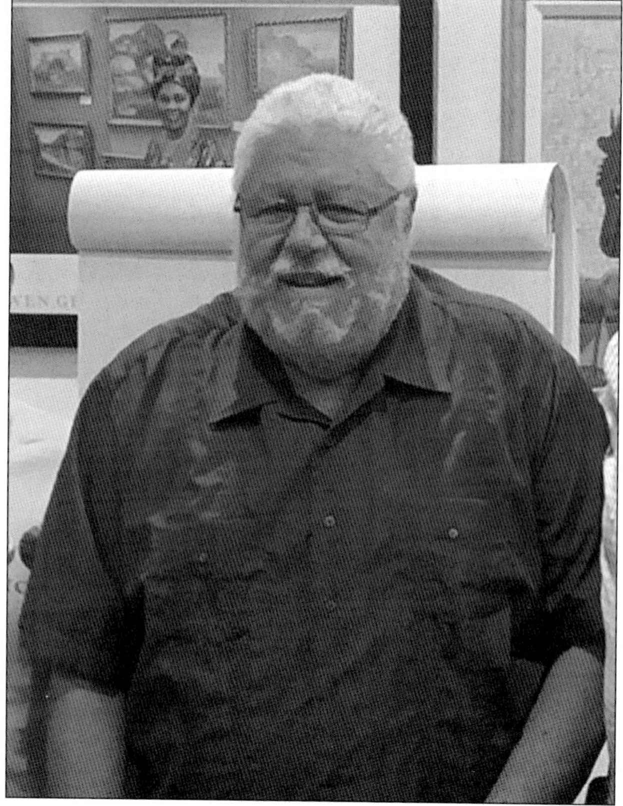

Dr. Patrick Bellegarde-Smith is an emeritus professor in both international relations and African American studies at the University of Wisconsin-Milwaukee. His focus was generally on the Caribbean culture and political economy. He has further conducted much research into the Afro-Caribbean religions and the Vodun. A most regarded peer, he presided over several learned societies and is a prolific author and even a Vodou priest himself.

Dr. Johnny Laforet is a Fulbright scholar and lecturer at Princeton University. He received his doctorate in French linguistics, second language acquisition, and teacher education from the University of Illinois at Urbana-Champaign in August 2016. In 2022, Dr. Laforet published his book *Haitian Creole Maintenance in the Greater Chicago Area*, which examines language maintenance and transmission by Haitian immigrants in the greater Chicago area.

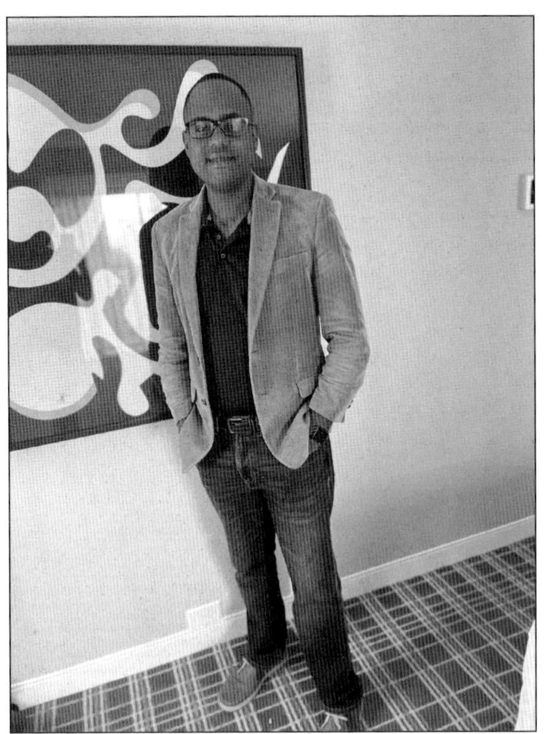

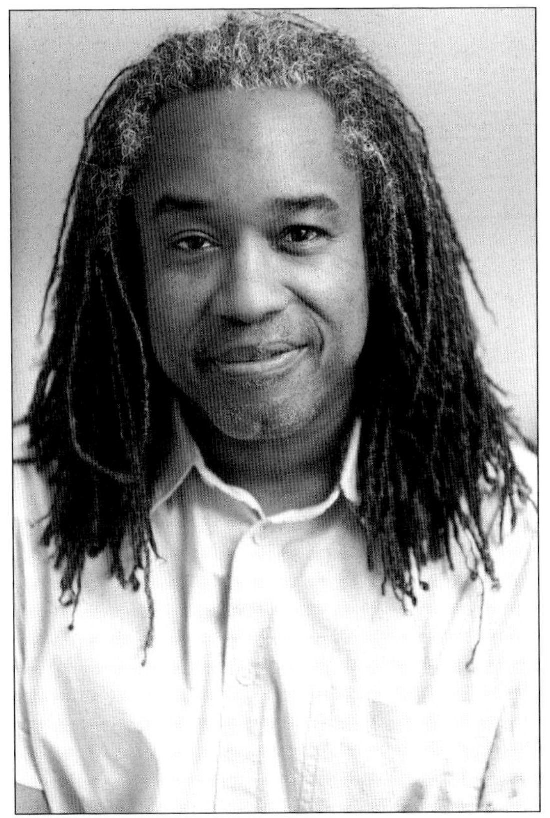

Mario LaMothe is an assistant professor of Black studies and anthropology at the University of Illinois at Chicago, where he received his doctorate in performance studies from Northwestern University. His work examines queer life and social justice in Haiti and the Caribbean, and he is a frequent collaborator on scholarly and artistic projects related to African diasporic women.

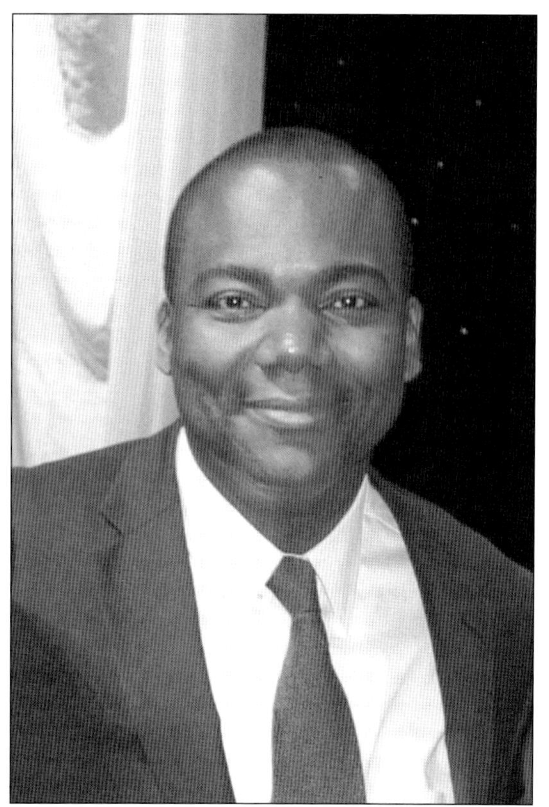

Jean Claude Brizard was born in Port-au-Prince, Haiti. He completed his education at the City University of New York. He served as the chief executive officer (CEO) of Chicago Public Schools from 2011 to 2012. He is now the CEO and president at Digital Promise. The company is a global, nonpartisan, nonprofit organization that focuses on accelerating innovation in education.

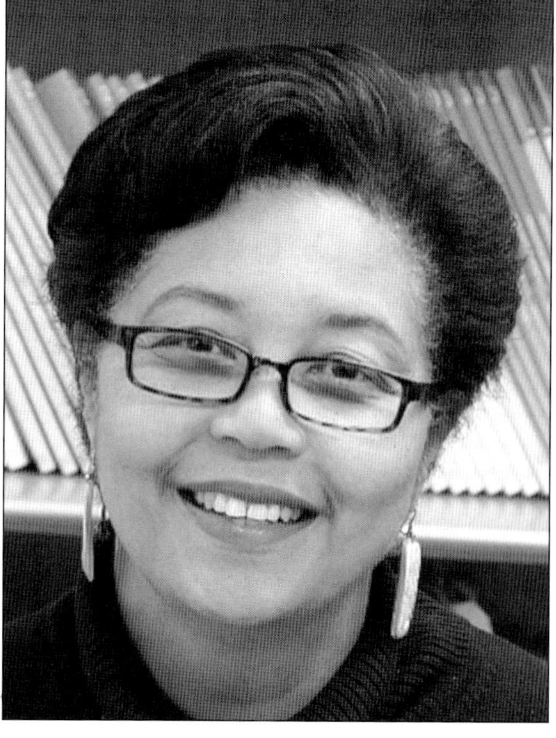

Nadia André was born and raised in Port-au-Prince, Haiti. After completing her postsecondary degree in bilingual studies at Christ the King School, she moved to Chicago, where she earned a bachelor's degree in computer science and a minor in international/intercultural studies from Northeastern Illinois University and a master's degree from DePaul University. She teaches French at DePaul University and North Park University.

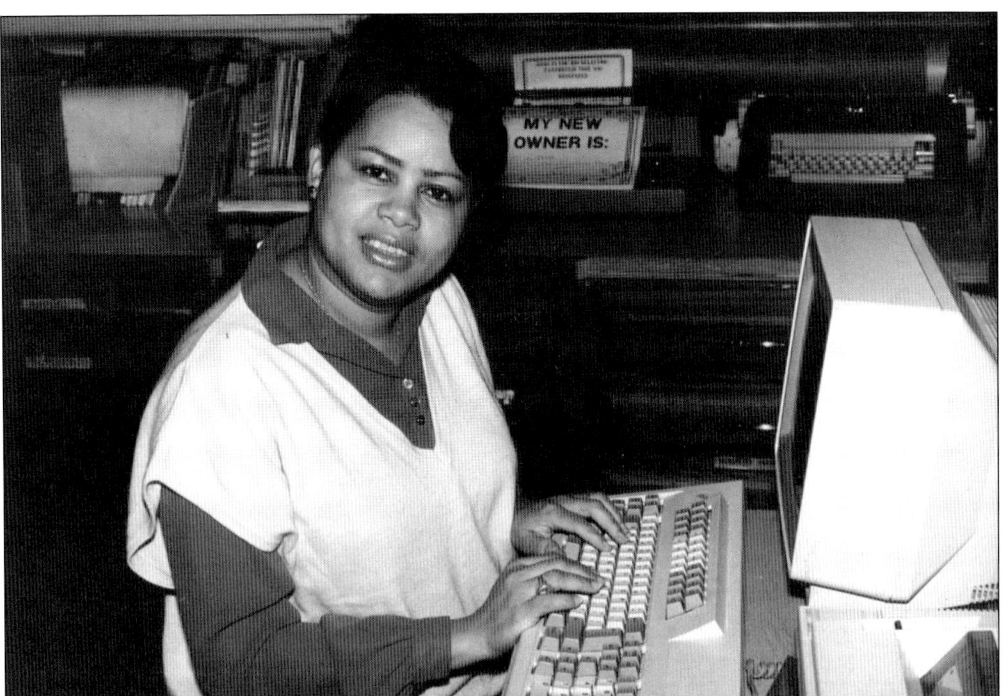

Aliette Marcelin launched her career in education in the 1980s as a certified teacher with the State of Illinois, holding a bachelor's degree in secondary education and a master's degree in teaching English as a second language and an endorsement in bilingual education in French and Haitian Kreyol. She retired from the Evanston School District after 25 years to later join the faculty at Oakton College in Skokie in adult education.

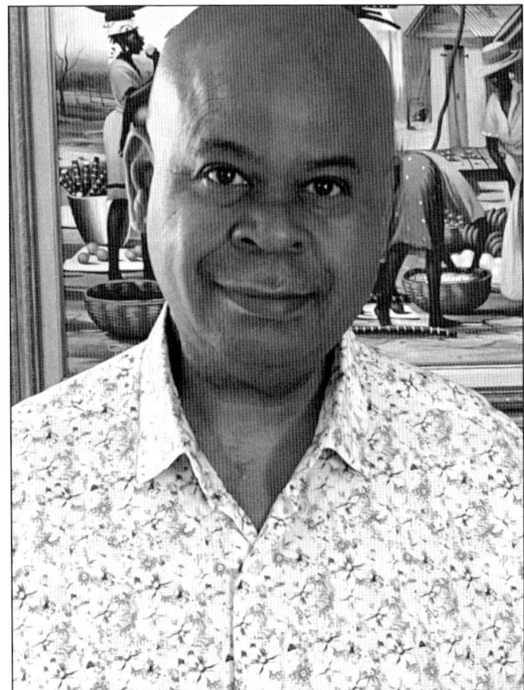

Michel Acacia, a sociologist who studied in Chicago, teaches Haitian Creole at the Haitian American Museum of Chicago and has taught at the University Caraibes and at the State University of Haiti. A member of the Société Haïtienne d'Histoire, he is the author of *Être ou ne pas être, La gestion de la souveraineté nationale en Haïti 1804–1934.*

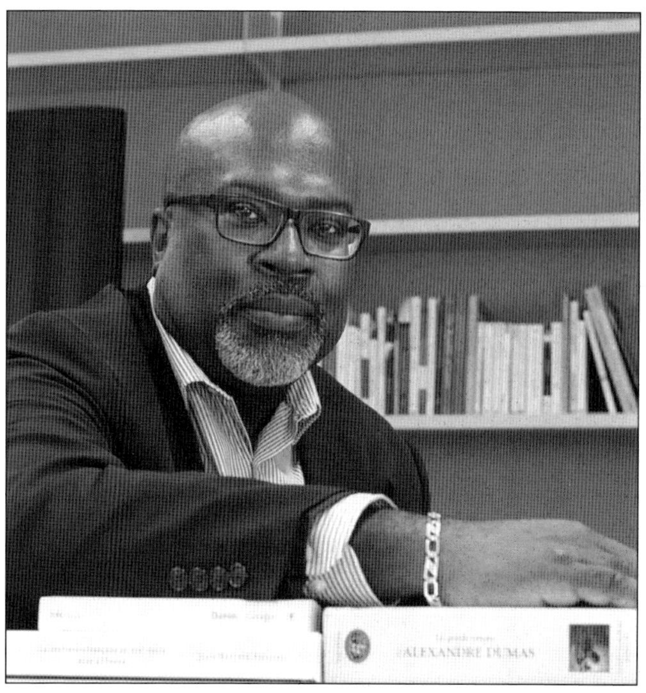

Daniel Desormeaux is the William D. & Robin Mayer professor of arts and sciences. He has held tenured positions at the University of Chicago and the University of Kentucky, which he joined after beginning his career at Dartmouth College. He has received numerous research awards, including a National Endowment for the Humanities Fellowship and a residential fellowship at the Franke Institute for the Humanities.

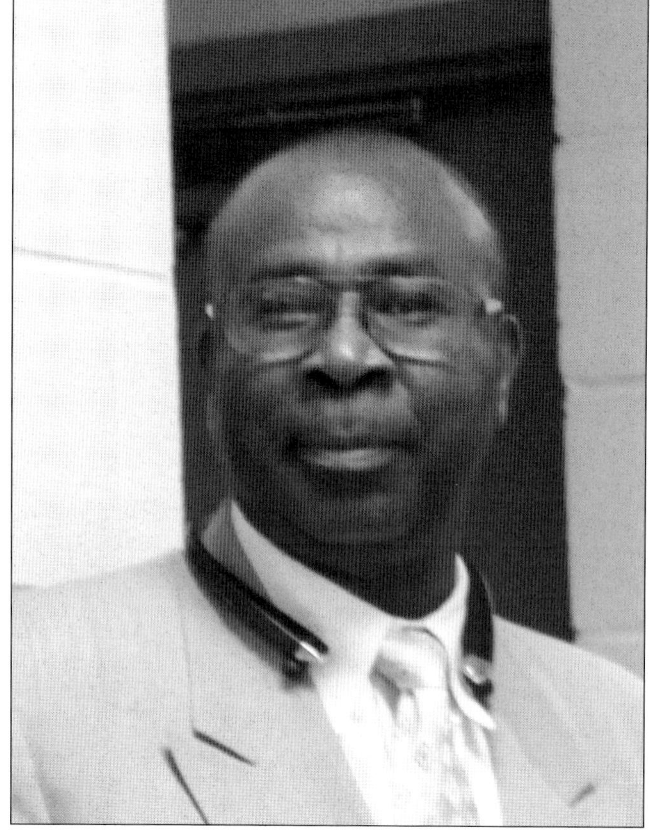

Dr. Jean Franco Valdemar is a native of Haiti and teaches as an adjunct professor at Trinity International University. He is a pastor at the Eglise Evangelist Bethel of Chicago and teaches music at various venues in the Chicagoland area. He is an active member of the Chicago Haitian community and dedicated to helping the underprivileged in his home country.

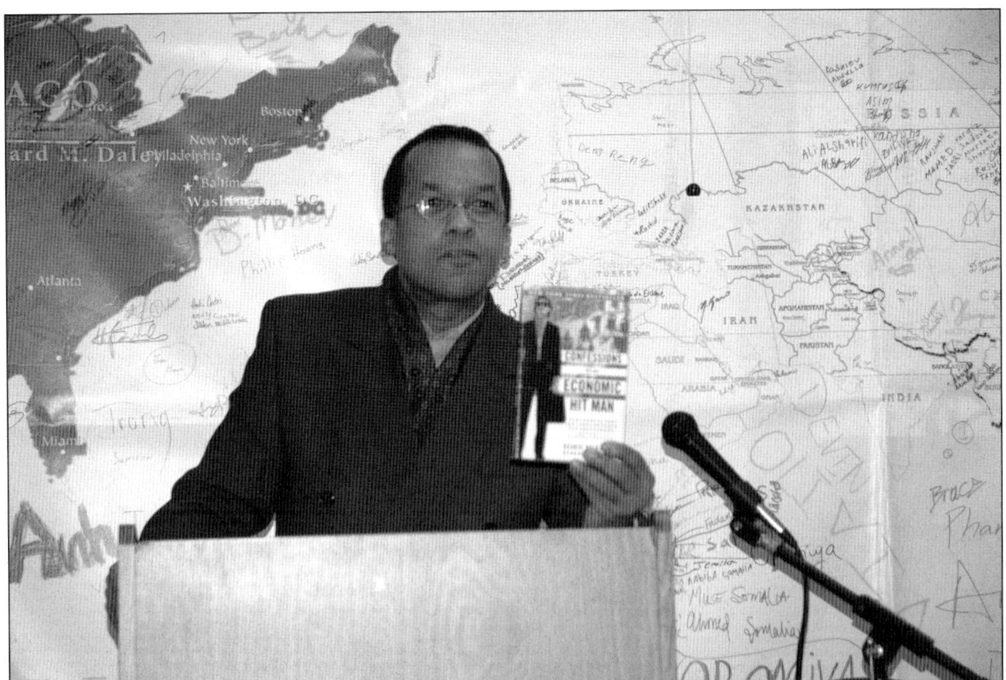

William Leslie Balan-Gaubert has received training in philosophy, history, psychology, and social thought. He has studied in Haiti, France, and the United States. He is a former lecturer in the Department of Romance Languages and Literature and the Center for Latin American and Caribbean Studies at the University of Chicago. He teaches critical thinking in the Collegiate Scholars Summer Program at the University of Chicago. (University of Chicago.)

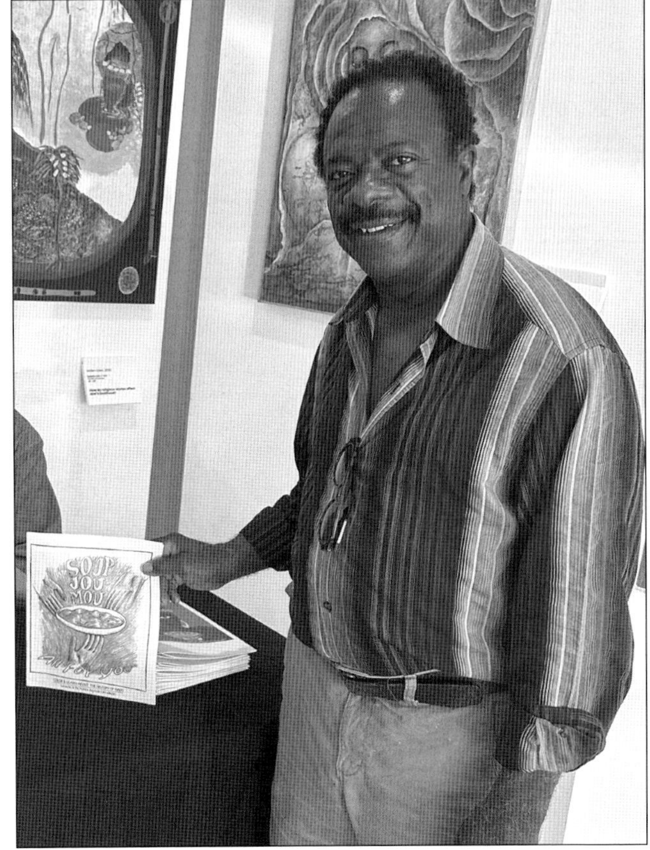

Marc Rosier is an educator at Chicago Public Schools and was a lecturer at City College of Chicago. He has extensive experience in the educational sector, both at the school level and the college level. He is also the author of *Chicago's Authentic Founder, Jean Baptiste Point DuSable or Haitian Secret Agent in the Old Northwest Outpost 17451818*.

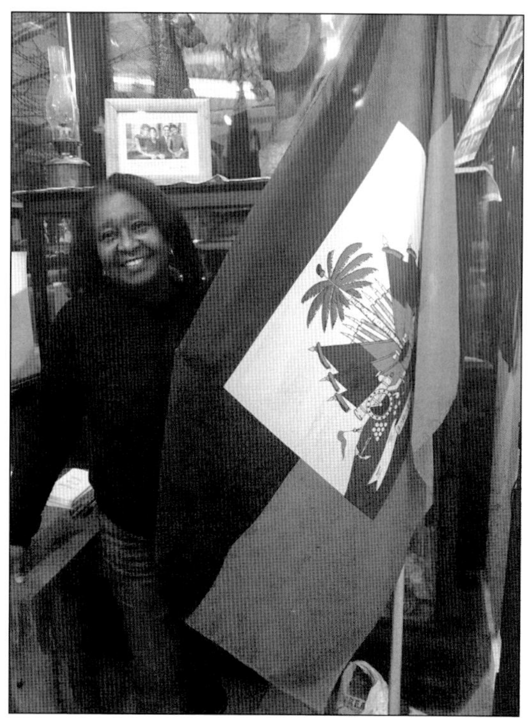

Elsie Hector Hernandez was born in Port-au-Prince, Haiti, and immigrated to New York as a child. She has been an adjunct professor in the departments of nursing and biology at the Chicago Community Colleges for the last decade or more. She obtained a nursing degree and a bachelor's degree in romance languages in New York. She received a master's degree in public health from the University of Illinois at Chicago.

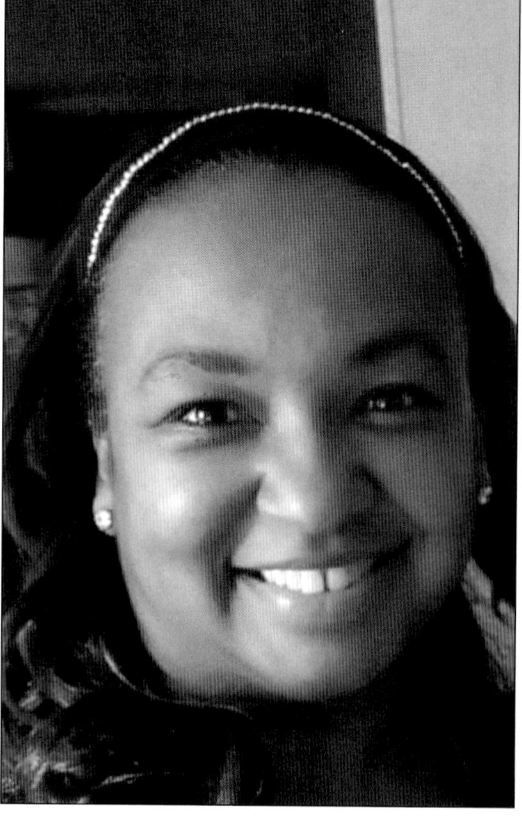

Myriam Souffrant was born in Haiti and immigrated to Chicago as a child. She has worked as a French, Spanish, and ESL (English as a second language) teacher in the public school system in the Chicago Suburb School District of South Holland and at the university level for the past 15 years. Her goal is to educate others to become internationally minded, socially conscious individuals with the attitudes of productive global citizens.

Five

Haitians in Culture, the Arts, History, and Community

In this multicultural American society, the contributions of the Haitian community in arts, culture, history, and sports are noticeable in the past and present. Nowadays, the younger generation considers themselves not as Americans but as Haitian Americans.

One of the most popular activities that the community enjoyed the most was the explosion of grand balls and festivals almost every month during the 1960s and 1970s. There were two nightclubs in the South Side that hosted major orchestras like Tabou Combo, Ska Sha, Coupé Clouré, Orchestre Septentrional du Cap, and others.

As early as the 1970s, Haitians have grouped themselves to lobby the City of Chicago so that a statue be erected in honor of Jean Baptiste Point DuSable, the first resident and businessman of Chicago from Haiti.

The period of the 1980s was the "Golden Age" of the Chicago Haitian community because the City of Chicago hosted several events. A radio program was produced in 1981 by Caricréole and the French Cultural Services of the Consulate General of France. The first Haitian Film Festival was also produced by Caricréole and the Film Center of the School of the Art Institute of Chicago. A featured presentation was made possible by the International House of the University of Chicago. A group of Haitian men produced the radio program *Bonjour Soleil*, which lasted more than two decades.

In sports, a Haitian soccer player, Franz Mathieu, led the Chicago Sting soccer team and won the national cup during the Soccer Bowl in 1981 and 1984.

In 1987, a major art exhibit was organized by the Chicago Cultural Center of the city in collaboration with The DuSable Black History Museum and Education Center and Nicole Smith, Haitian art dealer and gallerist. Not too long after, Marjorie Vincent, a young Haitian American woman raised in Illinois, became the first Black woman to become Miss America.

The 21st century is witnessing more and more participation of Haitians: Kwame Raoul became Illinois attorney general; Lionel Jean Baptiste, past alderman of Evanston, became a circuit judge; and Yolaine Dauphin was a state commissioner and is now an administrative law judge.

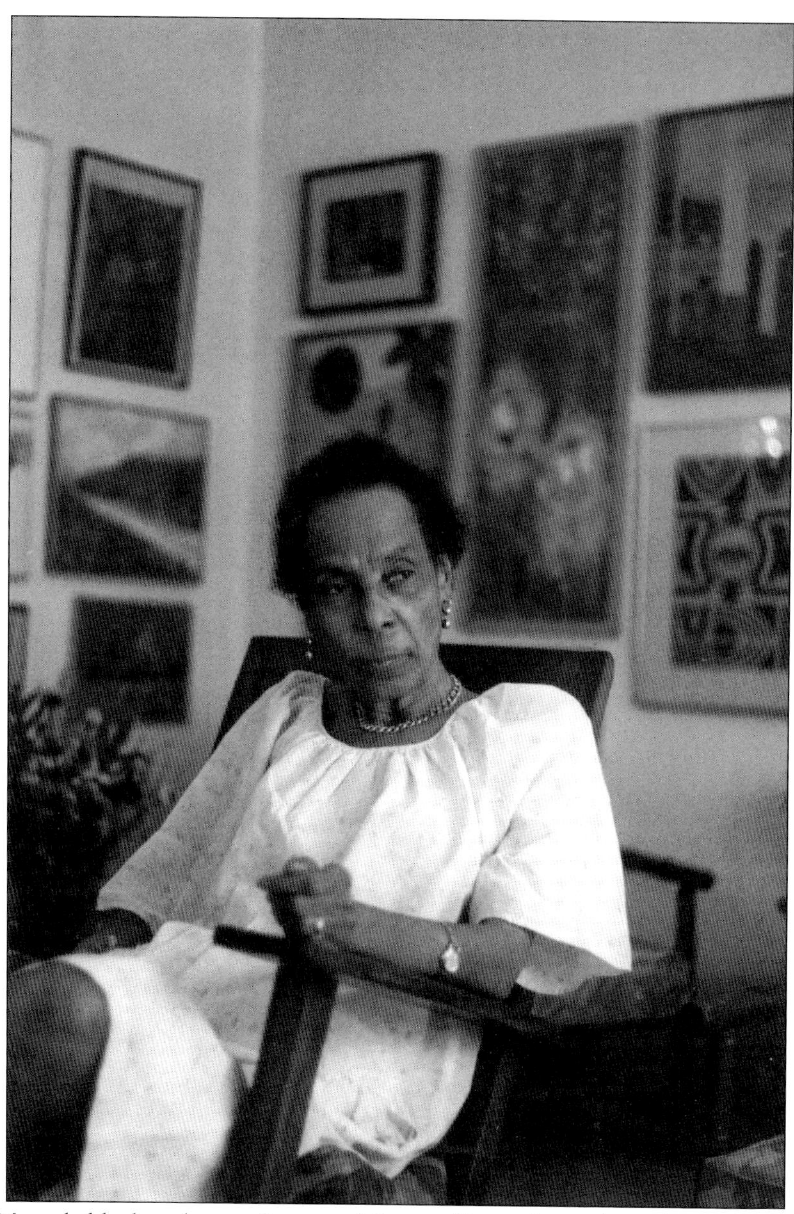

Francine Murat held a key place as director of Centre d'Art, it being the only institution in charge of promoting the artistic heritage of the nation, whether of local or universal character. At her side, Nicole Smith collaborated with her toward this end through programs that ensured that Haitian artists were also integrated into world artistic life. Besides that, their collaboration of talents aimed at nurturing the talent found in Haiti by giving a platform to young, emerging artists to grow and build their skills while showcasing the country's rich cultural heritage to the international community. Murat and Smith were responsible for workshops, exhibitions, and outreach to help increase awareness of Haitian artistic achievements and ultimately make the richness of the Haitian heritage known globally. Such a collaboration would go a long way in increasing Haitian art as well as bring the local creatives closer to the greater expanse of art and their work being understood for what Haiti's culture truly is: a global player deserving of respect and recognition. That gave way to highlighting how important Haiti's artistic expression and heritage are.

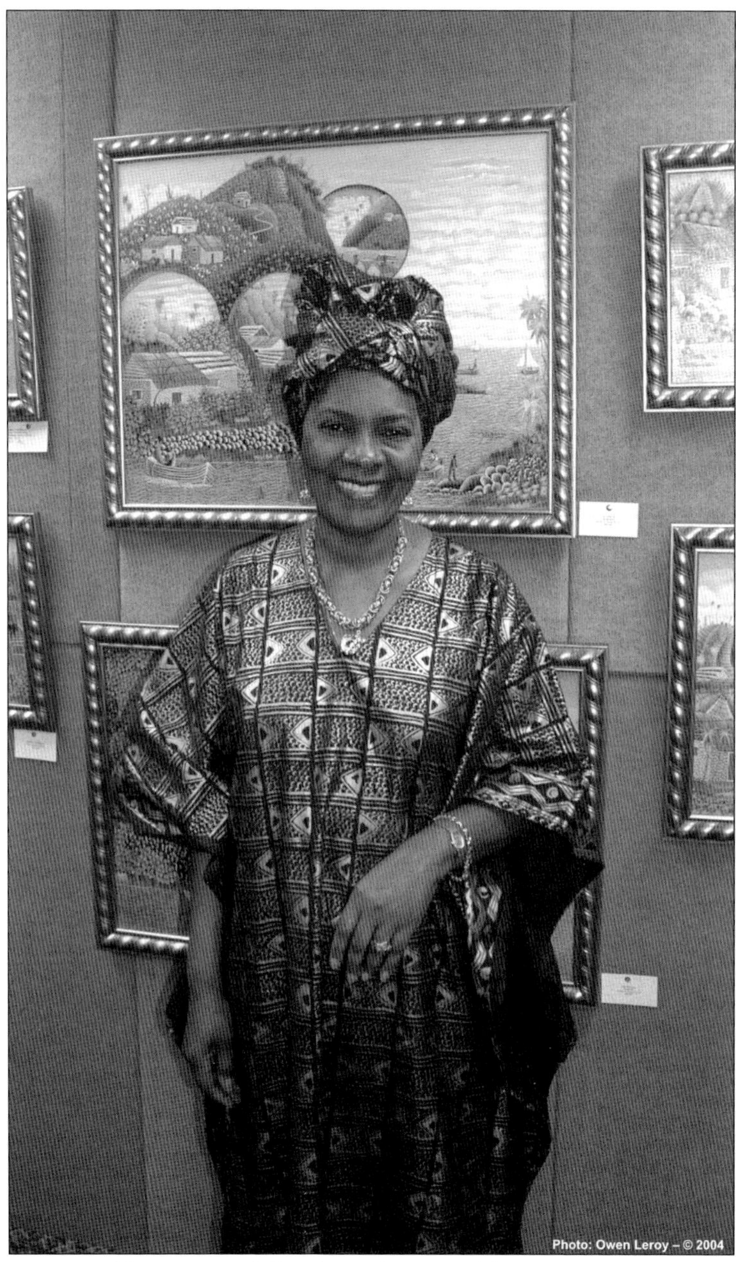
Photo: Owen Leroy – © 2004

Nicole Smith came to Chicago in 1973, where she started her career as an artist with Francine Murat, who had founded the Centre d'Art in Haiti. In the early years, Murat sold art out of her home and her car until it evolved into a successful venue. The determination and vision of her mentor inspired Smith to establish the Nicole Gallery, which was soon recognized as one of the best galleries in Chicago. This became a busy spot where Haitian art and culture would be displayed, reflecting her commitment to exposing the rich artistic heritage of her home country. Thanks to the Nicole Gallery, she provided a platform not only for emergent artists but also established ones, deeply caring for all the diverse narratives within the artistic community. Smith's passion and commitment to the arts have made an enduring difference in the cultural landscape of Chicago, bringing into the city the vibrant spirit of Haitian creativity. She passed away on March 29, 2016.

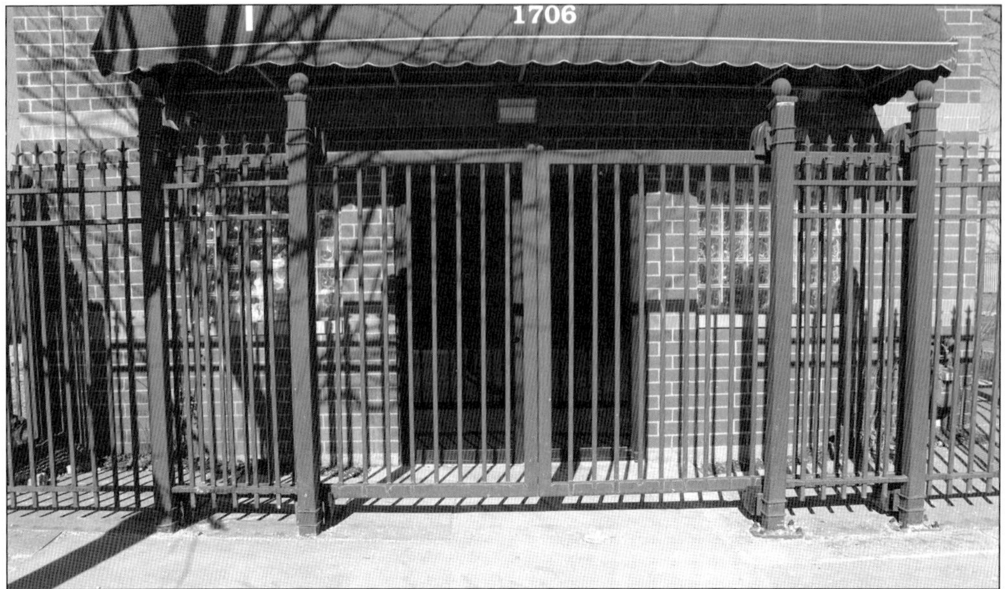

Where the New Jerusalem Evangelistic Church currently stands, 1706 East Seventy-Fifth Street, was once the Caribbean Village Club, owned by Raoul Armand, a hotbed of nightlife for the Haitian American community. Following its closure, Madame Lariviere bought the property, transforming it into the New Jerusalem Evangelistic Church, thus giving new life to the site and revitalizing that community space.

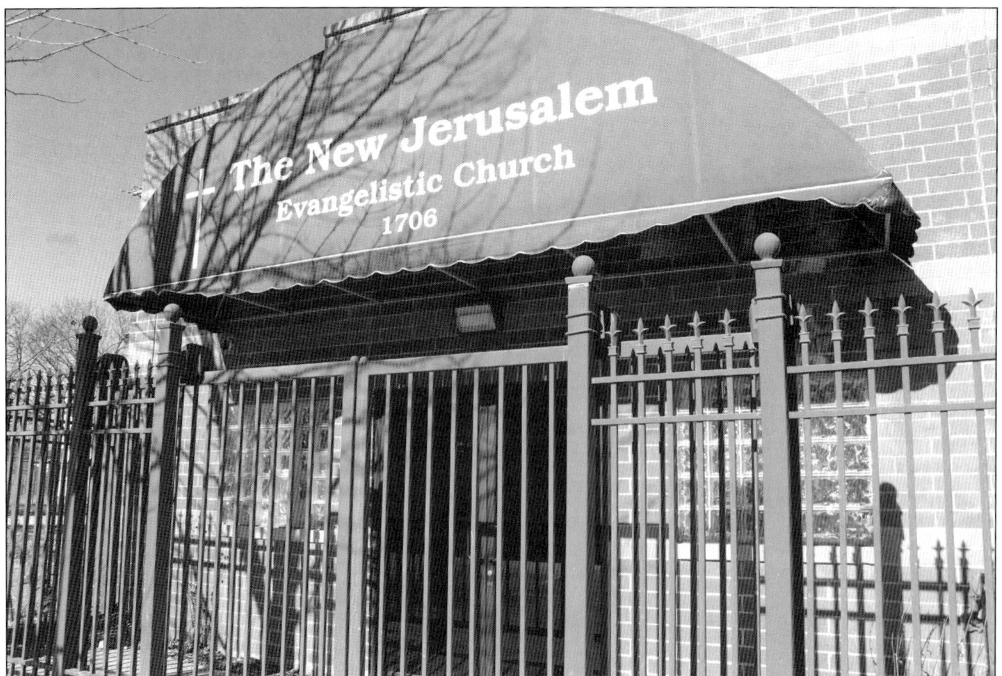

The Haitian New Jerusalem Evangelistic Church is a community-centric church on the South Side of Chicago that provides a place of worship and camaraderie. It builds spiritual development and relationships within its membership by fostering a warm, inviting place of worship for people and families to come together in faith and culture, sharing in numerous outreach ministries.

In Haitian society, foods have strong social and religious roles. Foods act to bind family and communities when prepared and consumed in feasts and celebrations. Foods have rich, deep meaning, inheriting conventional customs and beliefs. Through preparing and consuming foods, Haitians celebrate heritage, build relationships, and become part of who and what they are, emphasizing the key role played in heritage.

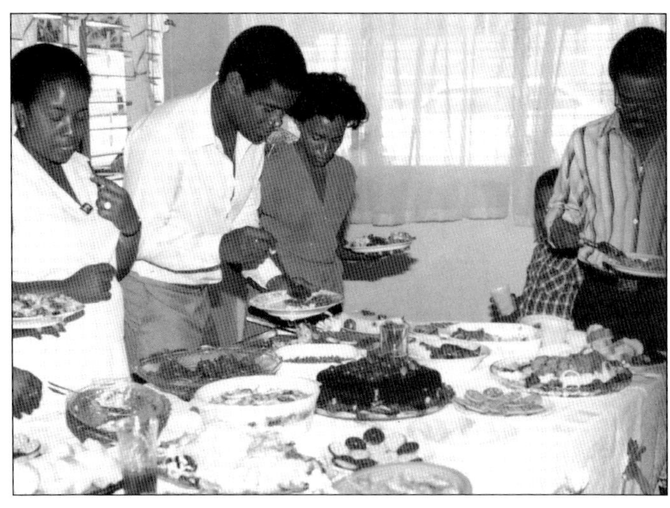

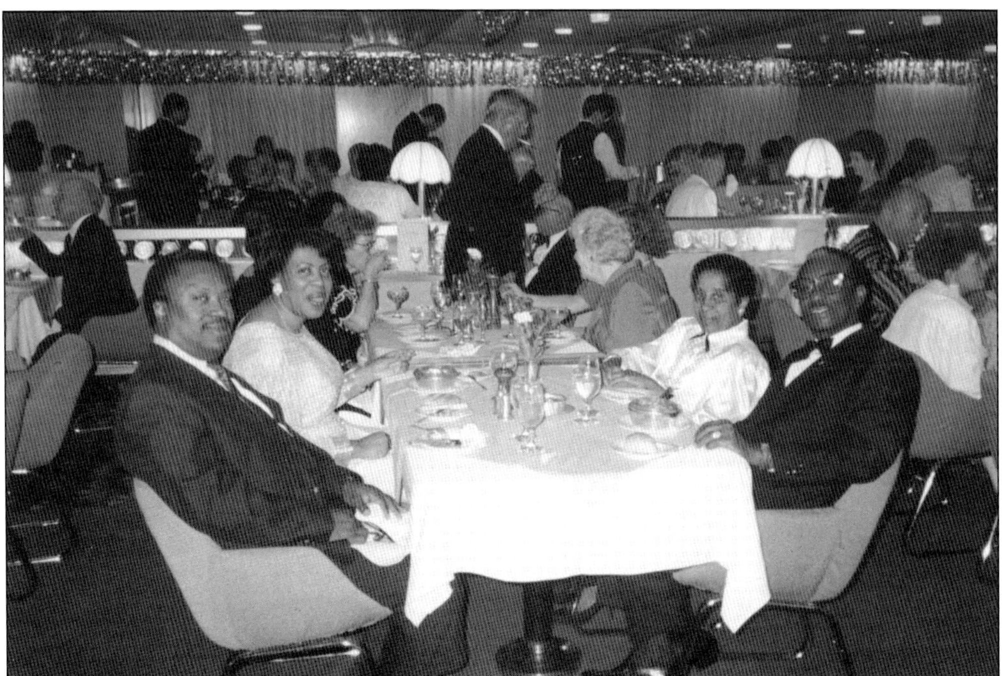

A distinguished group of medical professionals with a Haitian background joined a high-profile conference, with a view to providing expertise and contribution towards medical practice. Not only did such a conclave speak volumes about working professionally, but it also placed high value on representing and injecting diversity in medical discussions at a national level in terms of cultural contribution and diversity in general.

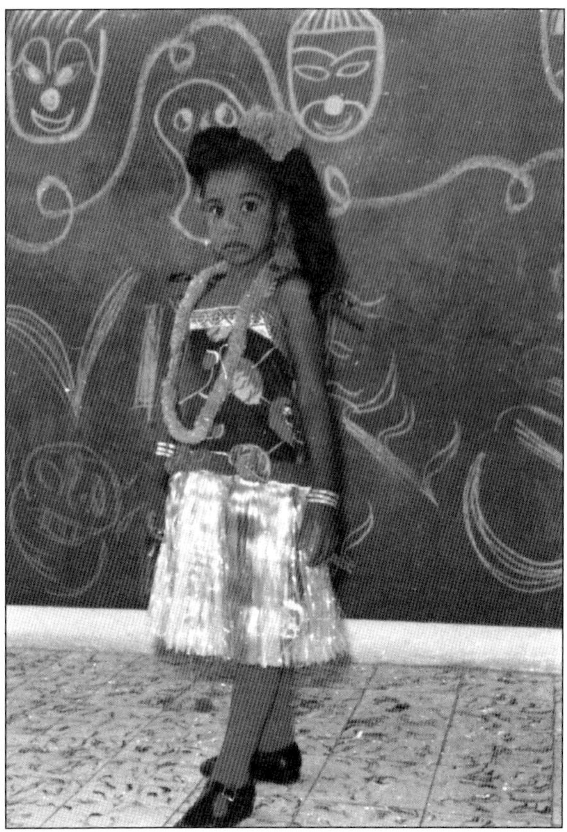

Carnaval is an important cultural and national event in Haiti and one that has been adopted, and new immigrants have been determined to maintain rich celebrations in new environments through dancing and music and multicolored marches, celebrating heritage and dispensing Carnaval's joyous, vibrant atmosphere and a new kind of community even in a new nation with a preserved cultural heritage.

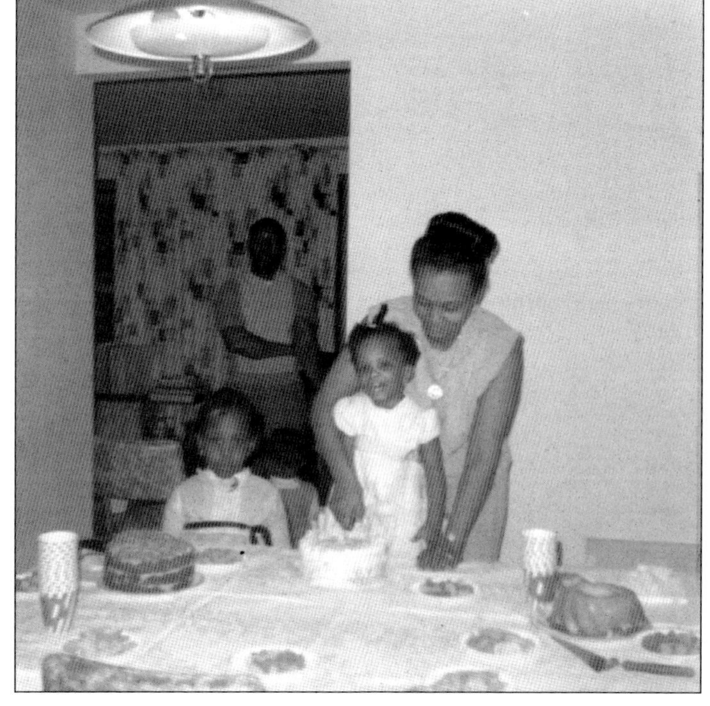

A birthday party in a Chicago residence rich with customs and celebrations filled everyone with smells of mouthwatering Haitian foods, laughter, and tunes. The smells of mouthwatering Haitian foods surround them in all directions in a room full of family and friends getting together for one's birthday and creating cherished memories with a strong heritage and a strong community backing it up.

A group of happy Haitian kids is having a birthday party together. Smiling and laughter surround them in an atmosphere when they sit together to have a glimpse of pleasure through amusement, tasty foods, and the thrill of celebrations. Colorful decor accompanies a happy atmosphere. Not only does a memorable session create a memorable occasion, but a strong tie between them deepens and strengthens their companionship and camaraderie.

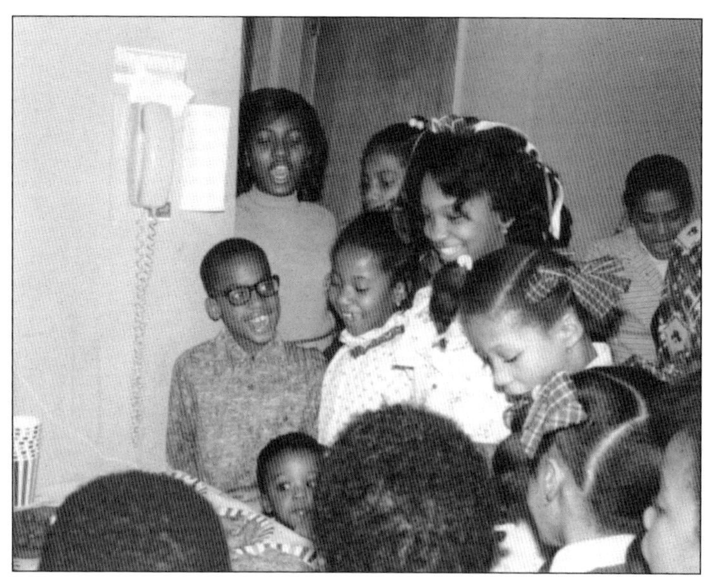

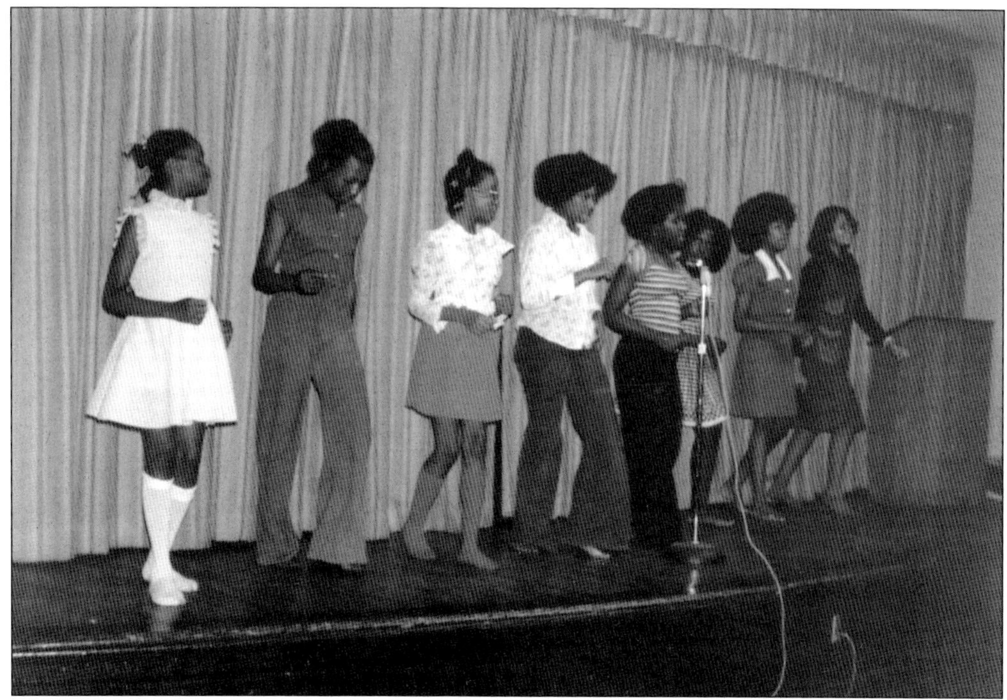

These youngsters in Chicago have been advised that preserving this type of heritage is no less than any sort of gold. Haitians may encourage the little ones for art, dance, music, or even theater performances, where the attachment to heritage and traditional traits among younger generations gets an opportunity for upbringing and exhibition. This has grown a united cultural community by bringing them to represent their diverse, rich cultures together.

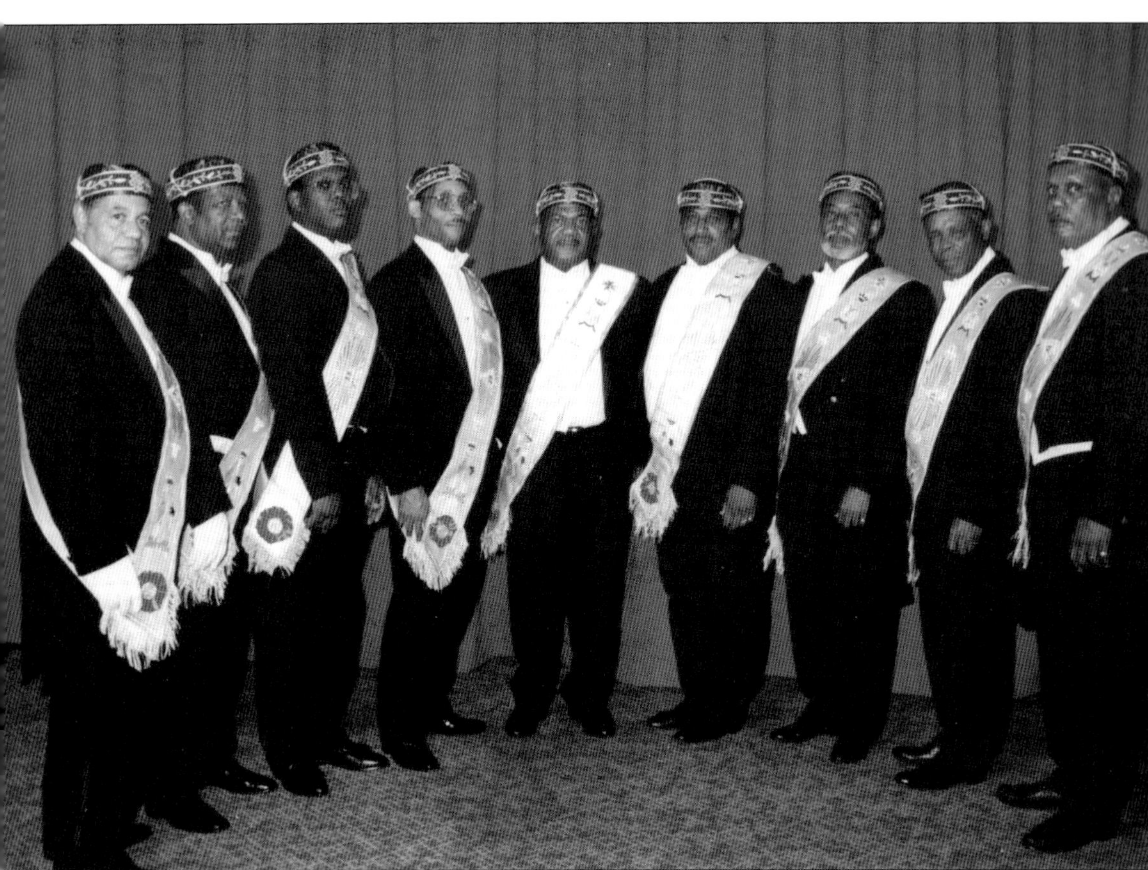

Freemasonry was first introduced in Haiti during colonial times, and its teachings gained widespread acceptance in the lives of many Haitians. In Chicago, a Masonic lodge for the Haitian community was organized in a continued practice of such a rich heritage. As portrayed in this photograph, its members actively engaged in Masonic rituals, developing a feeling of camaraderie and cultural heritage.

In Haitian society, communion forms part of important rituals in Catholicism. Communion unites believers in Christ with one another and brings a powerful sense of community and faith union. Engaging in communion both professes faith and devotion and instills values of union and unity, a key part of both its faith and cultural heritage.

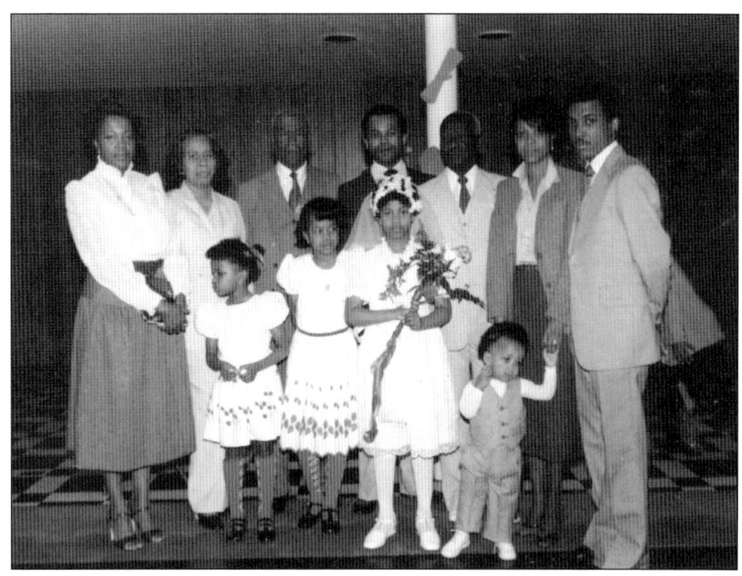

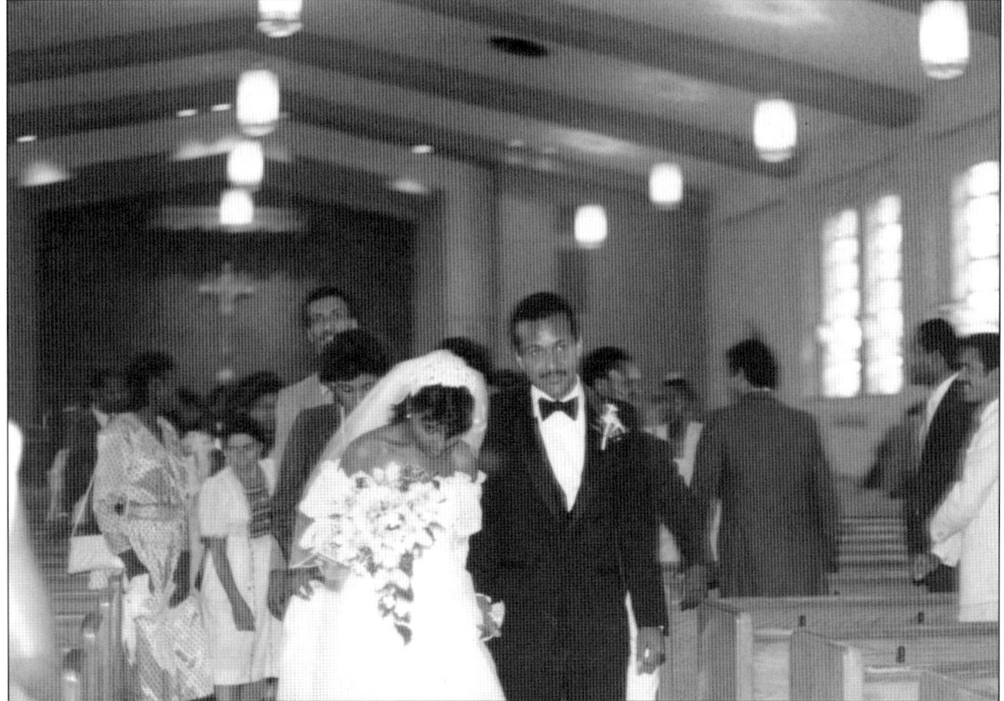

Weddings within the city of Chicago's community of Haitian heritage have a rich, full life that is a blending of strong heritage and modern trends. Bright colors, energetic tunes, and traditional foods can often be seen at such weddings, providing a joyous atmosphere for family and friends to rejoice together. The ceremony honors and amplifies unity and love, not just between the two getting married but also in their Haitian heritage.

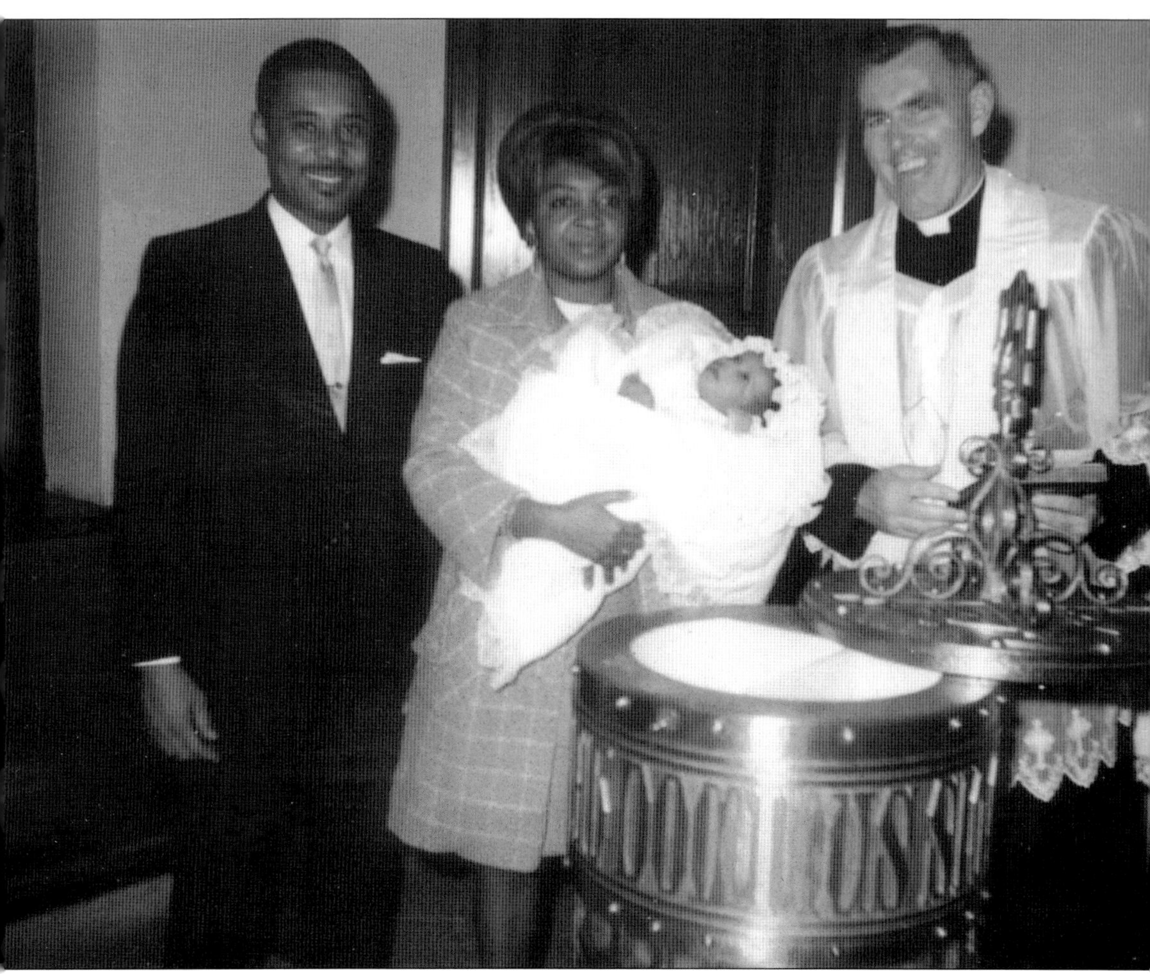

Christian baptism in the Chicago Haitian community is steeped with faith, ethnicity, and the spirit of belonging. The second most important life rite is one that initiates some essential elements in these children into the faith; families and friends celebrate such an important occasion. Thus, not only spiritual commitment but also reinforcing the bonding by continuously sharing the culture and traditions within the group. The event is packed with colorful ceremonies that represent the values and beliefs of the whole community, allowing its people to have a sense of belonging. In these ritual practices, the Haitian community establishes relationships between generations to come so that their heritage may be remembered and cherished. Such a collective experience will not only strengthen the faith of an individual but also create a unity and sense of support within the community, showing the resolute power of tradition in giving shape to identity and purpose. Ultimately, baptism in this context is more than a religious act, it is a celebration of life, faith, and cultural continuity.

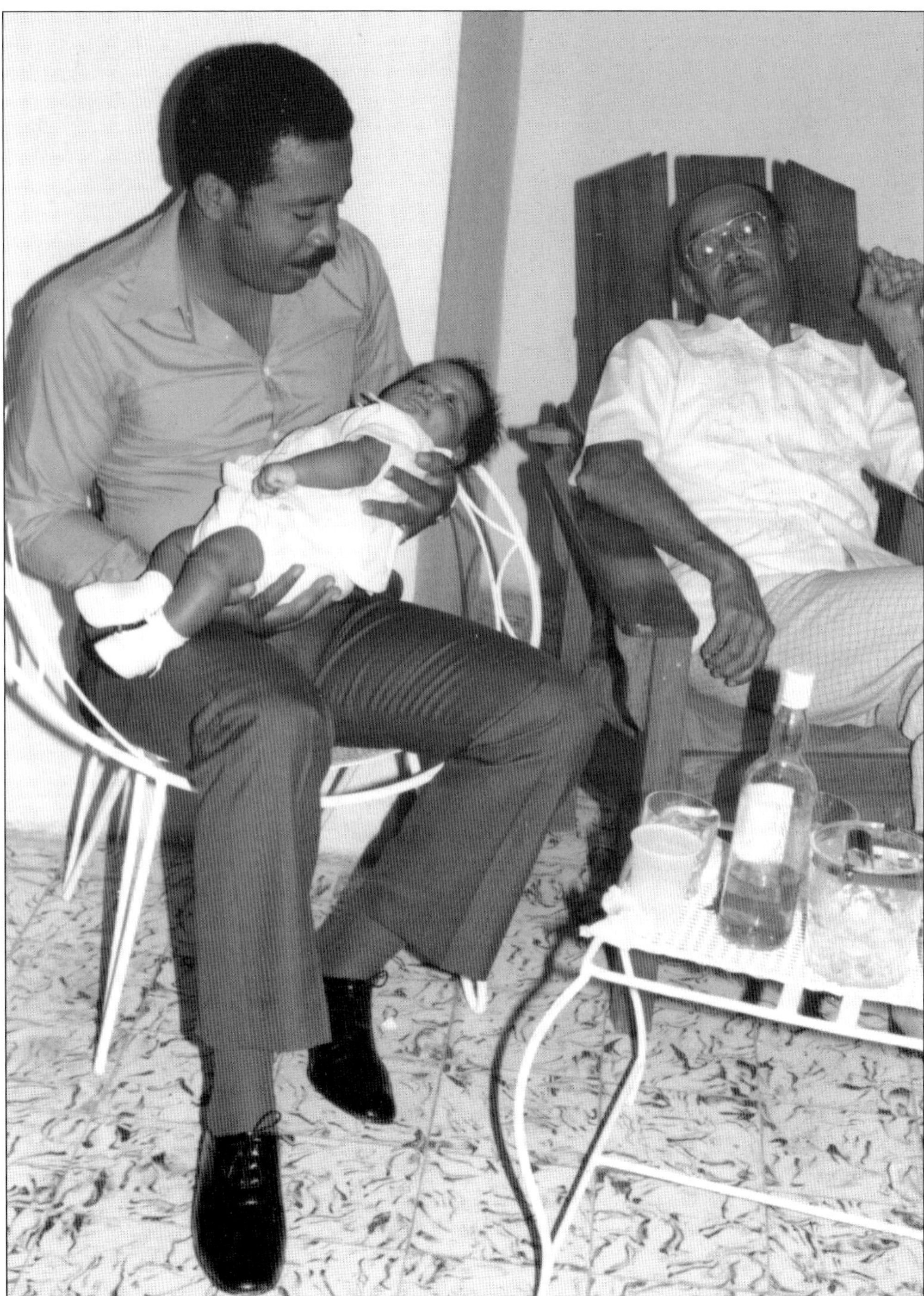

Fatherhood and childcare in Haitian society are both important, and familial ties and parental roles have a high value in its society. In many instances, fathers act in a protective and providing role, and in most cases, mothers have a role in care and instruction. This synergistic role strengthens family relations and community cohesion. Having balanced parental care is key to sustaining the role of Haitian culture in its society.

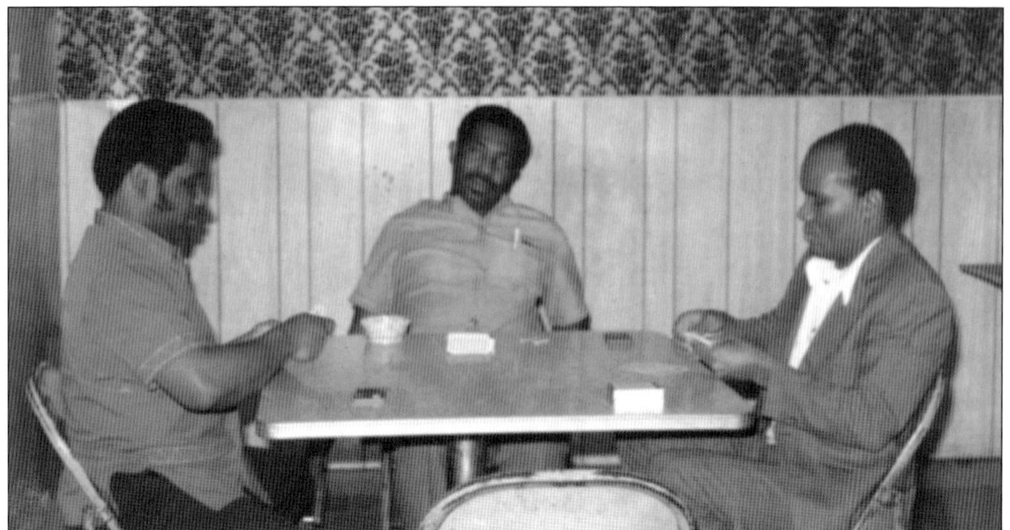

The folk games of Haiti have much to express about its rich cultural heritage, and most enjoyed card and domino games. Haitians take their favorite hobbies and leisure activities with them as they immigrate, and here, they share in the fun of a popular card game. It is a very lively social outlet, as friends and families come together to share laughter and stories through dominos or cards. The friendly competition encourages community spirit and strengthens relationships; thus, these games are very important in Haitian culture and social life.

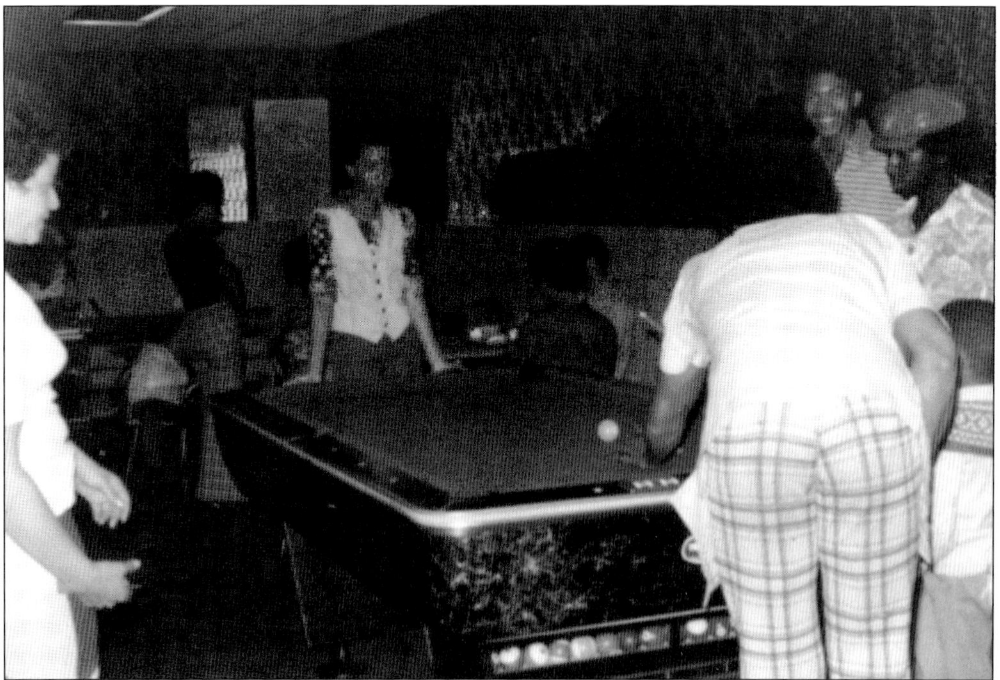

Pool is an important social activity for Haitians, creating a bridge and a sense of community amongst its players. Not a form of amusement, but one that creates strong-rooted community ties, its players exchanging tales, experiences, and encouragement for each other. By competitive yet friendly shared enjoyment, a bridge of shared and stated community is developed, enriching lives for its players.

Katherine Durham's dance techniques blended traditional Haitian rhythms with a more modern-day style, celebrating Haiti's rich cultural heritage. Her innovative approach preserved these traditions while introducing them to broader audiences and eliciting appreciation and understanding of Haiti's unique artistic identity. She did this as a means of honoring and giving a new life to the island's vibrant dance legacy. (Library of Congress.)

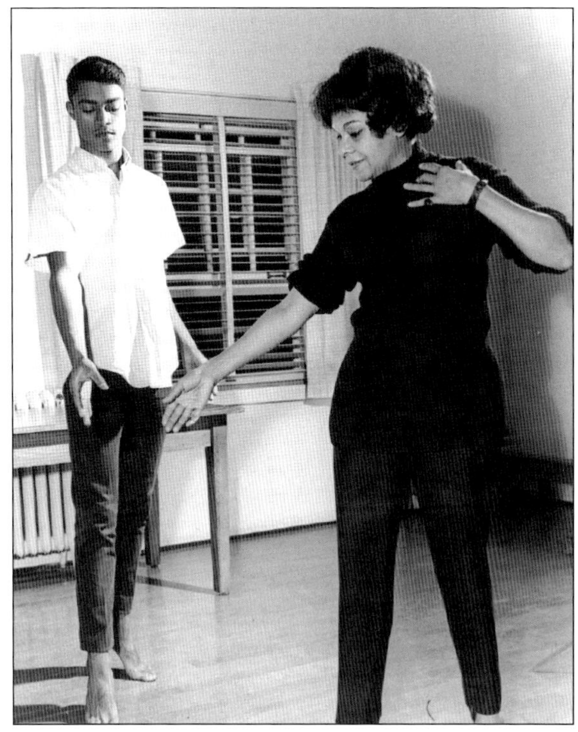

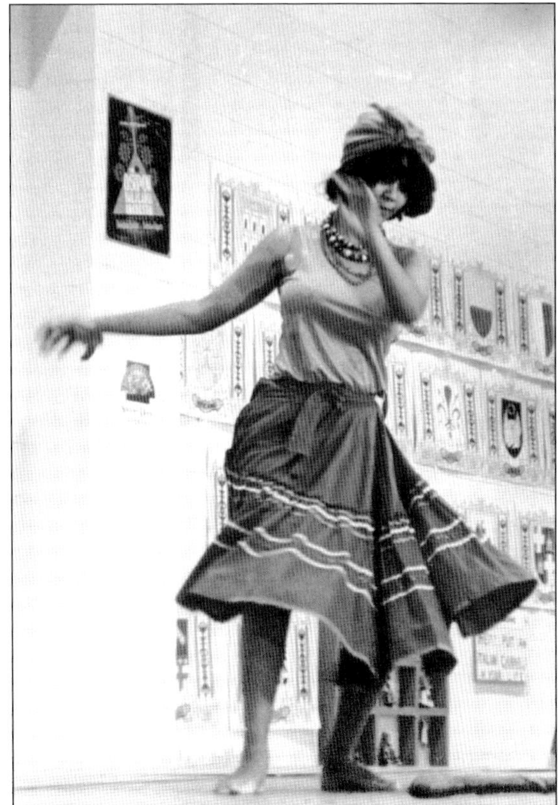

This 1976 image depicts a Haitian dancer in Chicago performing basic dance using traditional Haitian cultural movements. This special movement was adopted by Katherine Dunham, an American dancer, choreographer, anthropologist, and social activist, when she visited Haiti. This dance type became popularly known as a part of the Dunham Technique.

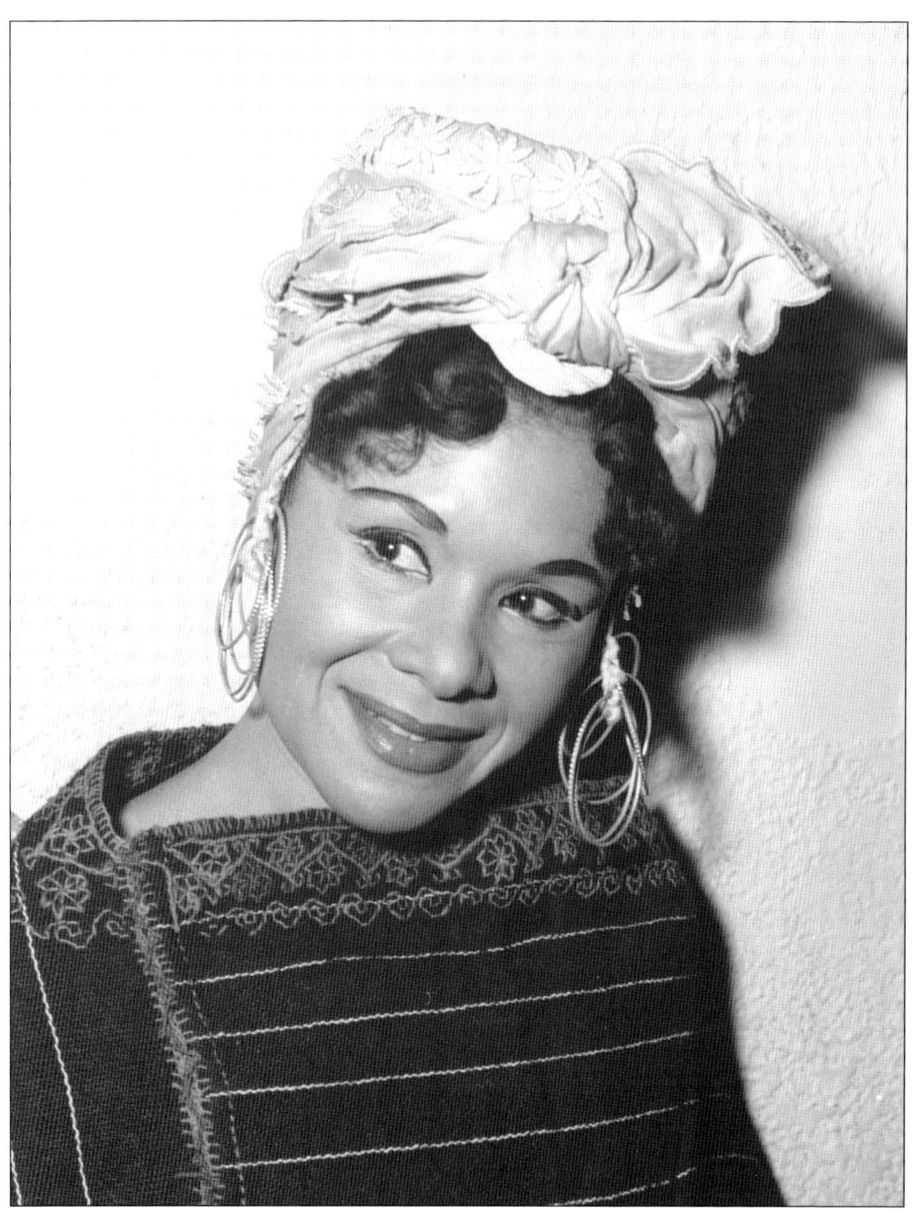

Katherine Dunham (1909–2006) was among the pioneers of African Americans in dance, choreography, and education. She was one who really transformed concert dance as it related to African Americans. Her innovative approaches and artistic vision opened the doors to the next generation. Dunham has been closely associated with Haitian culture since her student days in Haiti, and it deeply influenced her commitment to the cause of human rights. She felt that through the medium of art, much-needed social change could be catalyzed, and for that, her platform should be used to raise awareness for certain burning issues. One of the most powerful examples was her 47-day-long hunger strike back in 1992, protesting the mistreatment of Haitian refugees. With her pathbreaking career in dance and lifelong commitment to social justice, Dunham left lasting marks on the arts and human rights while inspiring generations of young people to follow their passions into commitments for equity and justice. Her legacy now stands as testimony to the power of art and activism. (Library of Congress.)

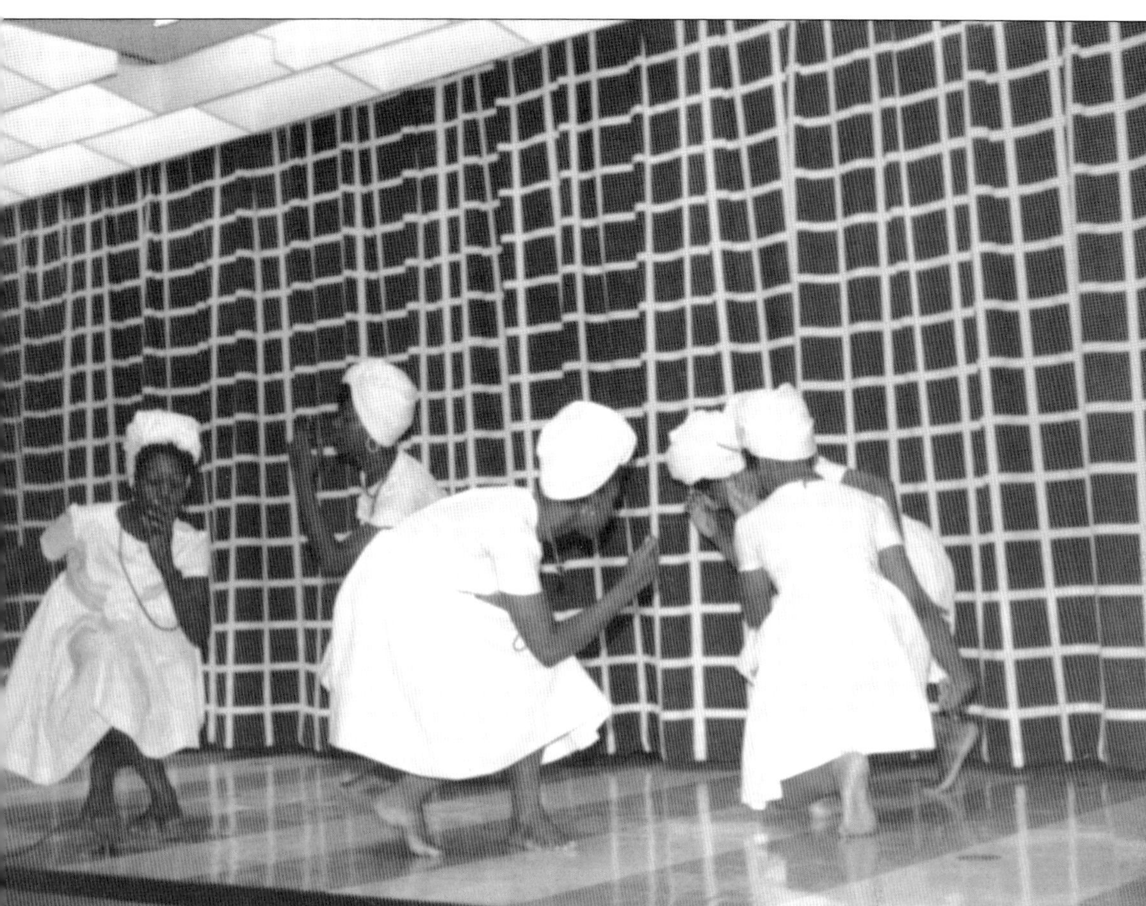

Haitian dance is a vital medium for the expression of identity and tradition. Many parents put their children into dance classes so that, even if immigration takes them to other countries, the rich cultural heritage of Haiti will be continued through generations. This commitment to cultural transmission is captured in the photographs from the 1970s, showcasing the dynamism and resilience of Haitian dance. These images do not just display the highly detailed movements and bright costumes, they also refer to the determination of this community to maintain their cultural roots. It is through dance that young Haitians learn to accept their heritage, a feeling of belonging that surpasses borders. In celebration through this form of art, it is not only a matter of paying their respects to their ancestry but participating in the continued evolution of Haitian culture, thus securing it for generations as a living, breathing form of expression.

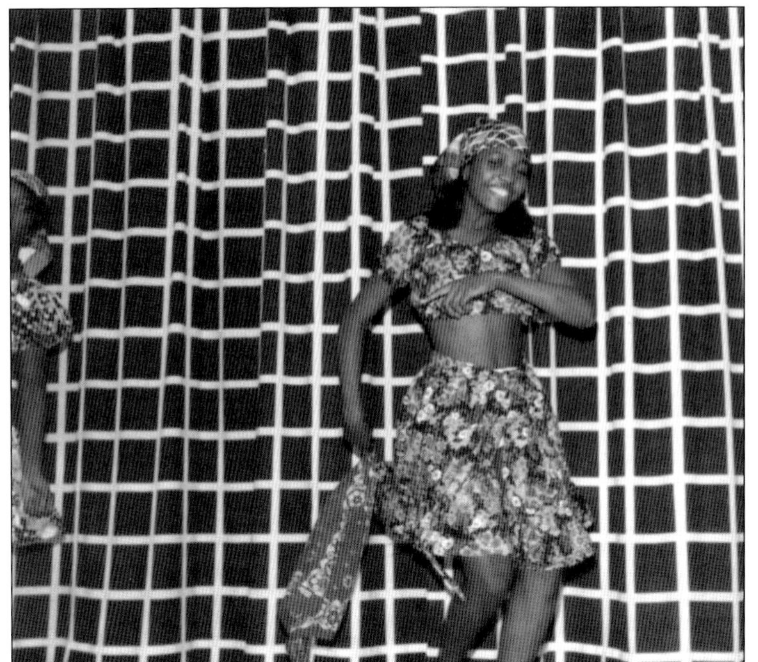

Dance is an important part of Haitian culture and a powerful medium through which heritage can be expressed. Many Haitian families encourage their children to take dance classes as a way to help them retain the rich traditions of their homeland. The photographs shown on this page, taken in the 1970s, document this cultural practice and attest to the need to pass such artistic expressions on to the next generation.

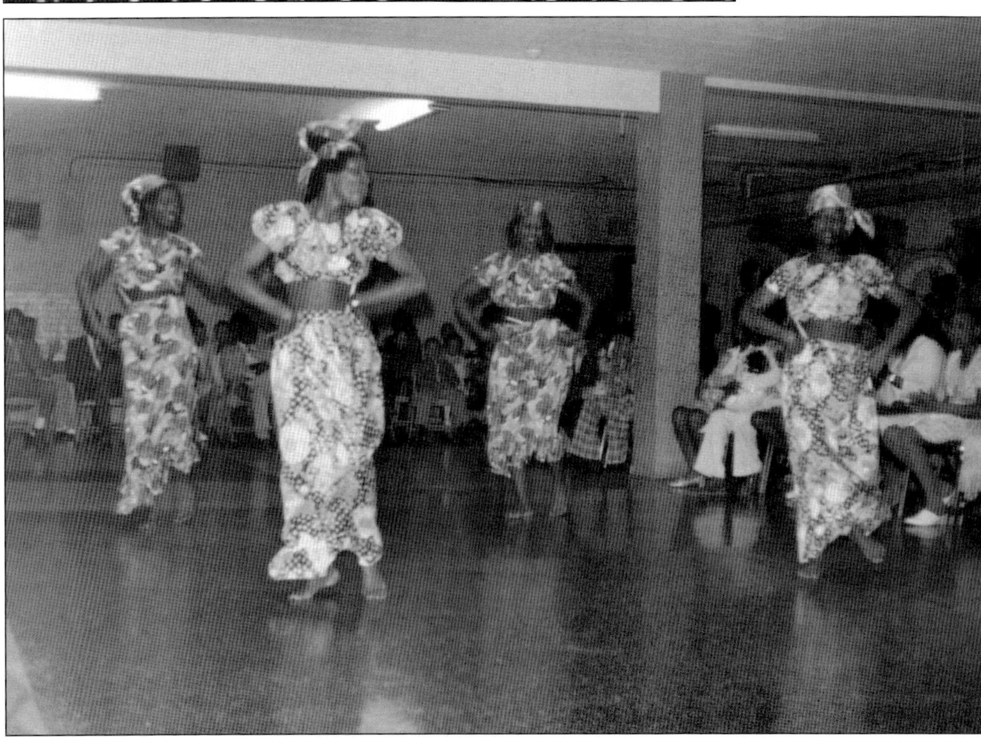

Dance holds an important position in society in Haiti, and it is a primary source of cultural expression for them. In an attempt to provide future generations with a relation to heritage, the Chicago community had taken an attempt at having kids attend dancing schools. In the 1970s photographs on this page, one can see communities in Chicago determined to maintain a rich heritage through dancing even under immigration sufferings.

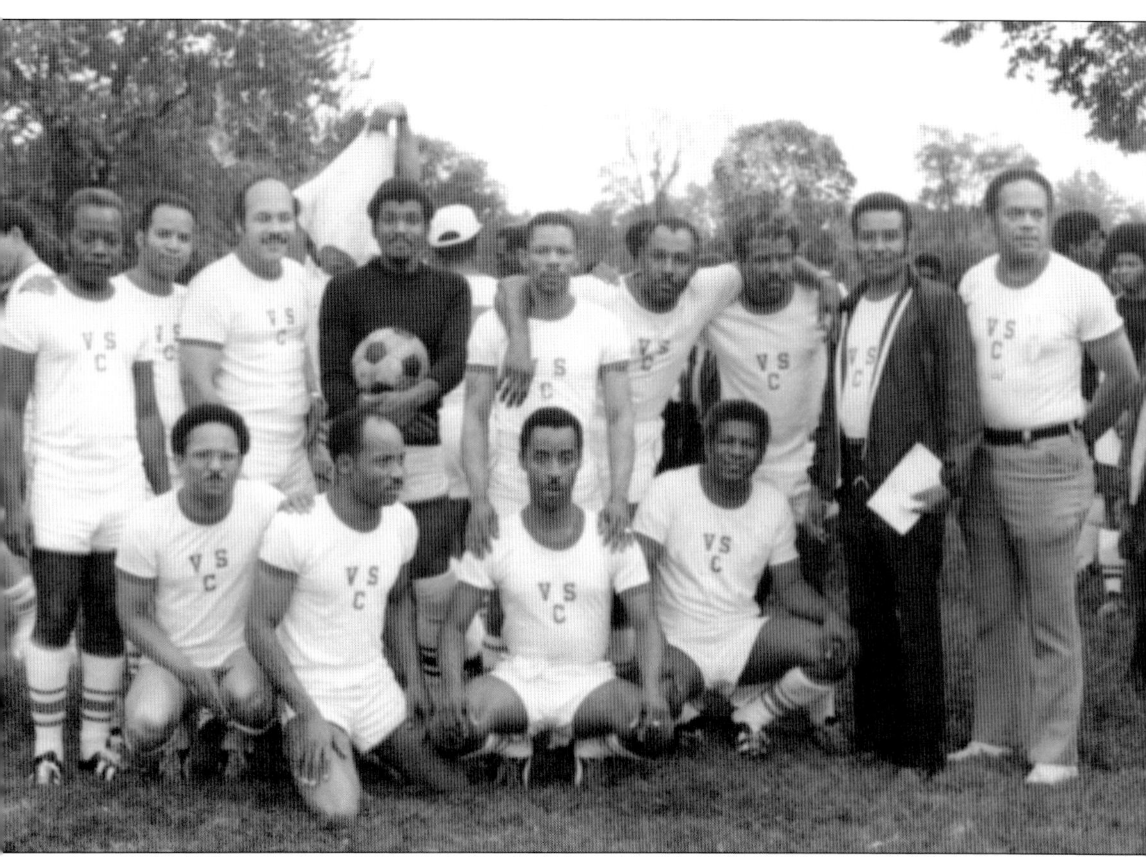

Edner Franck, affectionately known to many as either "Mr. SOS" or "Papi," was a founding Operation S.O.S., a Haitian and Haitian American serving nonprofit, board member and active advisory board member for over 25 years. The proof is in the multifaceted manner in which Franck was committed to community service, from designing structures for toilets for rural Haiti to sundry special projects. In addition to Operation S.O.S., one of his passions was soccer. For almost 10 years, he managed and ran the Haitian Soccer Club of Chicago, teaching a love for the game to people in the neighborhood. Franck's multifaceted efforts are a reflection of his deep commitment to bringing improvement into people's lives, be it through new infrastructure innovations or encouraging and nurturing the enjoyment of soccer. His work was symbolic of social responsibility and community involvement, through which he created significant marks in both Haiti and Chicago. Franck's legacy continues to inspire and to lift up people through his efforts.

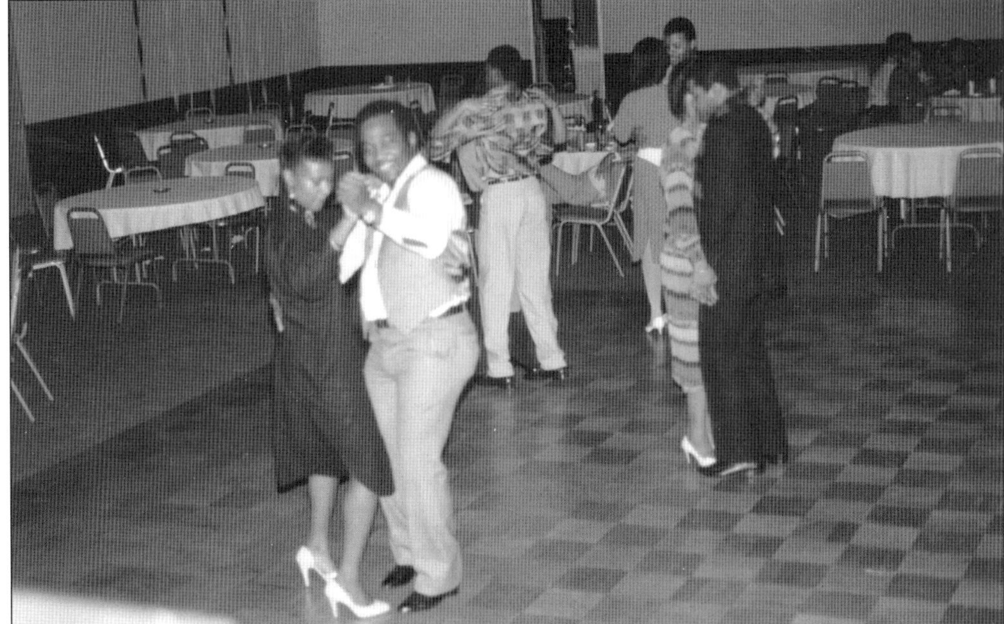

The dance, when it moved to dancing in dance halls, became a rich social activity and one through which dancers could celebrate and pass on their heritage. Dance halls emerged as vibrant centers for socializing, sharing memories, and enjoying heritage through performance in a warm, friendly atmosphere. Not only did the dance form a community, but it also passed a rich heritage and its value through a number of successive generations.

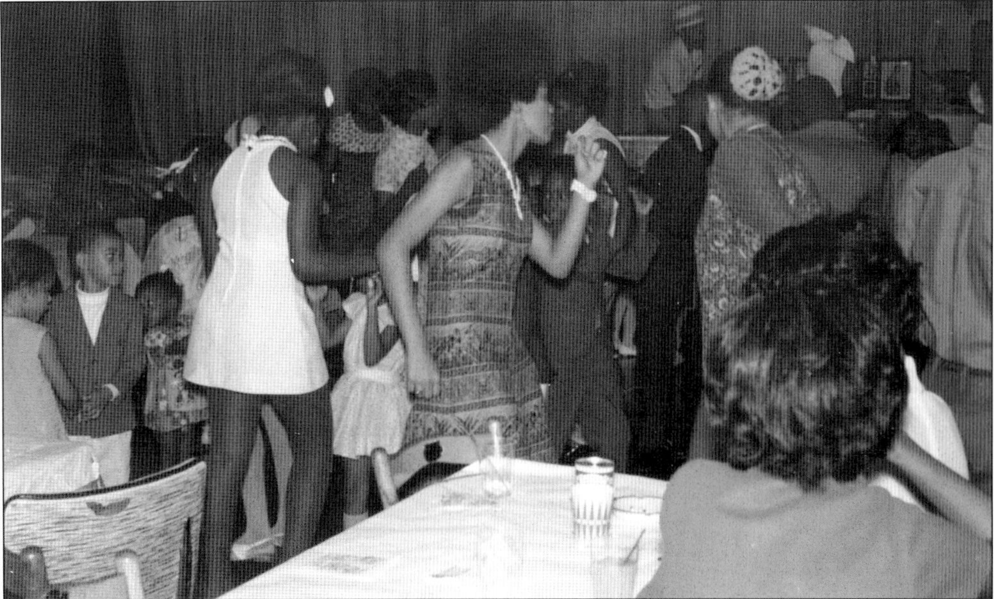

Spending weekends at dancing clubs is best captured with *konpa*, an energetic and rhythmic kind of dancing expressing happiness and celebrations. It not only unites everyone but also creates an actual energetic environment in which everyone feels free to present themselves. With a thudding beat in a room, dancers become a part of an environment, creating new friendships and memories under lights and glitz in a club.

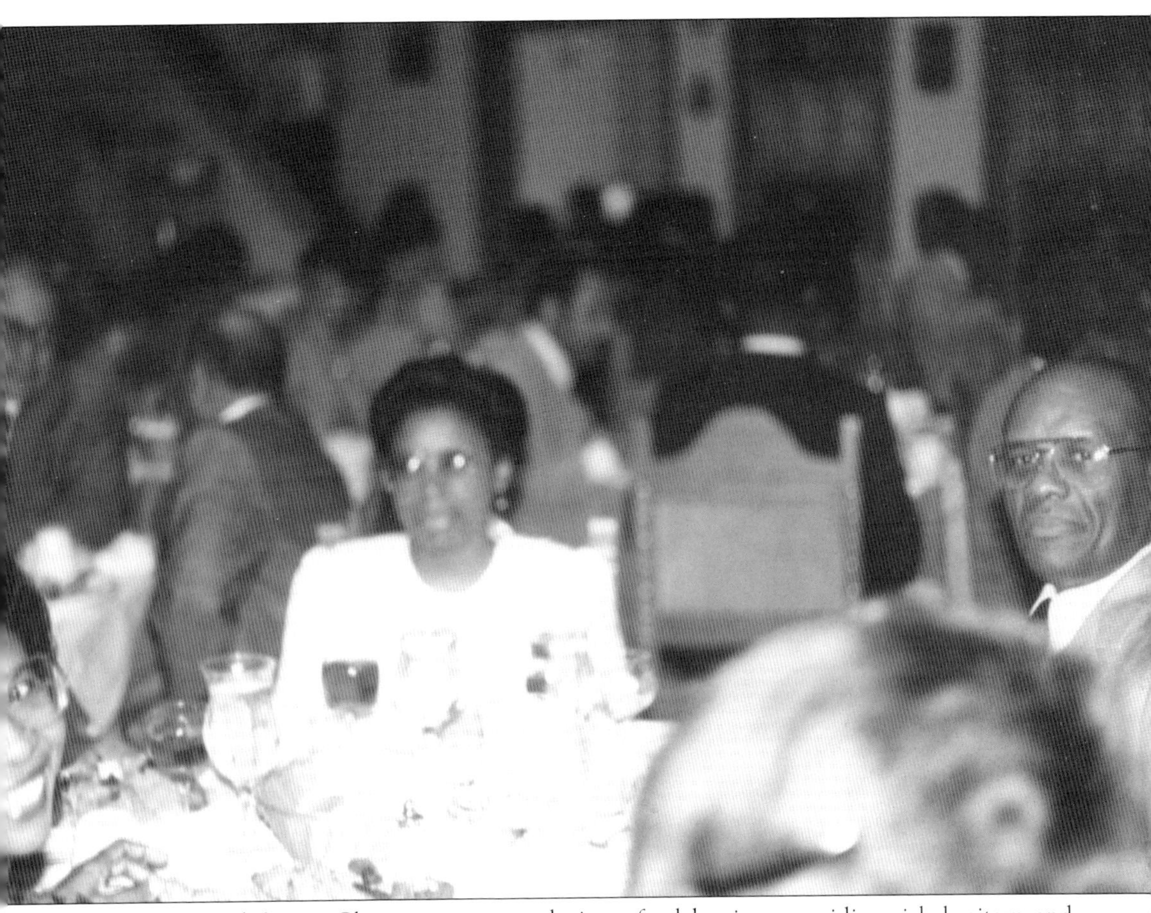

A vibrant social fete in Chicago was an explosion of celebration, providing rich heritage and rich culture. Participants savored traditional tunes, mouthwatering foods, and warm conversation, and, in the bargain, strengthened friendships and family ties. Not only did it have a one-of-a-kind aura in traditionalism, but it added a big boost in diaspora affiliations, injecting a whole lot of cohesion and a sense of group affiliation in urban heartland country.

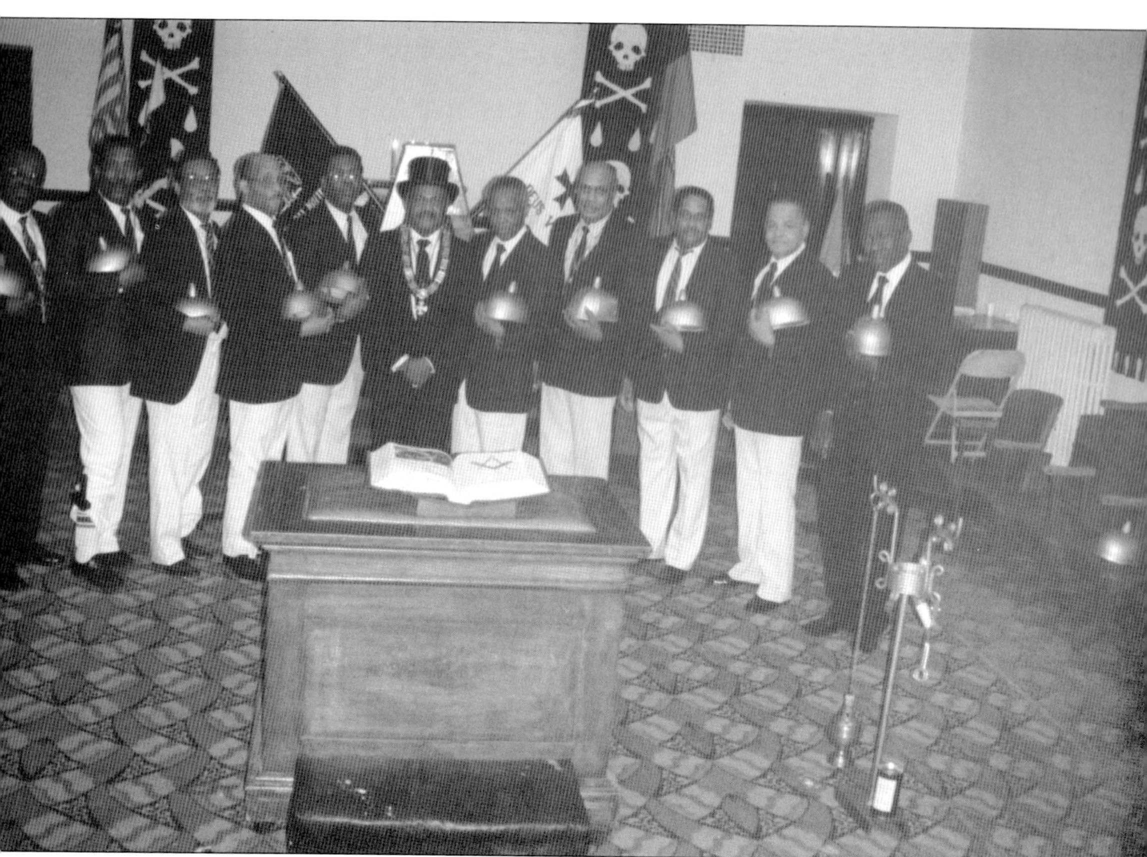

Freemasonry in Haiti first started during the time of early colonization, and over time, Haitians from different spectrums began to embrace these tenets quite warmly. Later on, Chicago formed a lodge from these very communities, again giving credence to the persistence that seemed inherent in this cultural heritage of Haiti. This lodge not only nurtures a sense of belonging among its members but also enriches the greater Masonic community through its unique values and cultural practices. It is through this organization that Haitian Masons of Chicago celebrate their shared history and ideals of brotherhood, charity, and personal growth. The lodge serves as a bridge of culture, linking the vibrant heritage of Haiti with contemporary realities here in the United States. This dynamic exchange elevates the experience of all Masons involved, creating an environment that is dynamic, where diversity in backgrounds is celebrated and honored, thereby strengthening the bonds of fraternity and community within the Masonic order.

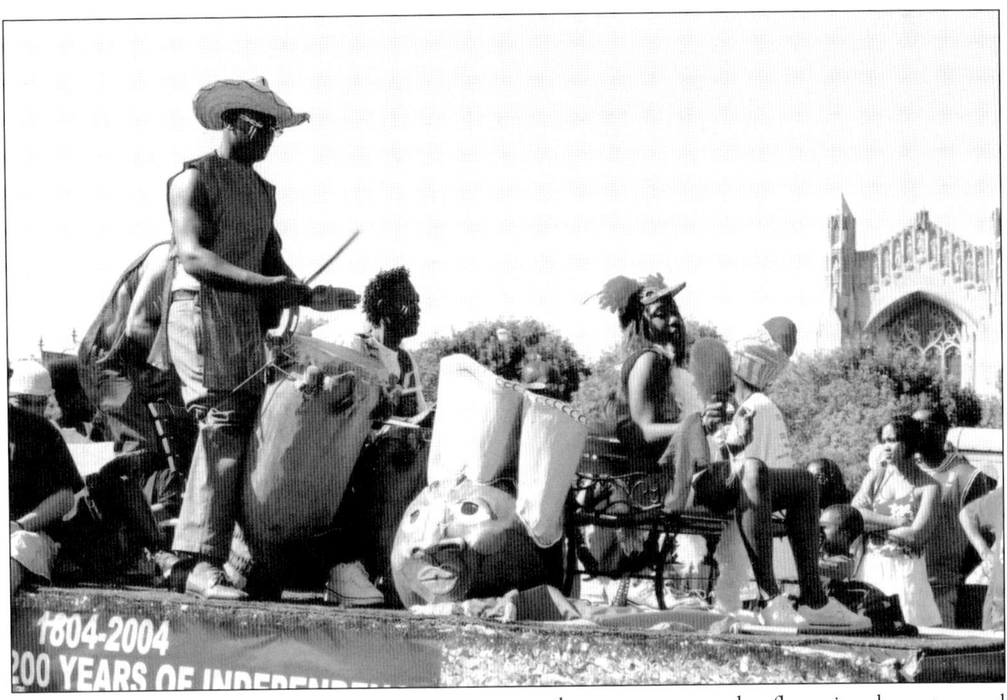

Carnaval is a national event in Haiti, an occasion that expresses and reflects its character and imagination. It is a practice that immigrants have embraced and sustained in a new format in new communities, not just to honor their heritage but in tribute to a shared community and a cultural mix, infusing surrounding communities with colors and energetic beats of Carnaval.

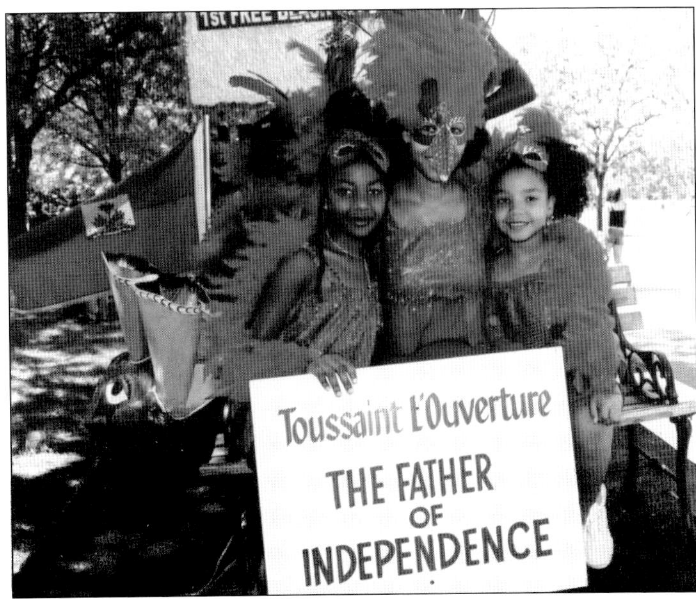

The Carifet, a new development in the 1980s, reached its height in 1989 with the Marshall Field's New Year's Parade. Bright colors of a vibrant Caribbean presence included African Americans and dancers representing Haiti, Jamaica, Trinidad, Tobago, and Belize. With temperatures at minus zero degrees Celsius, performers presented unforgettable performances, manifesting their cultural heritage and tenacity in enduring cold temperatures.

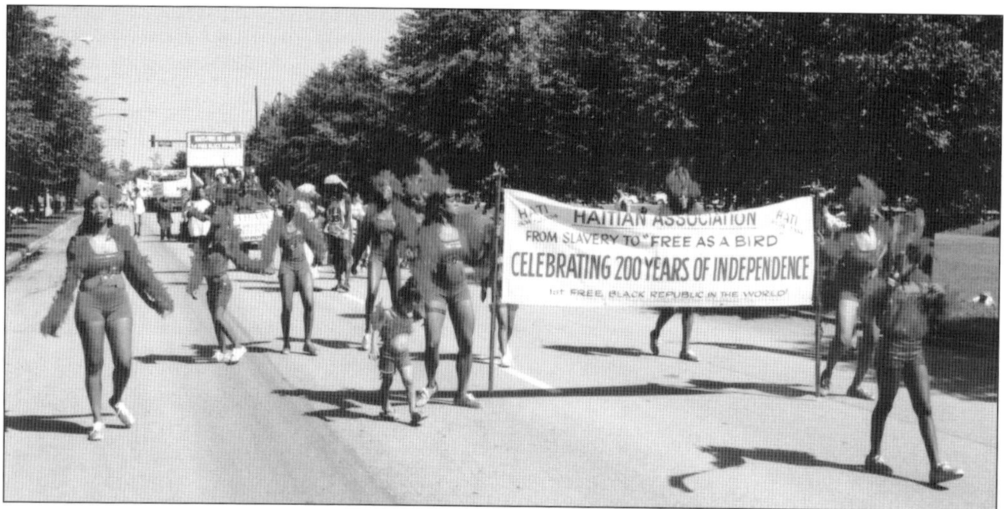

The Carifet festival, begun in the early 1980s, saw its best times in 1989 in the form of a Marshall Field's New Year's Parade, showcasing the energetic atmosphere of the Caribbean region. With dancers drawn both from African Americans and African nations such as Haiti, Jamaica, Trinidad, and Belize, cultures merged together through a single event.

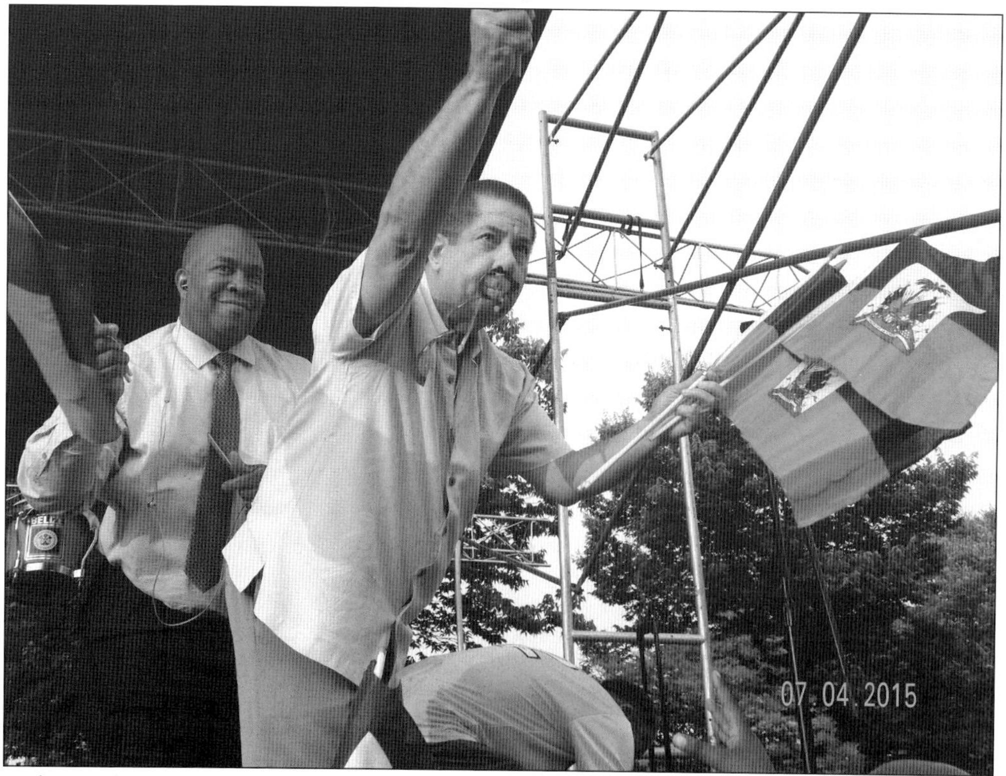

Lesly Conde, former consulate general of Haiti in Chicago, participated in a high-energy Chicago rally in commemoration of Haitian heritage and community. The activity united strong attendees in heritage celebrations and advocacy for significant concerns in Haiti. Conde's presence embodied the worth of a united Haitian presence abroad and stressed working for one's nation and union with fellow citizens in society at large.

This image features HAMOC's first-ever artwork to have been made in Haiti. This work was painted by Jean Yves Héctor at the age of 16. The work of Héctor is a witness to the museum in representing a range of new talent and a platform for underrepresented parts of the world, such as in Haiti. The work of Héctor is a vibrant expression of youth and heritage.

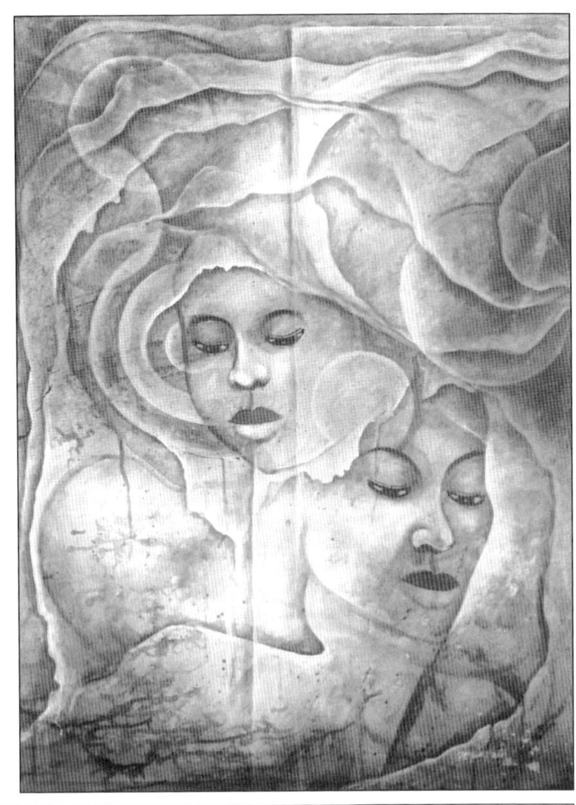

Fritz Millevoix, a Haitian painter, started out life as a street vendor, but in the early 1980s, a chance encounter with a gallerist, Nicole Smith, started him off on an international career path. By the 21st century, he became well-known in the Chicago art community, taking numerous high-profile accolades in the form of grants and awards from such groups as the Field Museum and the Museum of Science and Industry.

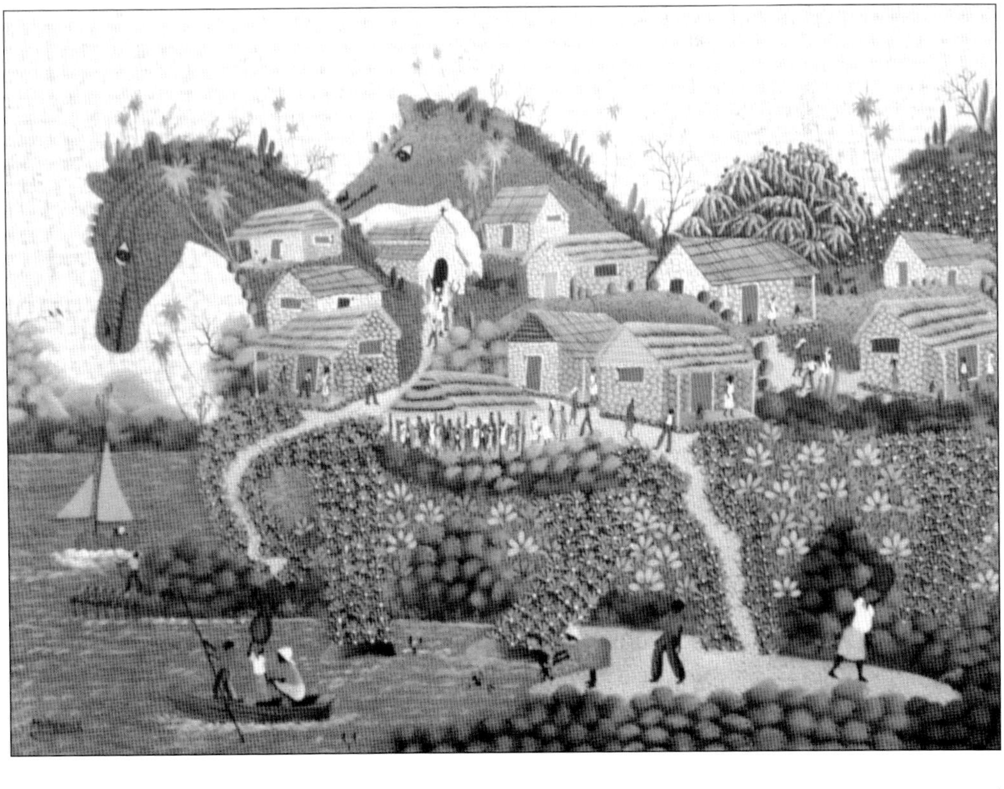

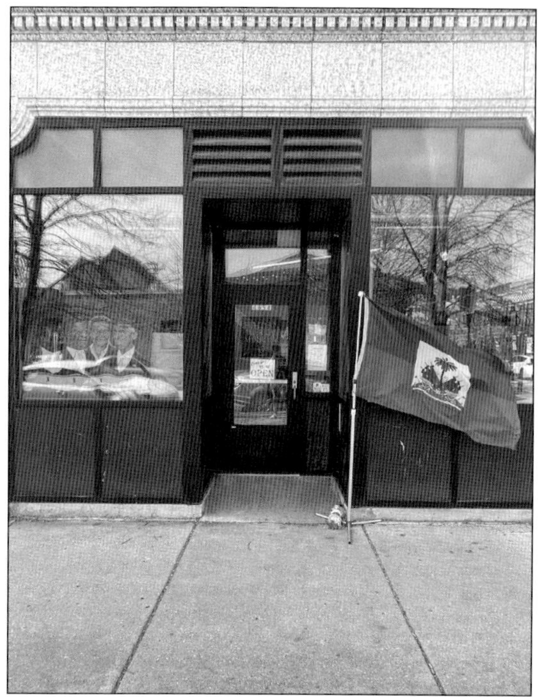

The Haitian American Museum of Chicago aims to preserve and promote Haitian heritage, community, artwork, and history throughout the city of Chicago. In Uptown, one of the city's most ethnically vibrant communities, it is a secondary such institution, following in the path of the Haitian Heritage Museum in Little Haiti in Miami, Florida. It is a significant location for community activity and cultural expression.

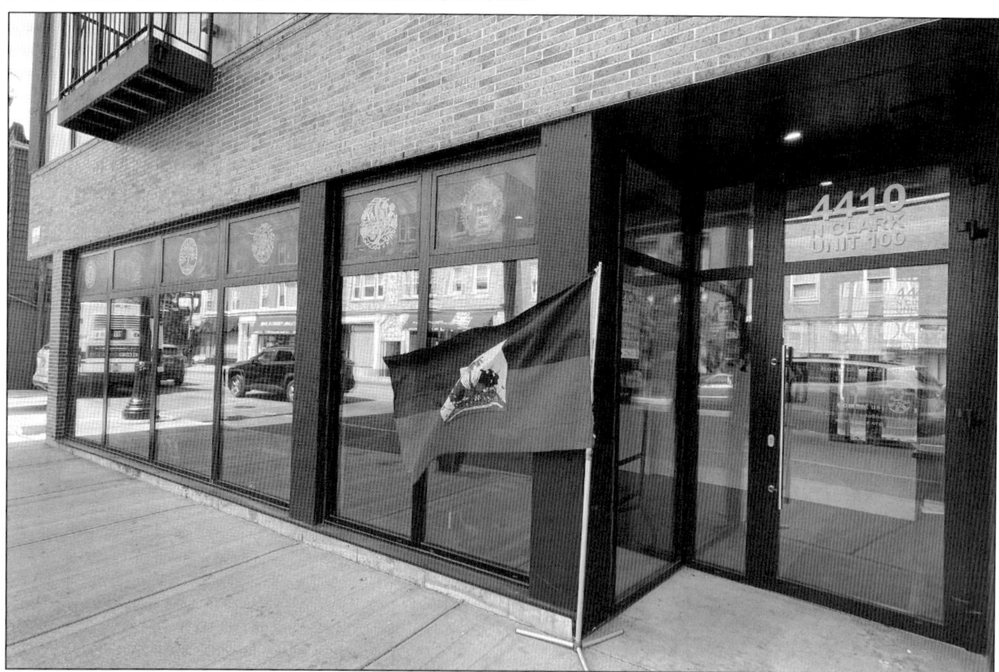

The Haitian American Museum of Chicago seeks to preserve and promote local and national Haitian heritage, community, art, and culture. Located in one of the nation's most cosmopolitan cities, the Uptown community in Chicago is home to the second such institution in the United States; the first is the Haitian Heritage Museum in Miami, Florida (Little Haiti). As a living, vibrant community and working hub for educational and cultural exchange, it is a community for everyone.

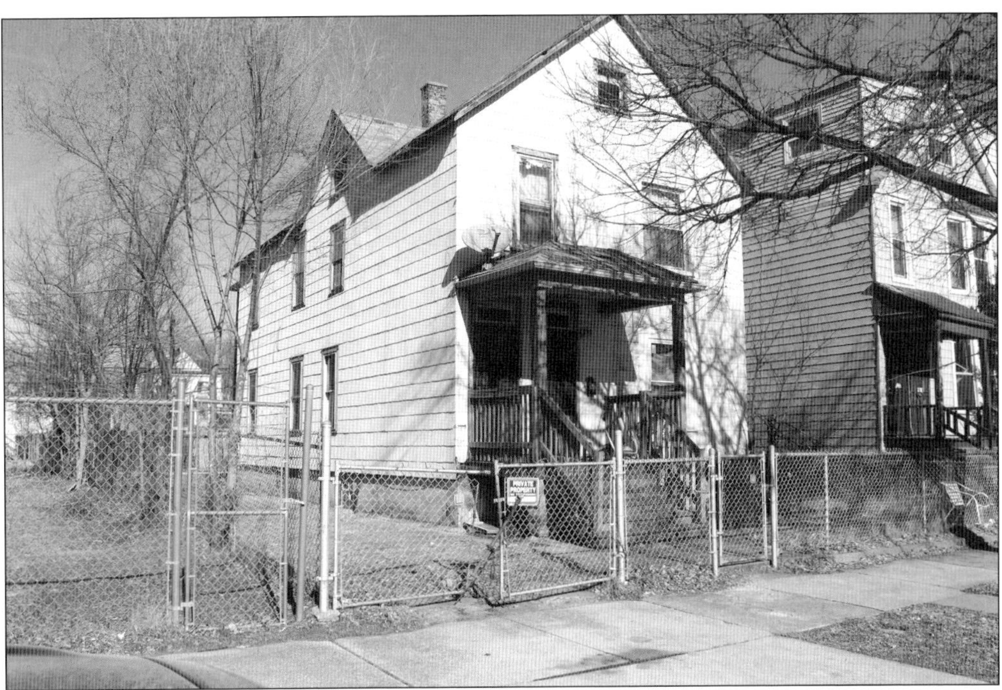

Paulette Masena's 1518 East Seventy-Sixth Place, Chicago, Illinois, 60619, home operated as an inviting haven for region-residing Haitian Americans. There, everyone mingled over board games, dancing, and food in a cozy environment. Masena's home was a valued social hub, creating a community and cultural solidarity for Haitians and a haven one could call one's own.

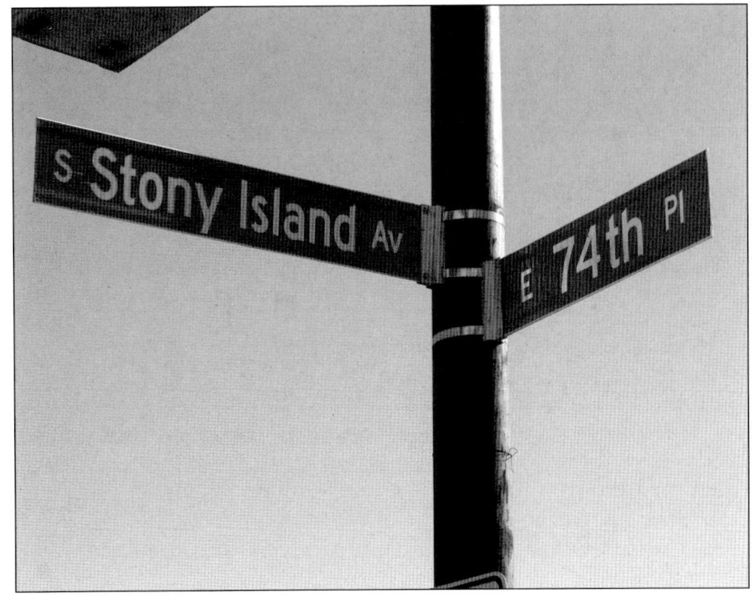

The Panama Club, located at 7416 Stony Island Avenue and operated by the Lambert family, was a high-class, 1960s-era Haitian saloon and nightclub. With its rich social atmosphere and cultural performance, the establishment grew into a cherished community hub, a reflection of vibrant Haitian life and customs, and created a community of visitors in a vibrant social atmosphere.

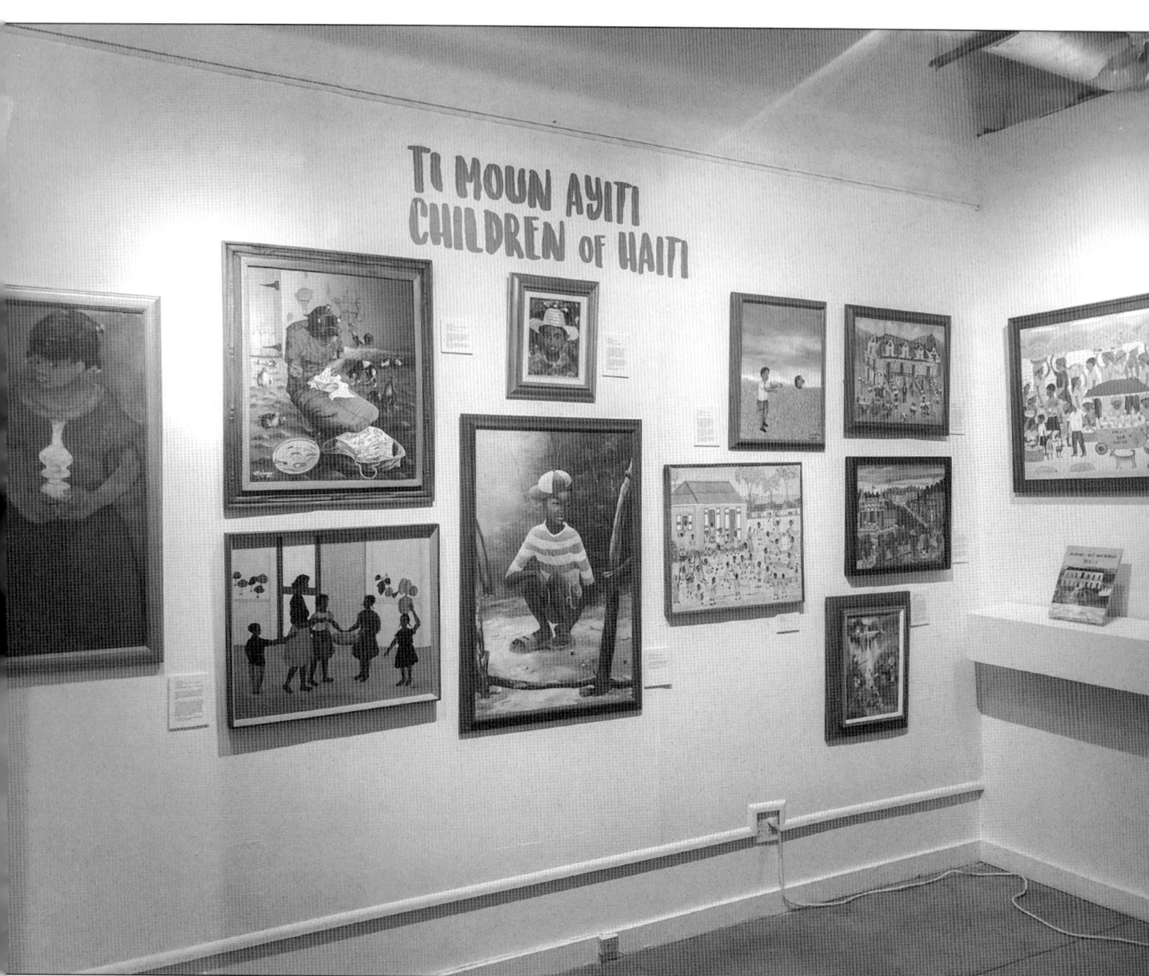

The Waterloo Museum for the Arts is proud to present, in conjunction with the Haitian American Museum of Chicago, the "Ti Moun Ayti, Children of Haiti" exhibit. The Waterloo Museum for the Arts is located in Iowa and hosts the largest collection in the United States of Haitian public art, with many exhibitions showcasing Haitian culture. The vitality of Haitian culture through the children of this poor nation comes into focus in this display of strength and spirit. Both institutions are committed to the development of an increased understanding and appreciation for Haiti's rich culture by diverse communities throughout Chicago and beyond. In this vein, they want to shed light on the exciting stories and contributions of Haitian children as major contributors to the cultural narrative. This is an initiative that has shown the beauty of Haitian art and works toward the linking of communities through recognition and respect for the special place that Haiti occupies in the world. "Ti Moun Ayti" carries much meaning, and with it, the museums will try to foster a deeper appreciation for Haiti's cultural legacy.

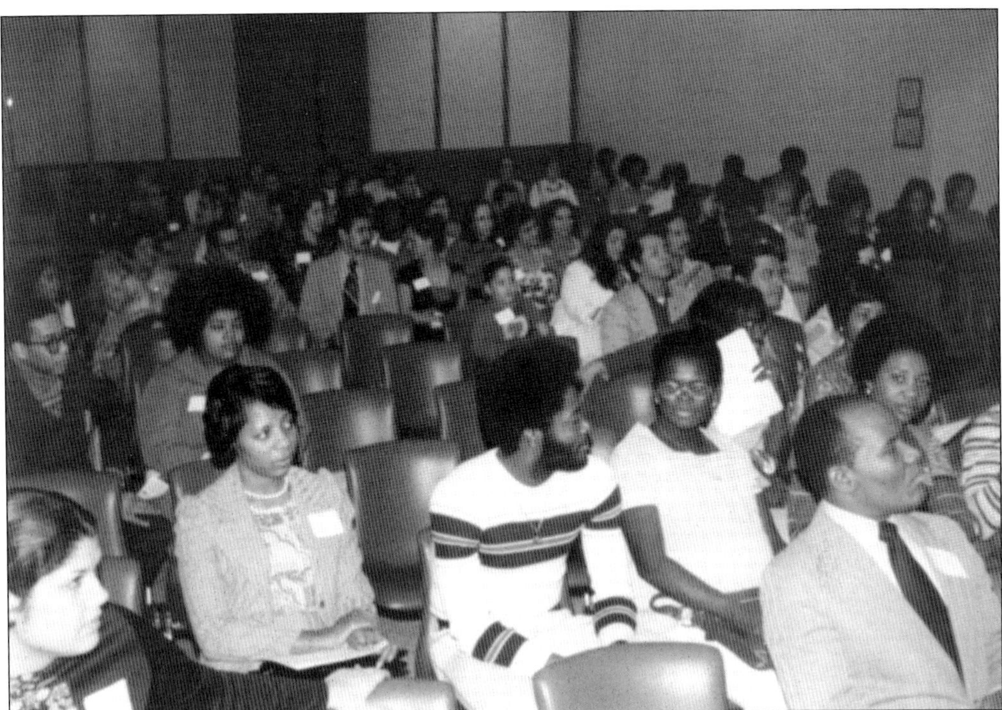

In the 1970s, a convention for the community of Chicago facilitated unity and dialogue between its citizens. It functioned as a platform for information and discussion about cultural heritage and for resolving and discussing diaspora concerns through debating them. There was meaningful dialogue amongst participants, creating a heightened sense of identity and solidarity and a united community during a transformation period.

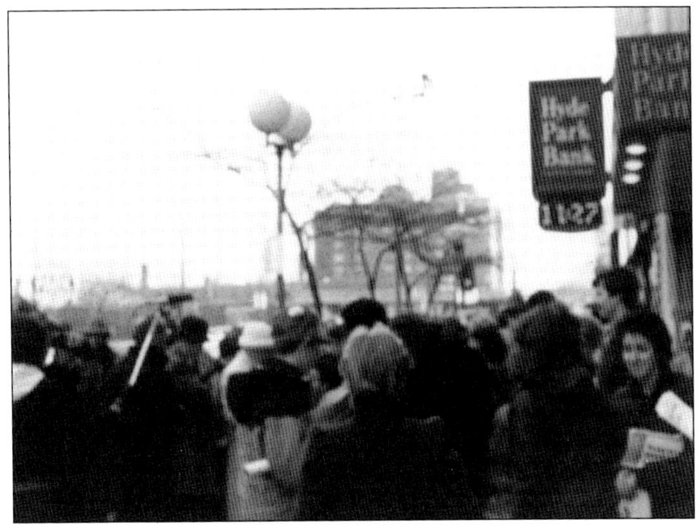

A significant migration of Haitians to Hyde Park has added to its diversity of cultures. This image showcases the multicultural neighborhood of this special community. What transpired brings out community solidarity and determination, an opportunity for them to practice their customs and seal their presence in Hyde Park through its social and family ties.

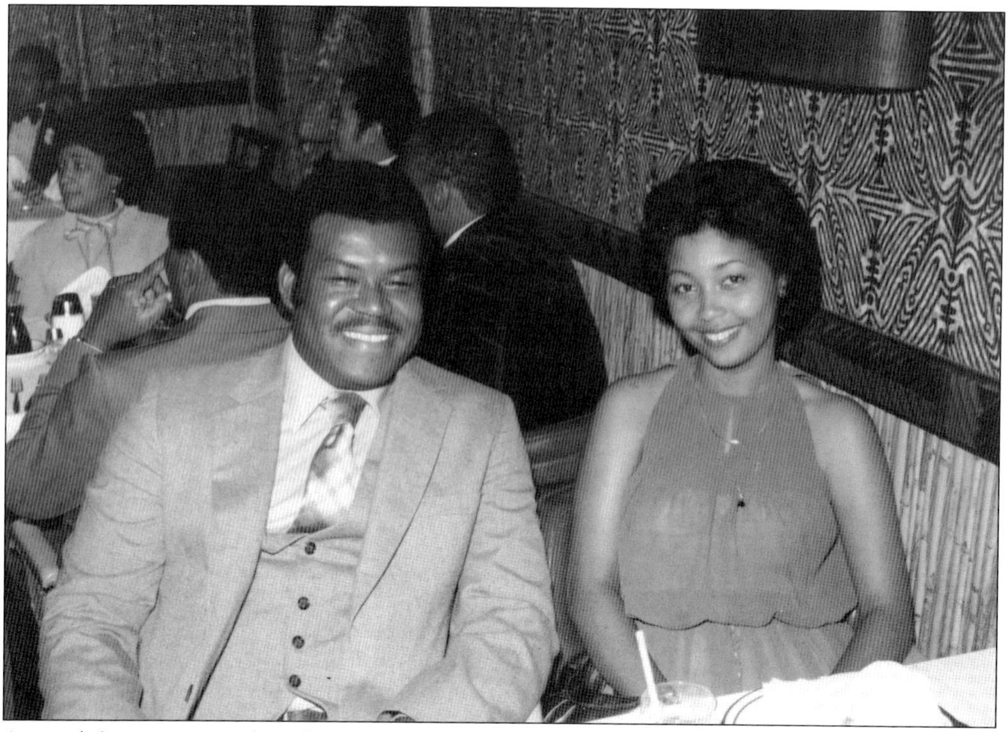

A social function united a vibrant community of settled immigrants in Chicago with a shared Haitian heritage. The social function provided a platform for community members to socialize, swap experiences, and celebrate a rich common heritage. Participants socialized, shared experiences of life, and bonded, creating a pool of solidarity and camaraderie in such a vibrant community. The social function displayed Haitian determination and success in the Windy City.

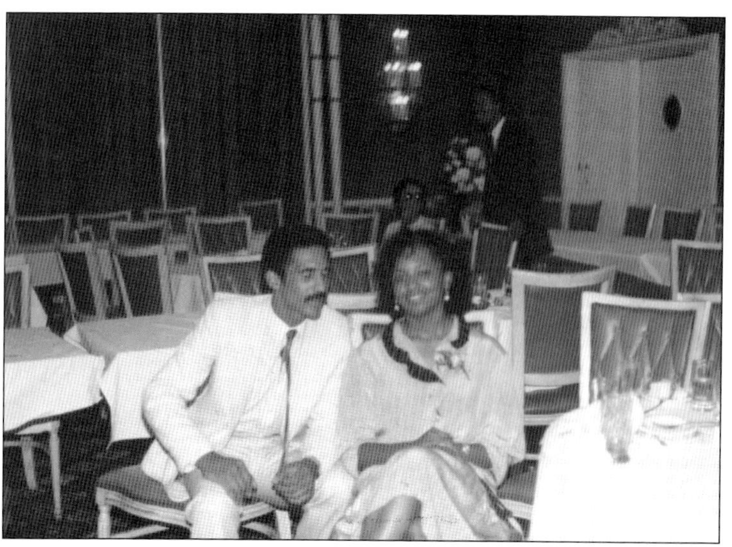

Young Haitians enjoy experiencing their new communities. Whether socializing in nearby parks, exercising with friends, or enjoying an exciting community party, it is important to them to create memories. Not only is it a unifier, but it forms rich experiences in terms of developing heritage and holding memories for a lifetime.

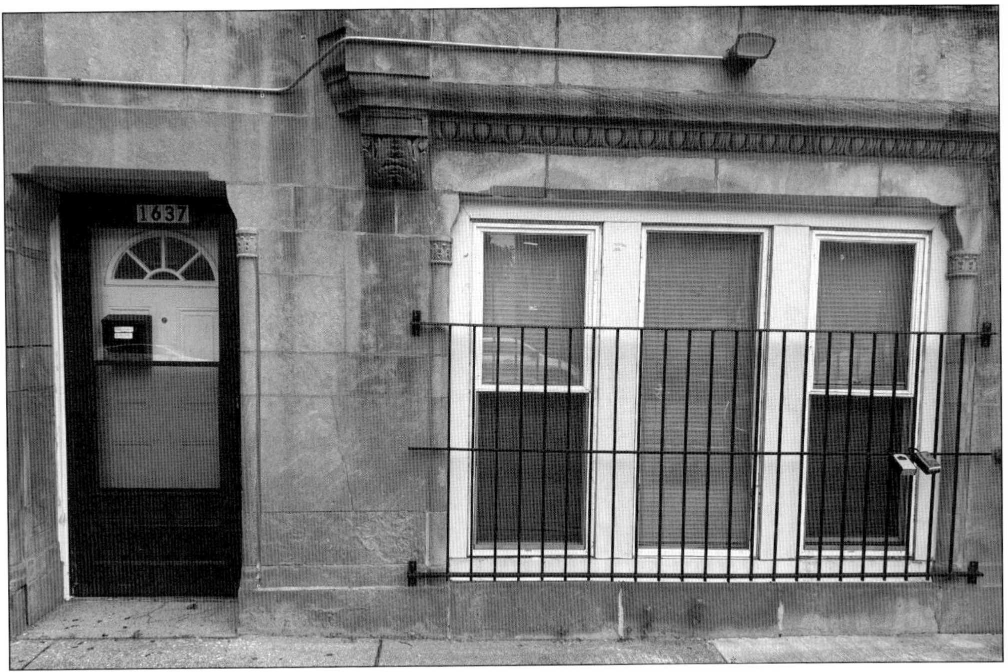

The Morse building has served as the Haitian Community Center since the 1960s to assist new immigrants. It is where residents and families take advantage of the different services, such as social and medical assistance. This center has also served as a starting point for the Haitian community to come together, share a supportive atmosphere, and gain all they require to move forward in their new home.

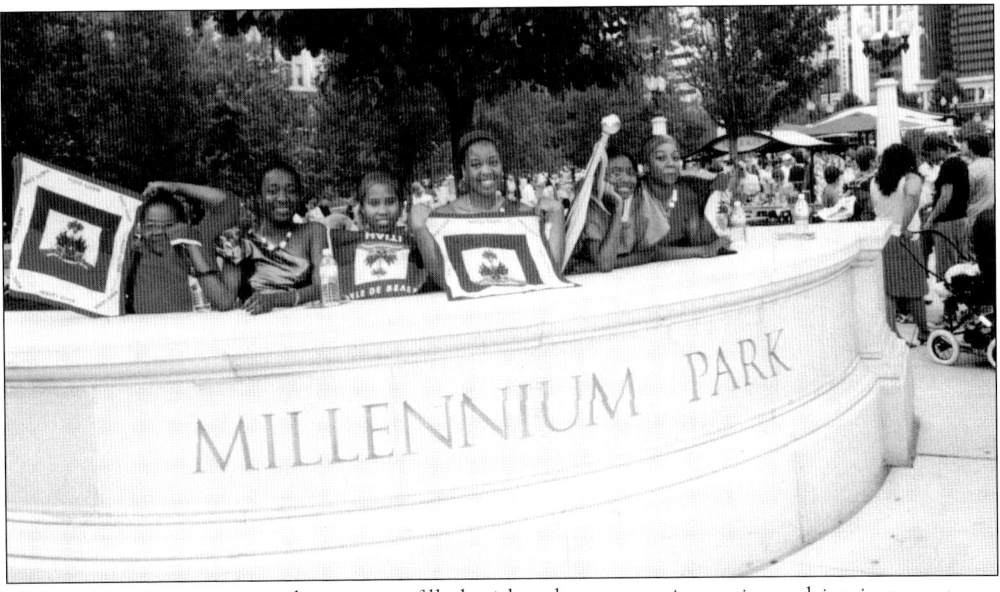

Carnaval in Haiti is an explosive time filled with color, energetic music, and intricate costume design. For new immigrants, perpetuating these events is critical in terms of cultural identity and community building. They organize events representative of Haitian Carnaval with the playing of *konpa* and *rara* music, folklore dances, and tales that add richness to their new surroundings through cultural diversity.

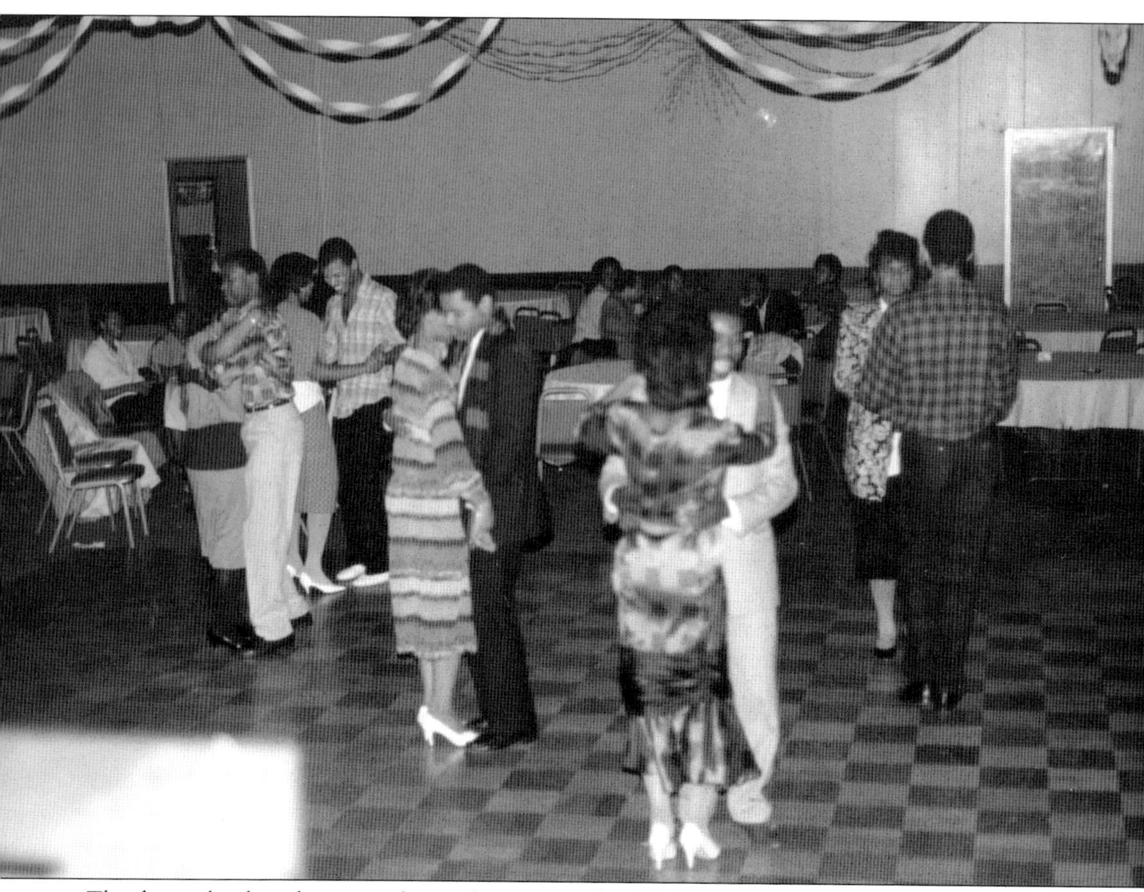

The dance developed into a rich social activity in dancing halls, in which dancers could maintain and celebrate their heritage. Dance halls then became social communities in which all joined together to celebrate both beat and emotion in dancing together. Not only did this enrich cultural life, but it also generated a community for its dancers, in which everyone longed for expression and motion through dancing.

Six

Churches and Religion

Haitians in Chicago are invisibly visible: most people do not know that a strong community exists in the Windy City, but when people do know, they can easily see how the historic community lives and thrives in diverse ways. Religion and church life are one area where Haitians in Chicago connect, collaborate, and hold on to their cultural heritage. This chapter explores the hidden historical network of Haitian churches in Chicago and the role of religion in the diasporic community's formation.

Religion and spirituality are central to Haitian culture on the island and in the diaspora. Despite the many misconceptions regarding Vodou, this spiritual legacy of ancient African religious traditions permeates the ways Haitians worship and think about their cultural identity. The majority of the Haitian churches are Christian-based: Catholic, Protestant, and smaller but growing denominations.

This chapter is largely based on research completed with two student assistants (Stephen Buban and Paula Pelletier) in 2018. Funded by the Mellon Foundation and Lake Forest College's Digital Chicago grant, the year was spent doing ethnographic and oral history research to create a map and recover the history of 14 Haitian churches in Chicago and the surrounding suburbs. Some of the church buildings are owned by community members, while others are rented for regular Sunday services (weekly or monthly). In this way, the story of the churches shows where and how Haitians are taking up space in the Chicagoland area.

These images try to capture the richness of the religious life of Haitians in Chicago. While not exhaustive, they fill a large gap in understanding the history of this community. Specifically, they show the importance of religion to diasporic community buildings. Church is about gathering, generational community, sharing food, childcare, Sunday school, and helping new migrants integrate themselves into the community and not feel so alone.

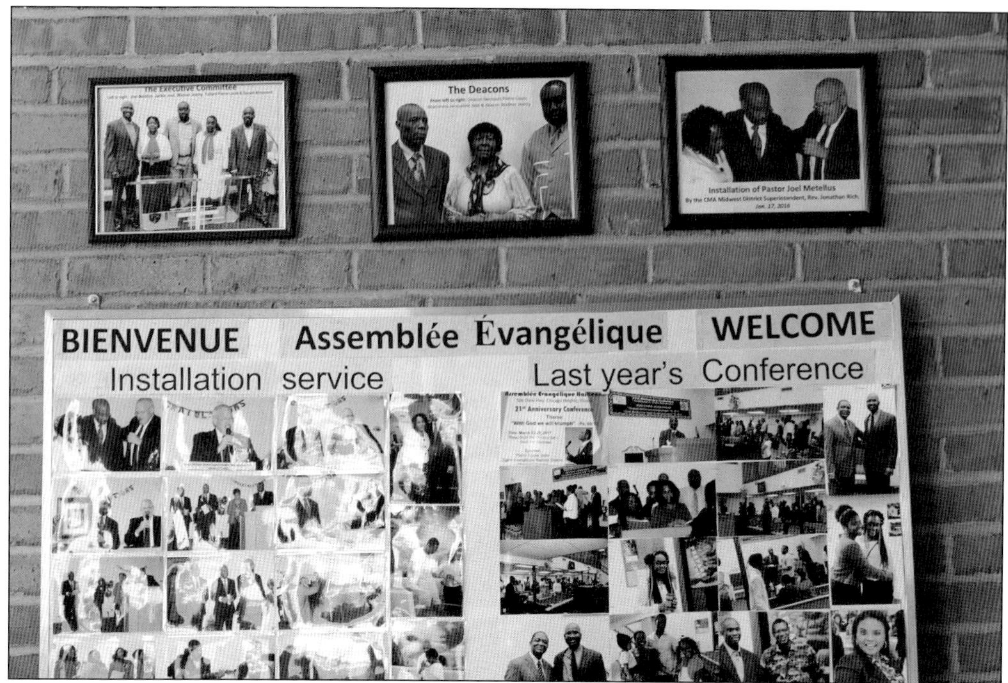

The Assemblé Évangélique Haitian Church is located in the south suburb of Chicago Heights. An evangelical church, it serves the growing enclave of Haitians in the south suburbs, many of whom moved out of the city beginning in the 1990s. Joel Metellus was the pastor in 2018.

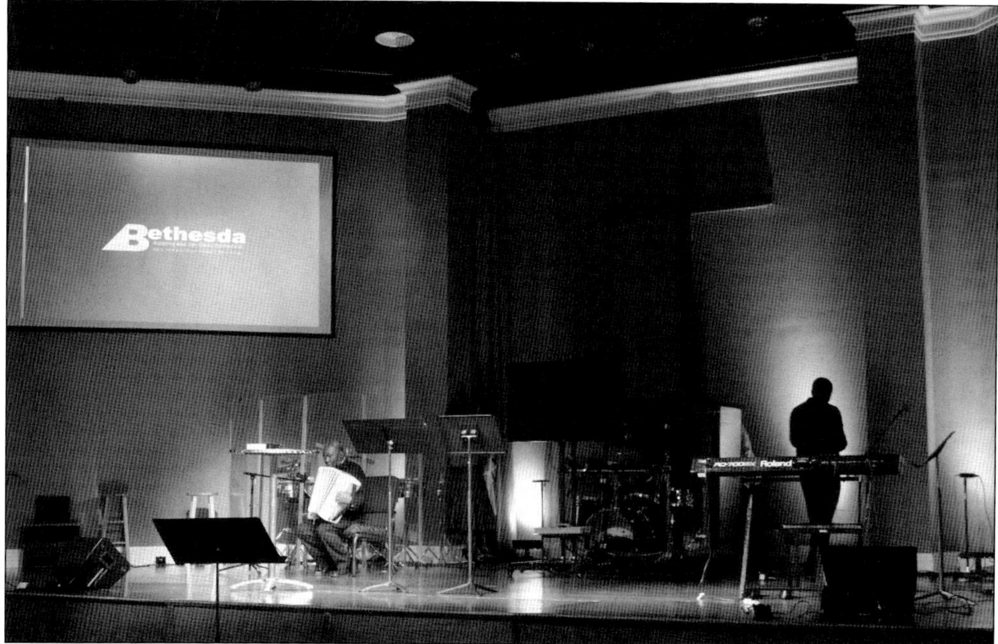

The Bethesda Haitian Assembly of God has rented a space inside the Northwest Assembly of God Church building in Mount Prospect since 2008. The church uses a mix of Creole and English in its weekly masses. In 2018, Marie Rose Michele served as the interim pastor to this locally based congregation.

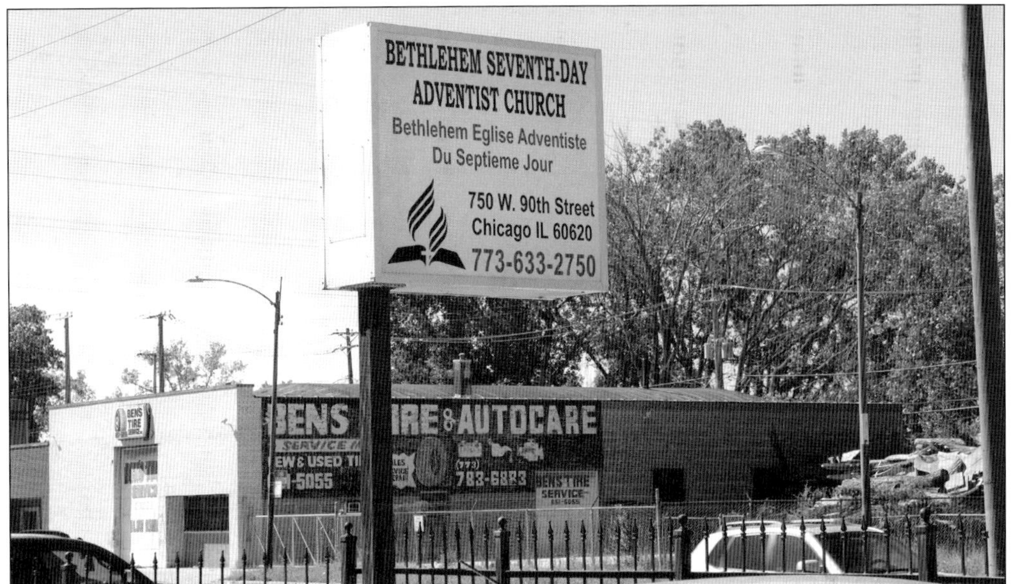

The Bethlehem Seventh-day Adventist Church celebrated its 50th anniversary in 2018. Like many of the other Haitian churches in the Chicagoland area, this congregation serves a multigenerational community that hopes to continue to engage the youth. The large basement serves as a communal space, where Sunday school and feasting after masses occur. As one churchgoer stated, "There are no Haitians without religion."

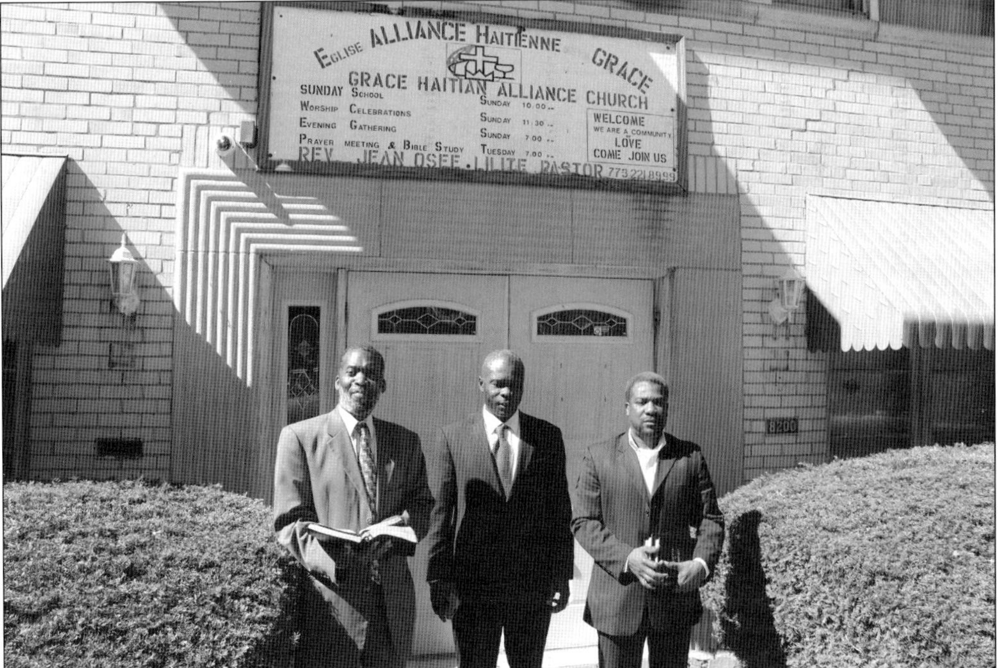

The picture, taken on June 23, 2018, shows the Reverend Humberto Almonord (left) of the Evangelical Tribe of Israel Church and Father Edward (right), with an unidentified gentleman in the middle. Indeed, the community's two spiritual leaders share their space with Eglise Haitienne De La Grace, testimony of the community's diverse spiritual populace.

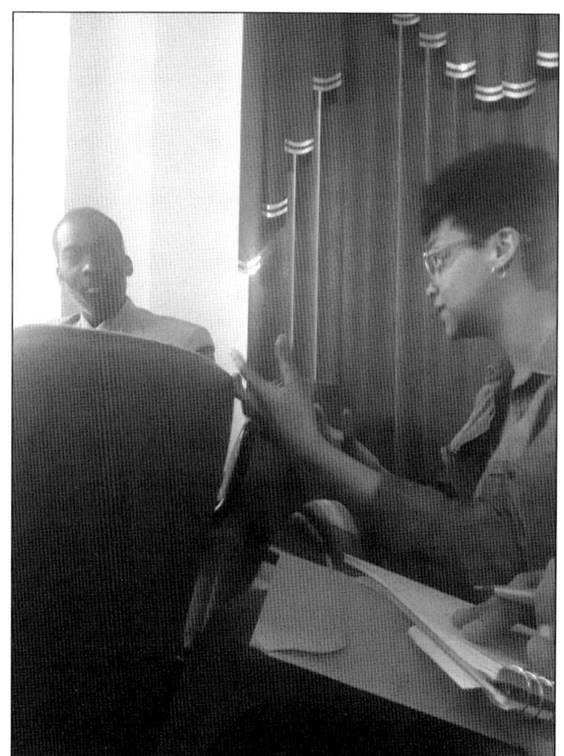

The two images on this page were taken in June 2018 when Dr. Courtney Pierre Joseph interviewed Reverend Almonord, the pastor of the Evangelical Tribe of Israel Church. This small but growing congregation shares a building with the Eglise Haitienne De La Grace on the South Side. They have a sister church in St. Marc, Haiti (the birthplace of DuSable), and they rely on the radio to share information across the diaspora.

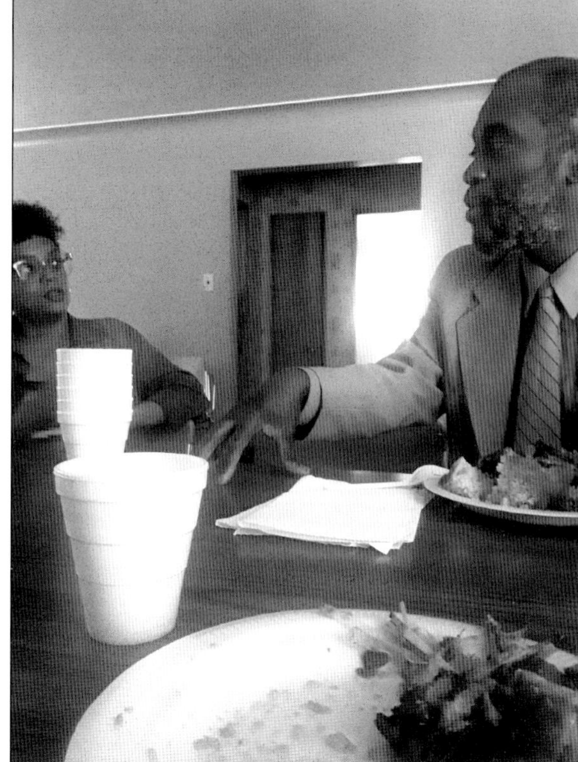

The Evangelical Tribe of Israel Church is located in Chicago and is a place for worship and companionship. It is open to people for spiritual growth and interaction in ensuring the lessons of the Christian faith are inculcated while reaching out to and sharing with the community.

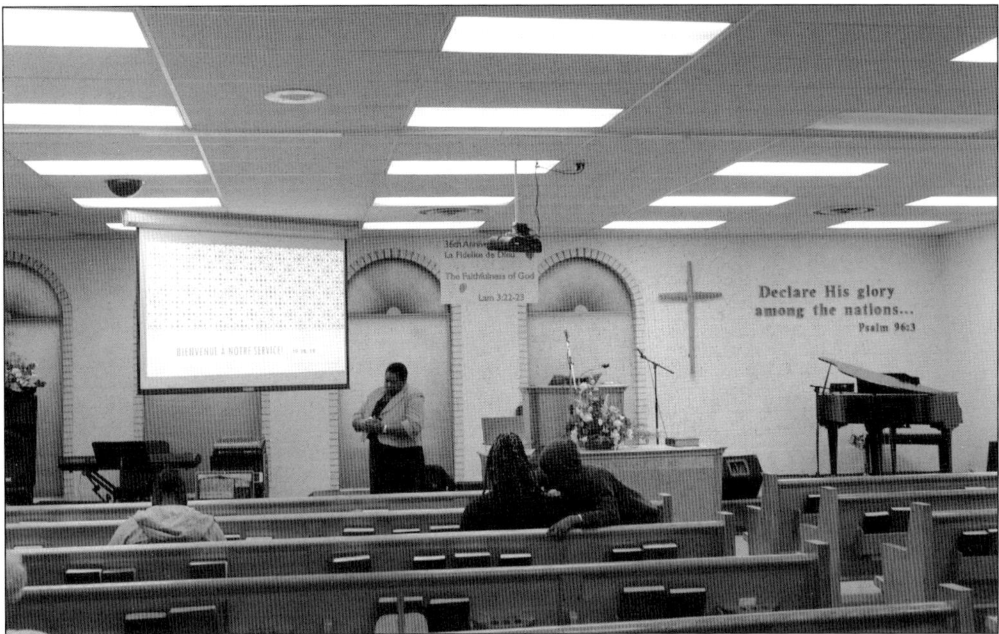

The two images on this page uncover a hidden gem of the Haitian community: the Bethel Evangelical Church/Eglise Evangelique Bethel, located in Des Plaines, a northwest suburb. This congregation moved west after being in the Rogers Park/Evanston area, and its church home is very large, giving room for its congregation to grow.

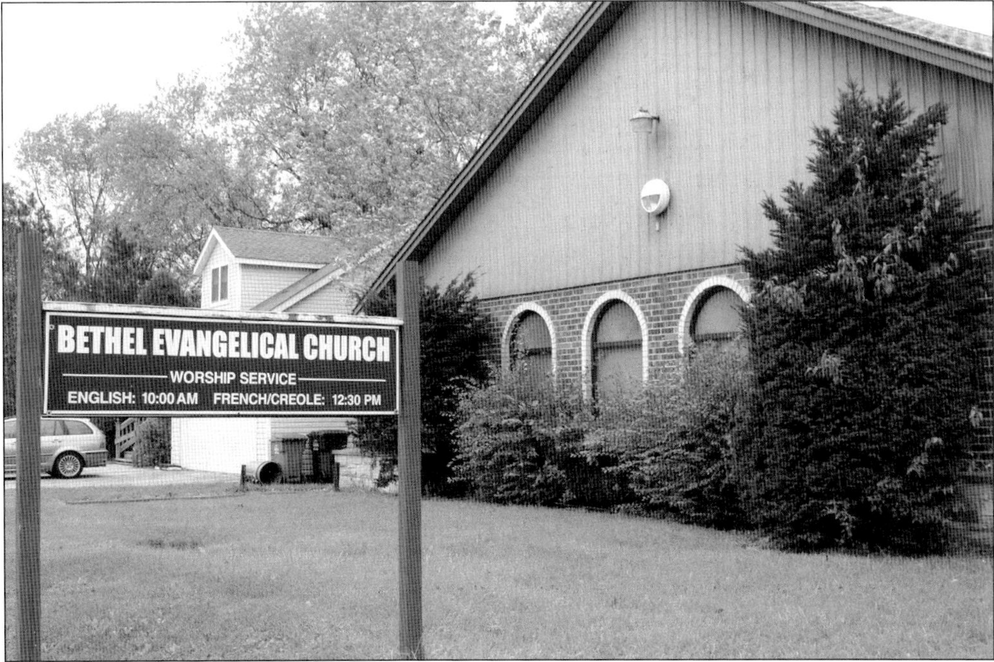

The Bethel Evangelical Church holds great importance and bears the name of Église Evangélique Bethel. It represents, for Haitians, a spiritual oasis that creates a sense of belonging among them, thus support. Empowerment is affected on a number of various levels through faith, unity, and resilience regarding its activities and outreach.

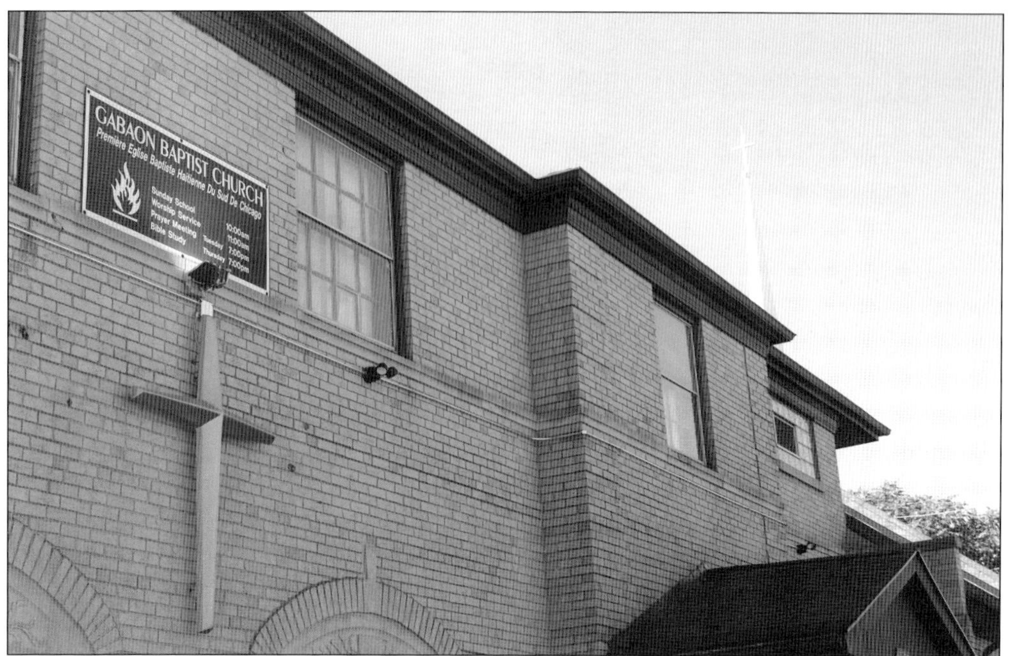

The richness of Haitian diasporic culture hits one immediately when walking into Gabaon Baptist Church. Located on the south side of the city, this congregation has been active since 1977, when it was founded by a Haitian couple. Masses are a mix of song and dance, in both English and Creole, which serves the Haitian and Haitian American base of the congregation and community.

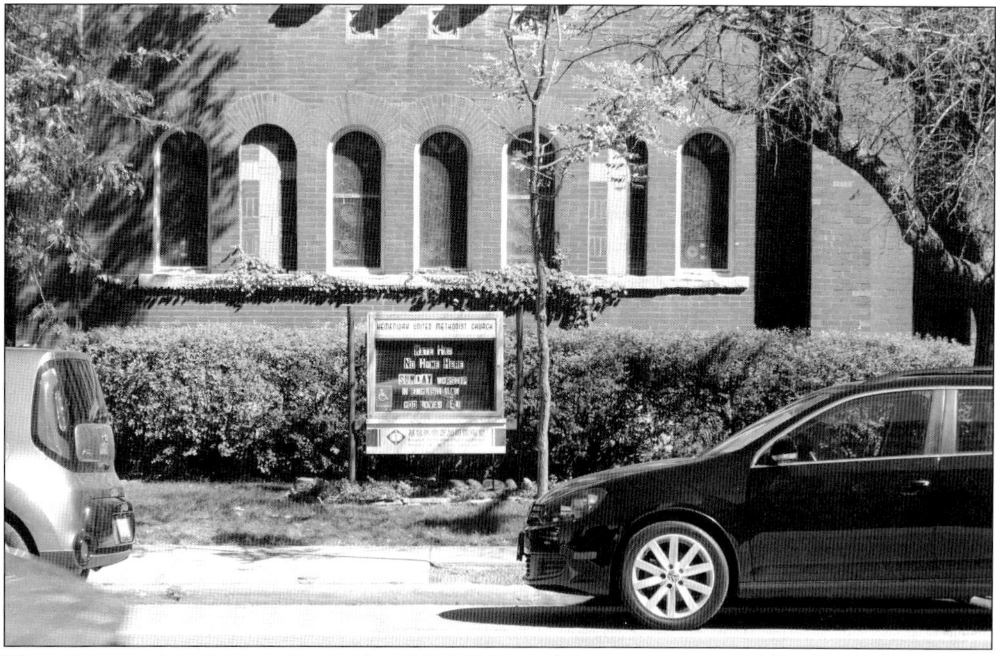

This photograph, taken on September 22, 2018, is of Evanston La Nouvelle Jerusalem Church, which worships at the Hemenway United Methodist Church. This represents part of the dynamic spiritual life found within the community. Thus, this particular church is highly responsible for creating an atmosphere of worship and fellowship among the members.

The Haitians have held a monthly Catholic service at Saint Mary Catholic Church in Evanston, Illinois, since the early 1980s near the border of the Rogers Park neighborhood. Like Our Lady of Peace, it is battling a shrinking congregation. Yet, its mission work keeps the congregation connected to each other and Haitians on the island.

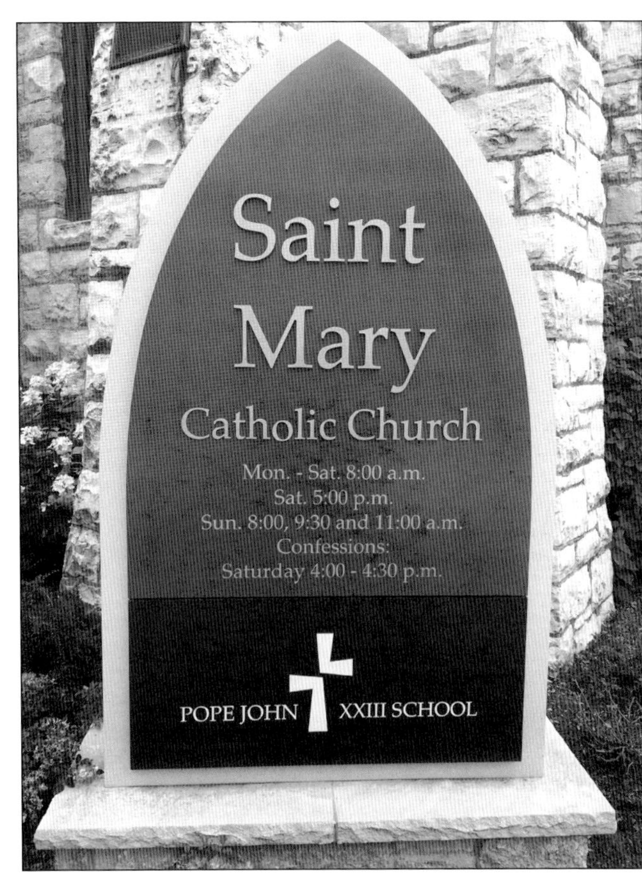

The North Side Church of God/Eglise De Dieu Du Nord has been active since 1979. Reminiscent of the storefront churches of decades past, this church is housed on North Broadway Avenue among shops and such. Pastor Jean Bertrand, a Haitian migrant to Chicago in 1977, has led this large congregation for many years. The church bus, among other communal initiatives, has clearly kept this diasporic religious community thriving.

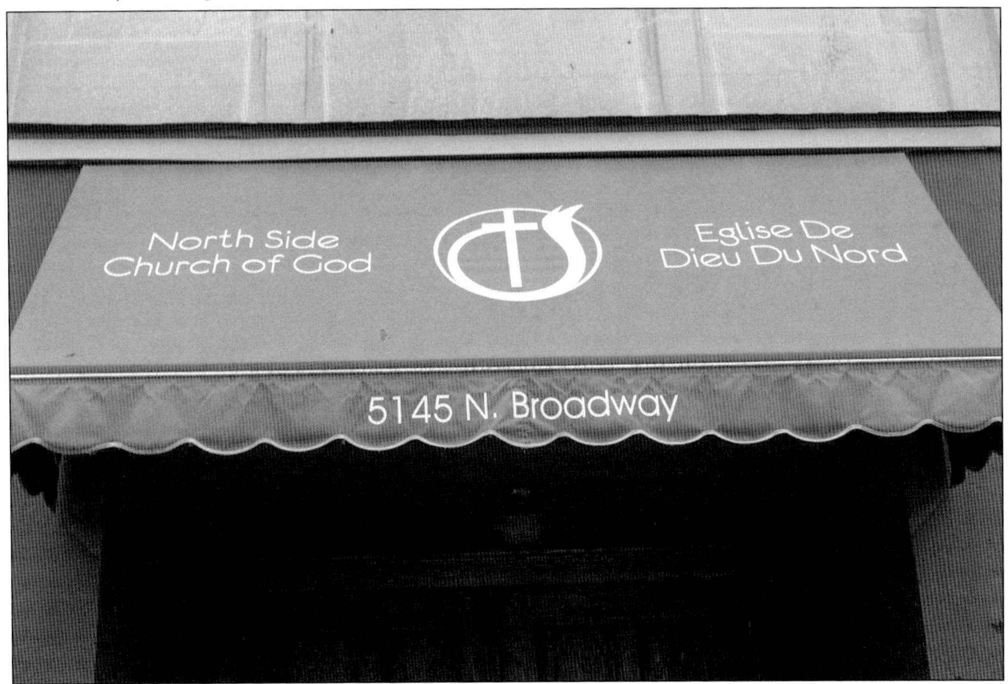

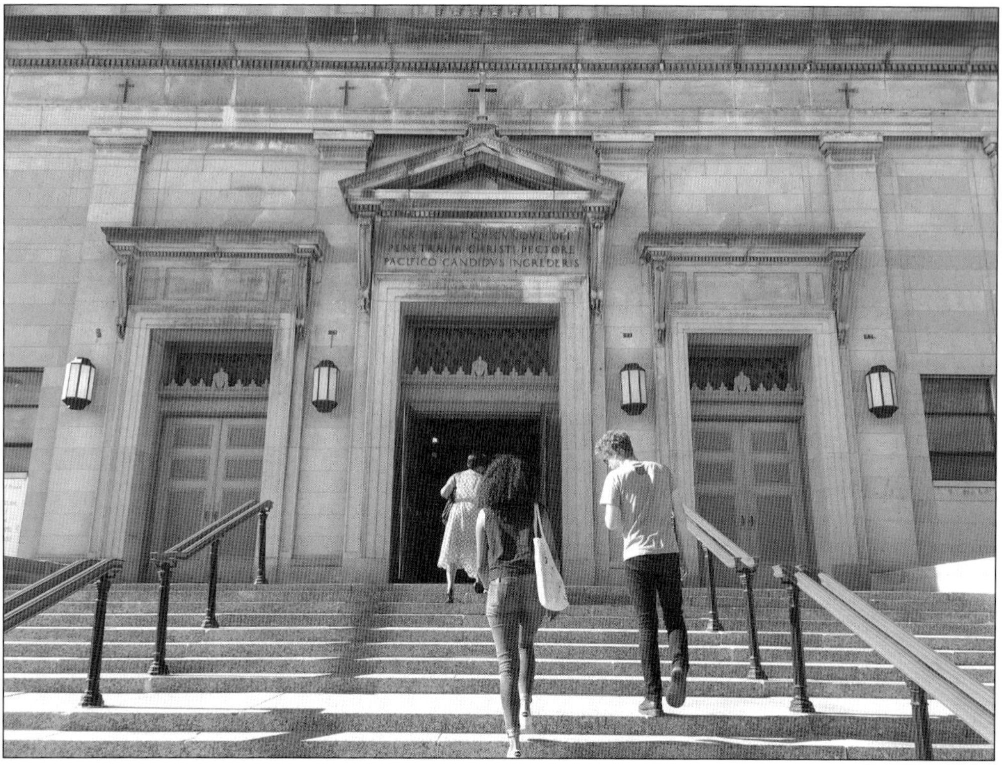

The two images on this page capture Our Lady of Peace Church, where one of the few Catholic masses takes place for Haitians on the South Side. In 2018, there were concerns about the future of this congregation; an aging population of current churchgoers and less interest in Catholicism among younger Haitians and Haitian Americans has meant the services only bring about 20 to 30 people on average.

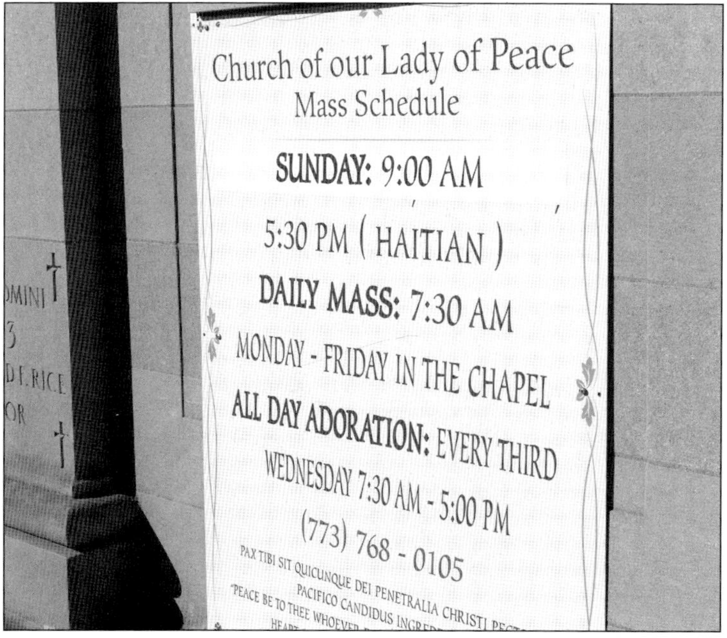

Our Lady of Peace Church has been a spiritual home for the Haitian Catholic community, where a sense of belonging and cultural bonding is very high. Through spirited worship and keeping in touch with traditions, this congregation invites all its members to celebrate faith and heritage, binding these ties even more strongly within one another and the community.

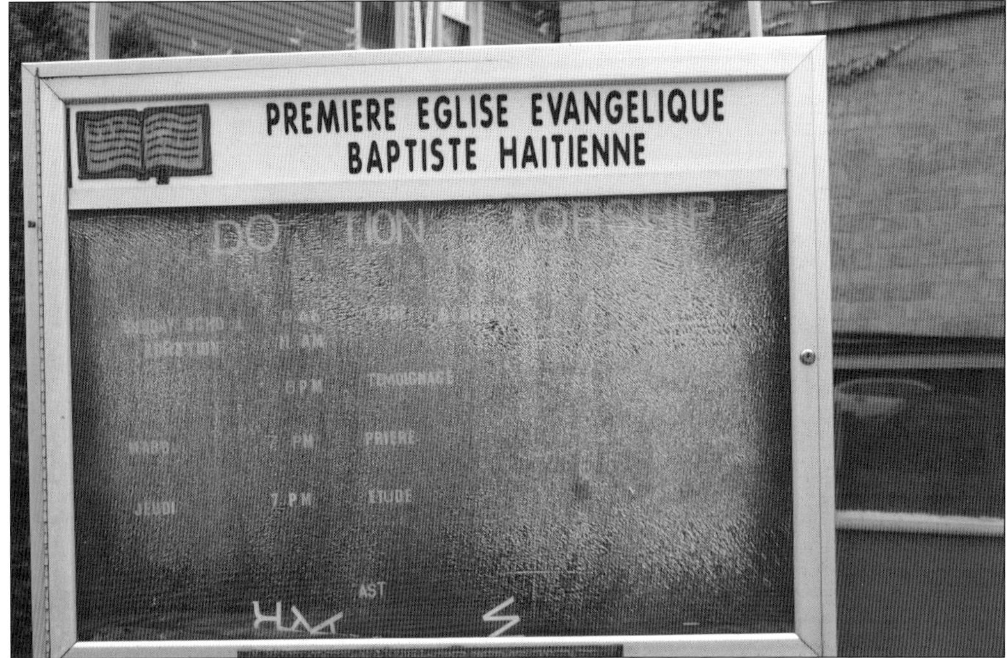

Première Église Évangélique Baptiste Haïtienne, established in 1976 and pastored since 2018 by Samson Adrien, is a vibrant Haitian church located in Evanston. Rich history is reflected in the church's stained-glass windows that honor its first deacon, and a full band worships together in French, English, and Creole alongside the devout congregation.

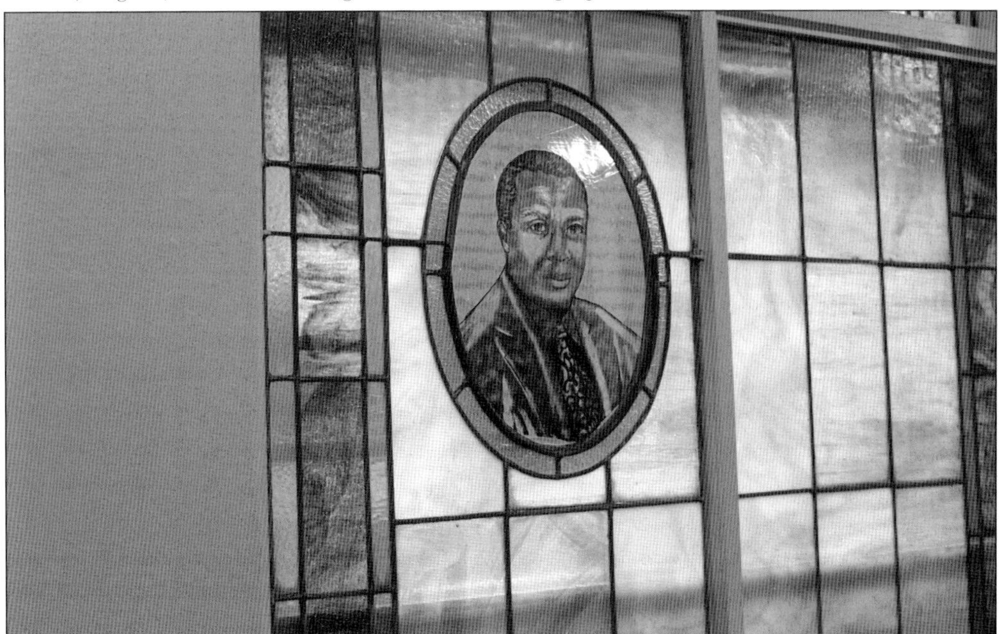

Première Église Évangélique Baptiste Haïtienne, or First Evangelical Haitian Baptist Church, has faithfully served the Evanston community since 1976. It provides a spiritual home to so many through faith, fellowship, and a connection to one's culture, fostering that within its members while adding to the diversity of this neighborhood.

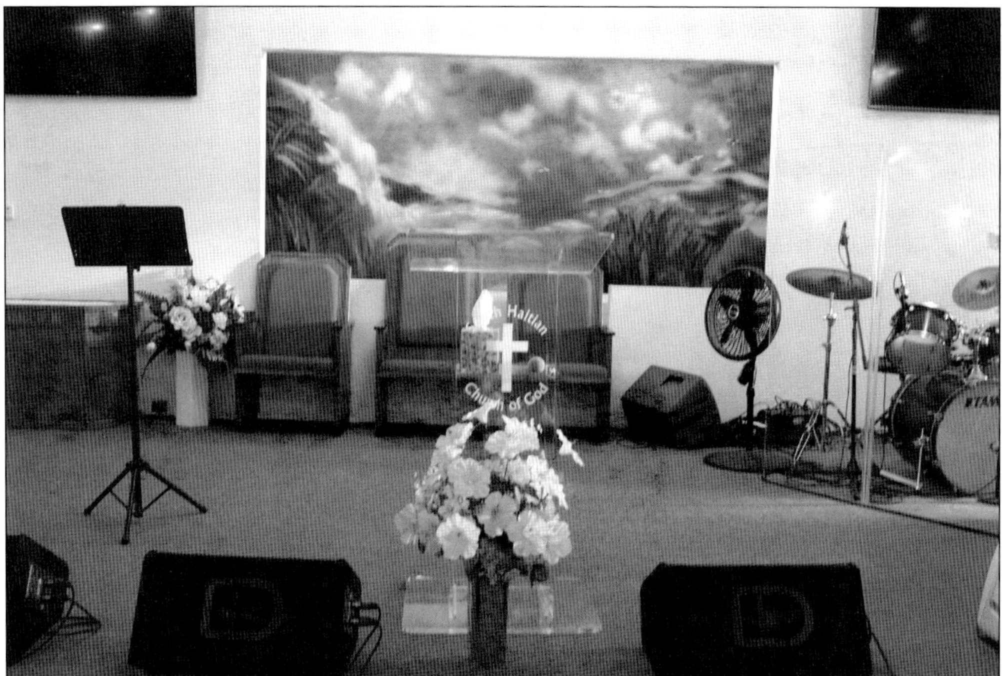

The Haitian Church of God, also known as the Eglise De Dieu Haitienne, has been active since the early 1980s but only at this location since 1994. After being led by Pastor Dumasrais for many years, he handed the reins to Pastor Edwin in 2017. Like many of the other Haitian diasporic church services, one will see a multigenerational congregation worshipping in both English and Creole.

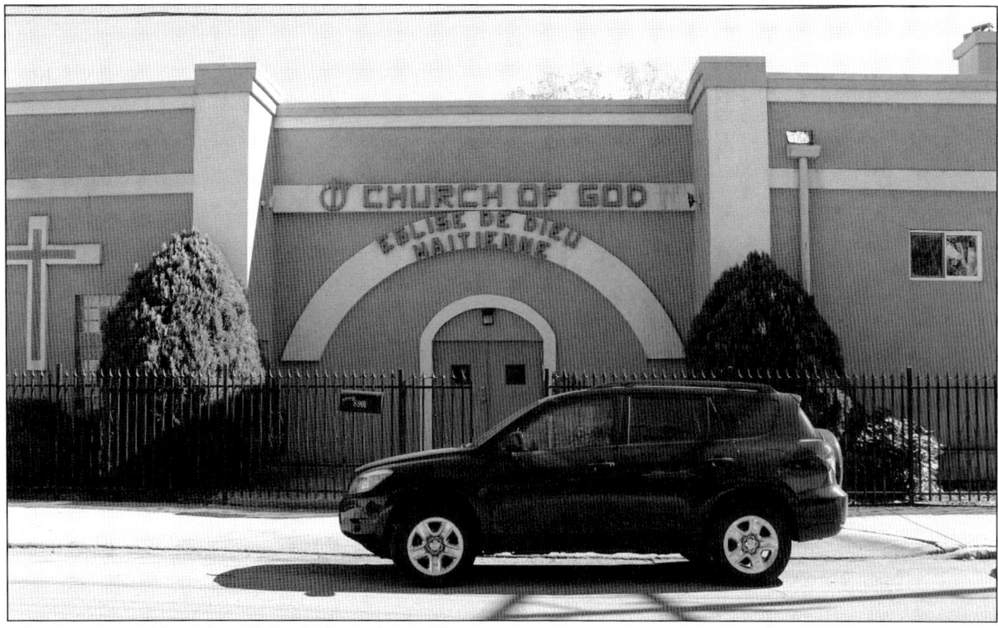

The Haitian Church of God, based in Chicago, serves as a very active house of worship and fellowship for members. It aims to offer spiritual guidance and support to its members, hence creating great bonds and harmony among the congregation. With many programs and activities, it seeks to develop cultural heritage and enhance spiritual needs in the community.

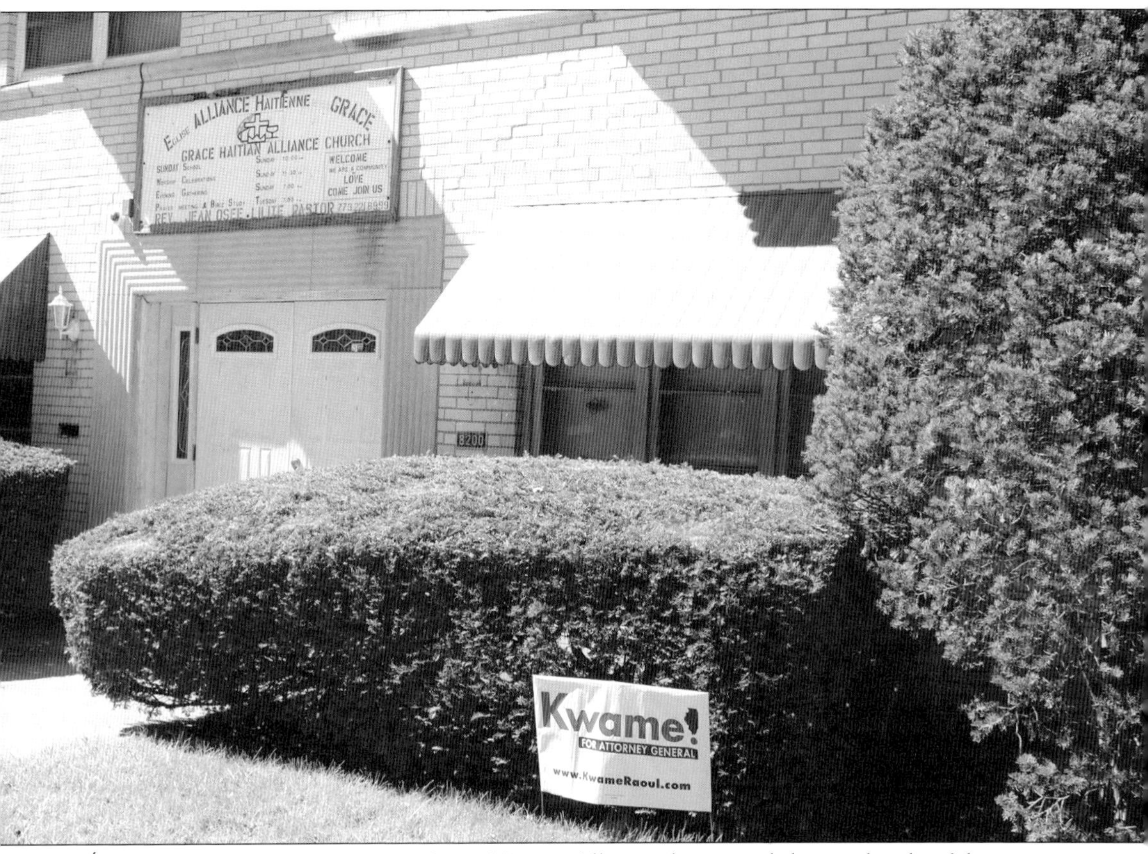

The Église Alliance Haïtienne Grâce, Grace Haitian Alliance, has served the south side of the city for decades. This church shares its building with the Evangelical Tribe of Israel Church, which considers Saturday a good day to conduct services, freeing up Sunday and allowing both groups to peacefully coexist. Under Rev. Jean Osee Lilite's dedicated leadership, who has led this growing congregation for nearly two decades, the church boasts over 100 members in its congregation. The Grace Haitian Alliance provides a spiritual home to its members and has brought together and supported many members of the Haitian diaspora in the area. The church, through outreach programs and events, promotes cultural heritage and addresses the needs of less fortunate people, further reinforcing its mission of faith and service. The longtime commitment of Reverend Lilite and the congregation is a reflection of enduring strength and resilience in their community, touching the lives of many.

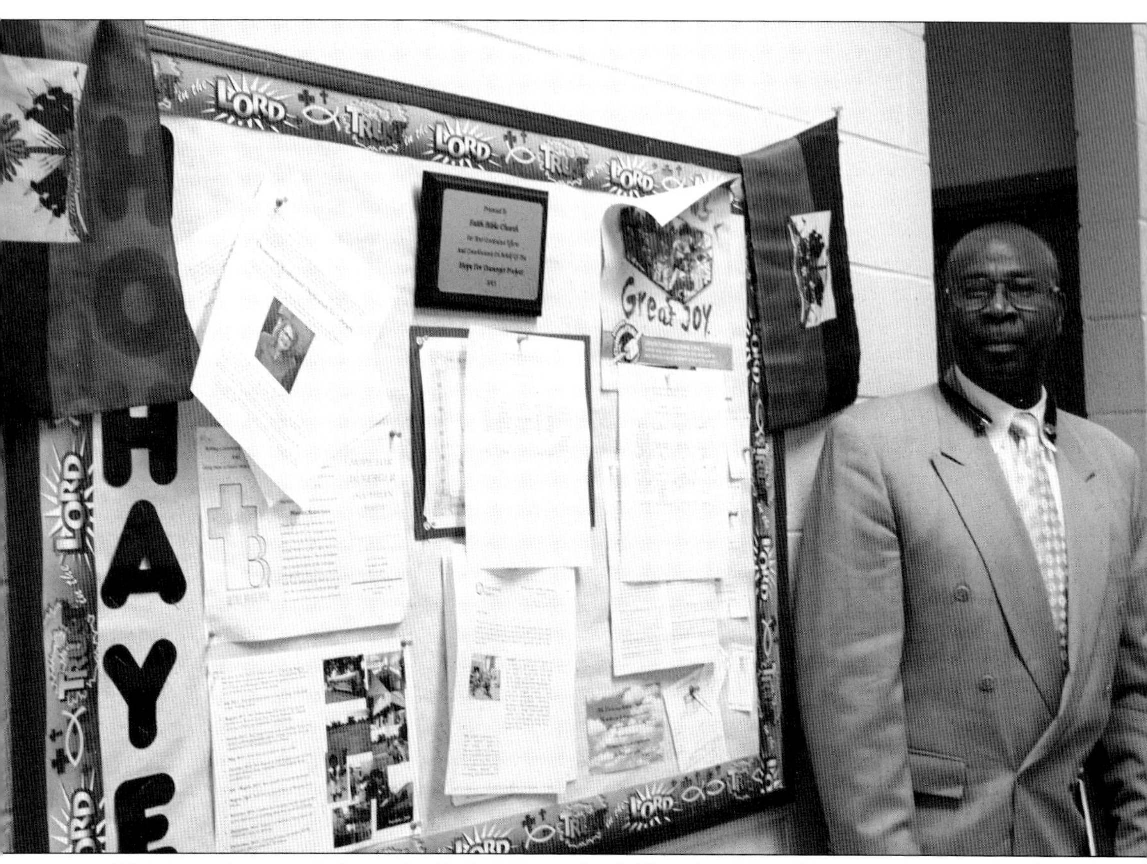

This is a photograph from the Bethel Evangelical Church of Des Plaines, taken on October 28, 2018, with Pastor Franco Valdemar. The church is a real focal point of community life, known simply as Eglise Evangelique Bethel, and acts as a source of spiritual growth and bonding within the community. Under the guidance of Pastor Valdemar, this congregation has grown in its core emphasis on Christian values and is also active in outreach and community service. This welcoming attitude brings people and families of all backgrounds together in worship and fellowship. It is not a moment in time but a portrait of the community, sworn to faith and camaraderie. The congregation, every time it gathers to worship, is also reminded of its common mission: to spread love, hope, and compassion throughout a world so desperately in need. Pastor Valdemar is committed to his flock in such a way that he inspires others to live their faith actively and meaningfully within and outside the church.

Seven

Haitian Leaders and Activists

The Haitian leaders and activists in Chicago come from a long line of revolutionaries that dates back to the turn of the 19th century, when Haiti established itself as an independent nation. Chicago Haitian leaders have a passion to effect change in their community and the city at large. With the migration of Haitians from Haiti to Chicago following the end of the US occupation, a vibrant community has emerged in both the North Side and South Side of Chicago.

The Haitian community was formed through the maintenance of networks and the establishment of institutions such as churches and community-based and professional organizations. Some of the early leaders helped newcomers from Haiti acclimate by using their social networks to connect them with appropriate services. Services for Haitian immigrants were sometimes provided through Haitian institutions that were established to build and sustain connections among Haitian immigrants and the homeland. With the increase of Haitian immigrants to Chicago, community leaders created organizations providing immigration, social, and legal services.

Additionally, Haitian leaders continue to help promote Haitian culture using their voice in the arts and media in Chicago. Chicago Haitian leaders have also raised the visibility of the community through political avenues and activism. For example, elected leaders have advocated for assistance for Haitian refugees seeking asylum in the US overall. Haitian leaders and activists continue to play an important role in maintaining the Haitian culture in Chicago and promoting the advancement of the Haitian community through the various positions they occupy, such as business owners, radio hosts, school officials, lawyers, advocates, and more.

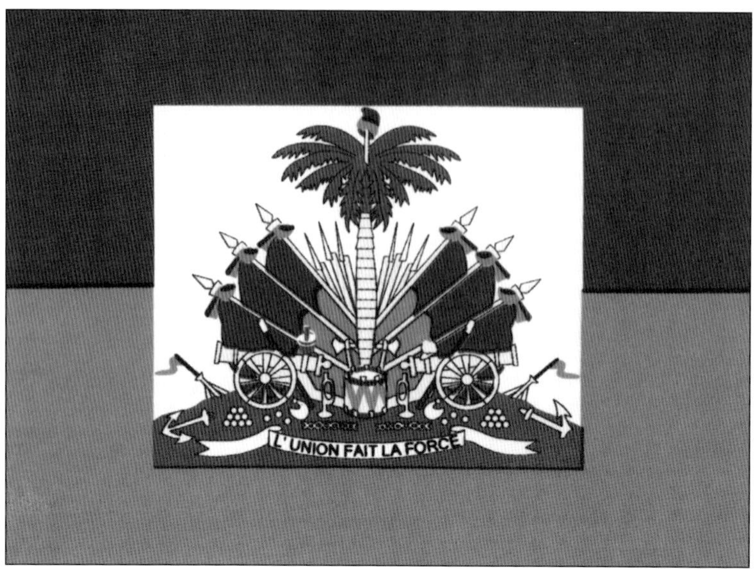

On May 18, 1803, the Haitian flag came into existence, according to a pre-independence decree by Jean Jacques Dessalines, the first Black revolutionary. On this day, every year in Haiti, the country and even its diaspora within Chicago celebrate it. It has a blue top, red bottom, and an image of a coat of arms with the motto "L'Union fait la force."

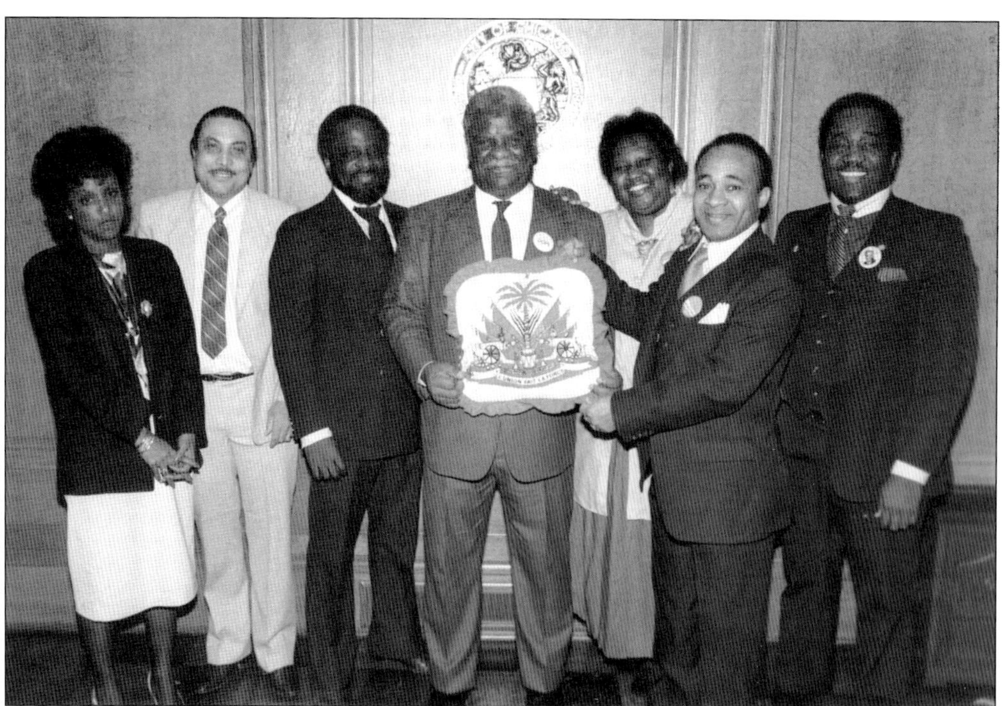

A delegation of Haitian leaders came to city hall here in Chicago and presented a replica of the coat of arms of Haiti to Mayor Harold Washington. The Haitian flag contains a palm tree with a liberty cap and a trophy of weapons. The motto on the flag is "L'Union fait la force," or "Union is Strength." Apparently, that just about sums up the entity of the Haitian people. (Harold Washington Library.)

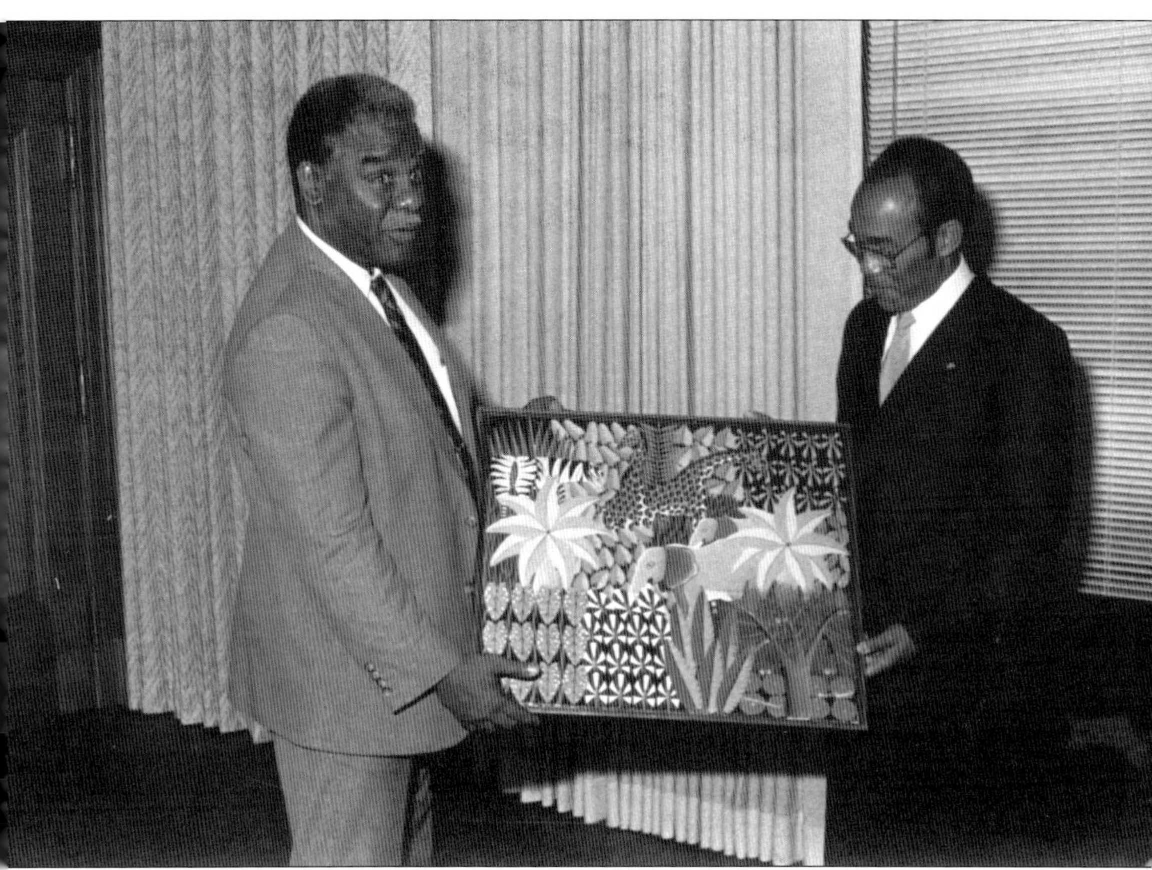

One very engaged community leader presented Mayor Washington with a vibrant Haitian painting, representative not only of the rich tapestry of Haiti but also of the depth of the connection between the mayor's office and the local Haitian community. It speaks volumes to the working relationship and mutual respect that define it. The vivid colors and detailed work of this painting represent Haitian culture, serving as a poignant reminder of the importance of diversity and community engagement. It represents how art can bring different cultures closer together, enabling an understanding and appreciation of each other. While it hangs on the wall in the mayor's office, the painting symbolizes an ongoing commitment to nurturing this bond, encouraging future initiatives that celebrate cultural heritage and promote inclusivity. By such actions, Mayor Washington reassured his commitment to serving all communities within. (Harold Washington Library.)

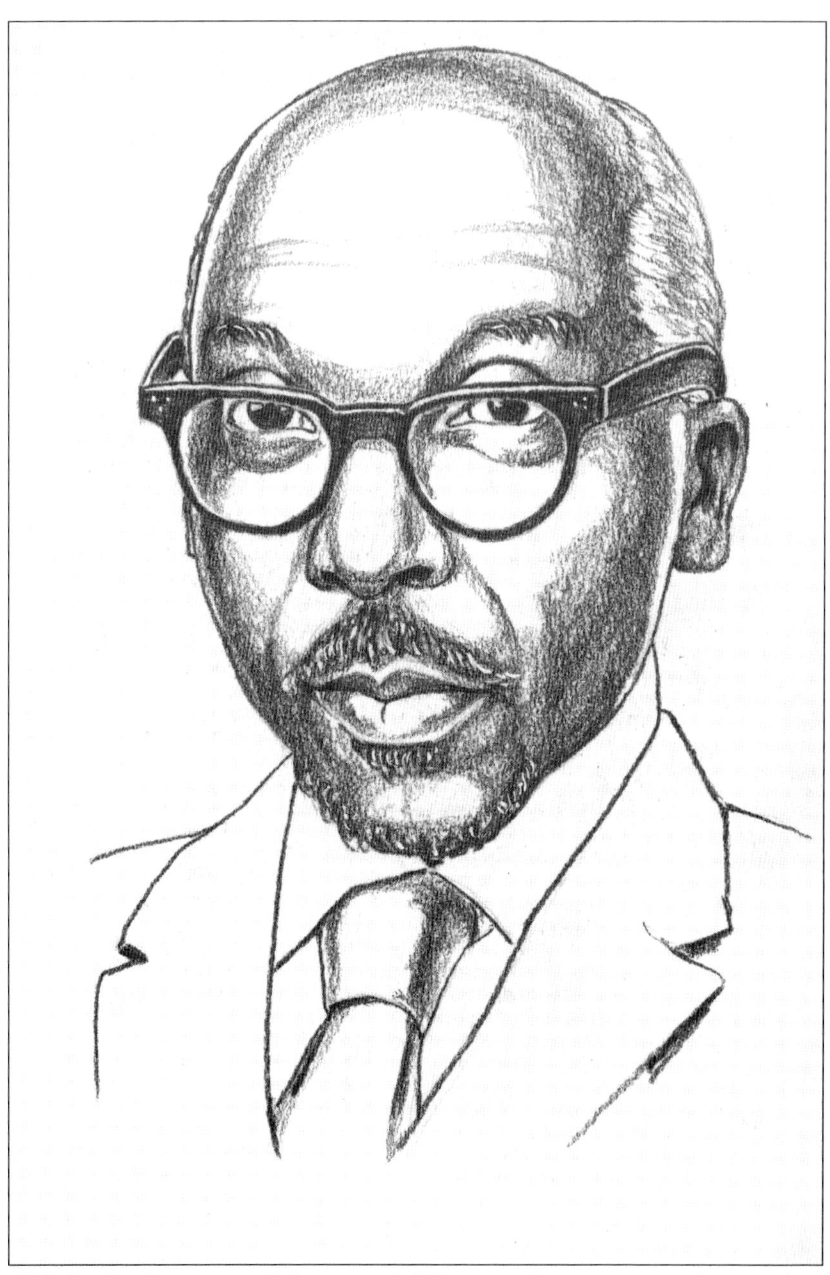

Dr. Metz T.P. Lochard was one of the powerful Haitian educators, journalists, and civil rights activists from 1896 until 1984. He had ties with the *Chicago Defender*, serving as associate editor and chief editorial writer for a period nearing 60 continuous years. Throughout his career, Lochard not only contributed to the paper's editorial direction but also played an integral part in its board of directors, ensuring that African American voices were heard at a time when mainstream media often overlooked their stories. Apart from his journalism contributions, he taught at various universities, shaping the minds of future generations. Lochard was an uncompromising force for civil rights and education, which has made him an important figure in the call for racial equality and social justice. His legacy continues to inspire those committed to giving voice to marginalized people and standing up against injustices in today's world. (Vivian G. Harsh Research Collection.)

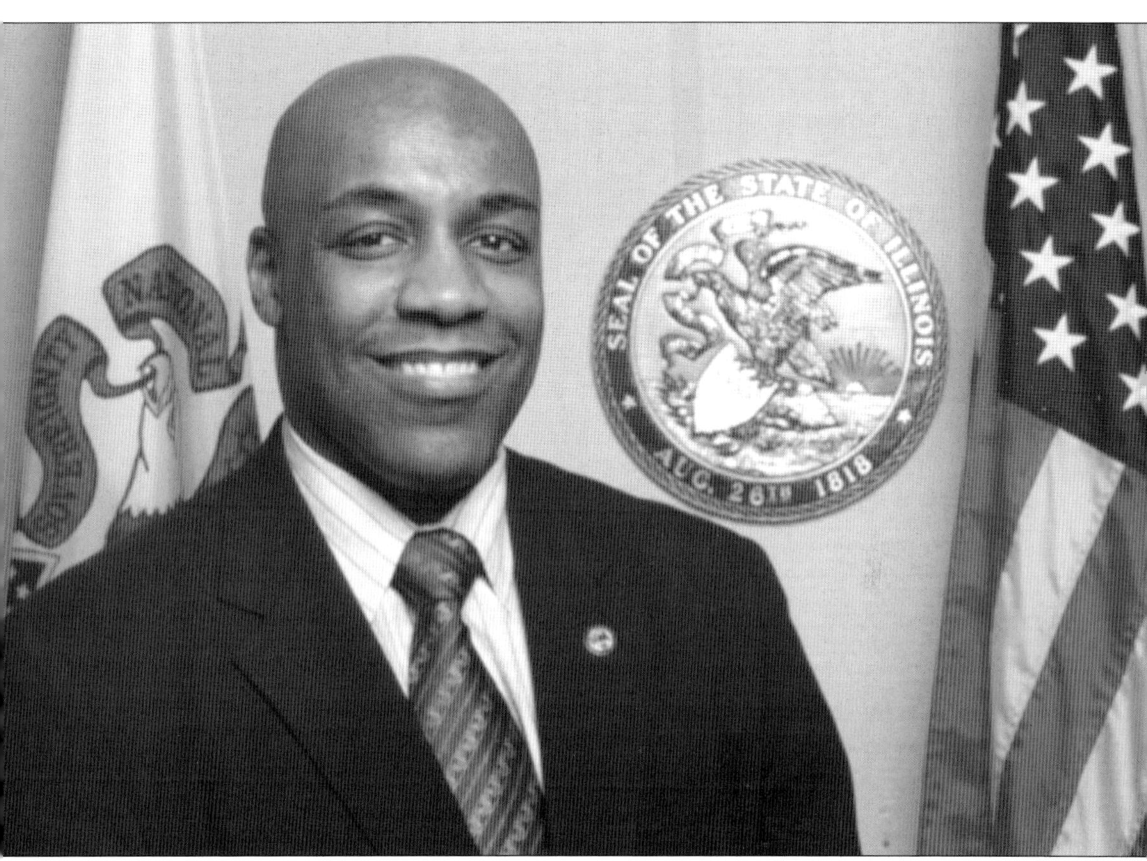

Kwame Raoul was born on September 30, 1964, and is a Haitian American attorney and politician who has been serving as the 42nd attorney general of Illinois since 2019. A member of the Democratic Party, he earlier represented the 13th district in the Illinois Senate between 2004 and 2019, leading such legislation as social justice, criminal justice reform, and economic development. Throughout his career, Raoul has demonstrated great dedication to community service and the legal profession. As attorney general, he pursues equity and justice in policies and programs that help in the well-being of Illinoisans, especially the underrepresented communities. His leadership is a testament to the impact of public service, truly capable of altering lives. This is very important in strong advocacy for reforms that bring equity to legal platforms. Raoul's work will continue to inspire change and better lives for so many throughout Illinois.

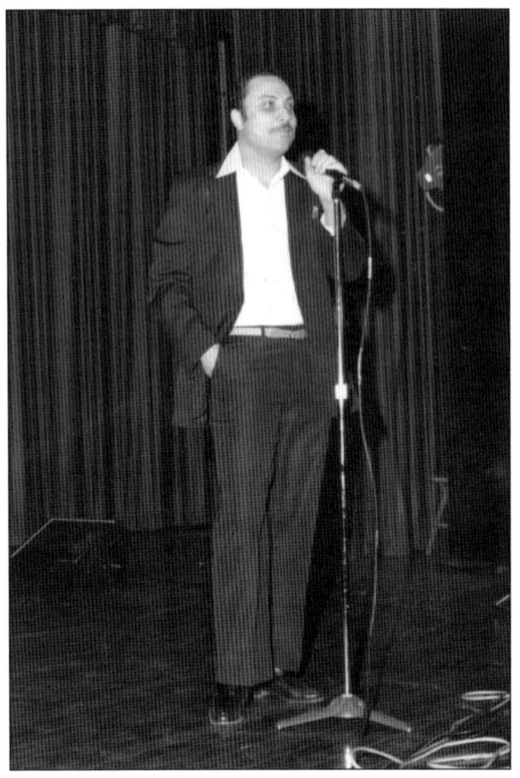

Robert Pressoir, the most prominent leader of the community, emerged in the 1970s; he played a significant role in organizing the Haitian Northside Community Center. His shipping company initiated business, and he played an active role in the establishment of the first local media, such as radio and television, to improve communication and cultural visibility for Haitians, indelibly etching his impact within the community.

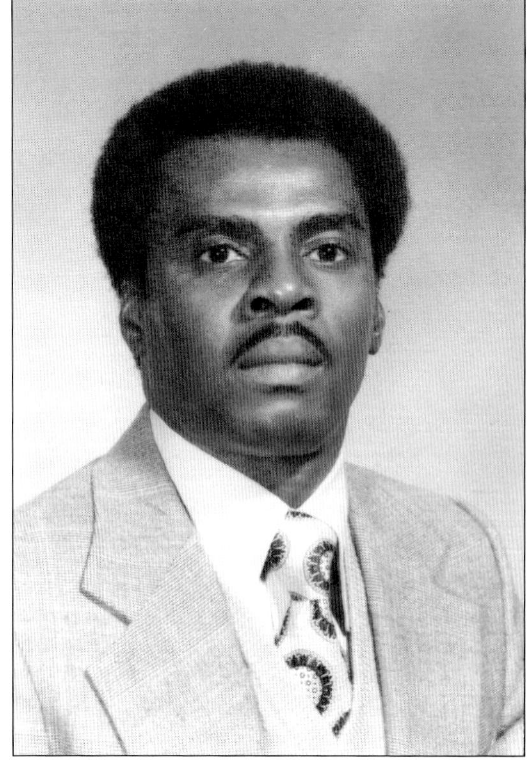

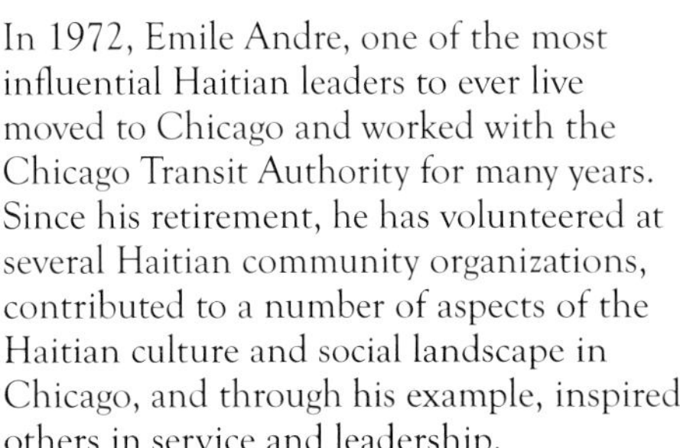

In 1972, Emile Andre, one of the most influential Haitian leaders to ever live moved to Chicago and worked with the Chicago Transit Authority for many years. Since his retirement, he has volunteered at several Haitian community organizations, contributed to a number of aspects of the Haitian culture and social landscape in Chicago, and through his example, inspired others in service and leadership.

Having had a long, exhausting day at work, the newly immigrated Haitian leader to the community dropped into his apartment seat, finally ready for his dinner. Fumes of the special dish cradled around him as he thought about his own problems and dreams that were held onto for the community.

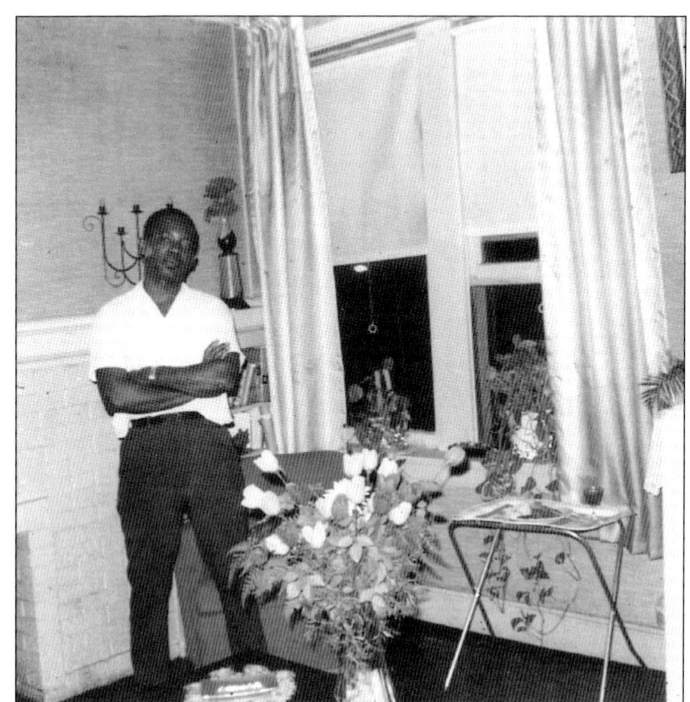

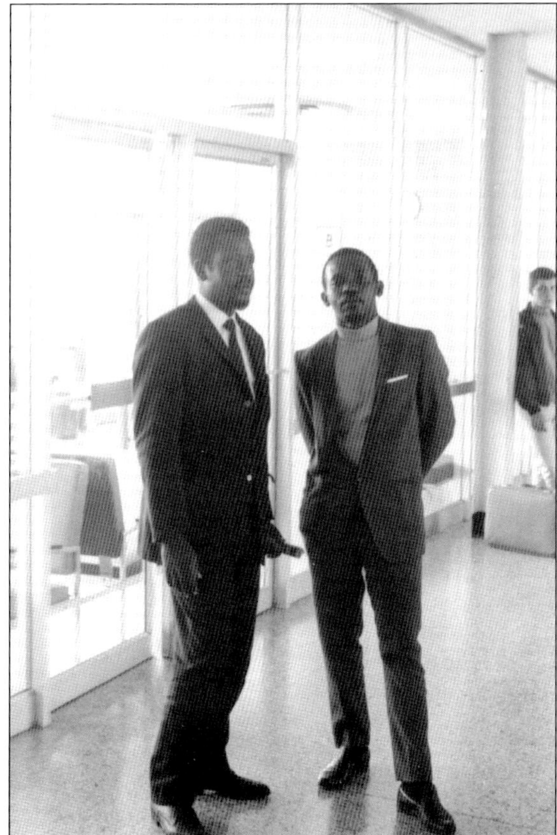

In the 1970s, prominent Haitian leaders held a meeting in a hotel in Chicago. People passing by stopped to watch them. Confident and engrossed in the discussions, they showed pride in their culture, and the improvement of their community was shown. It was a showcase of solidarity among Haitians on foreign land, and this act inspired onlookers who had seen their meeting.

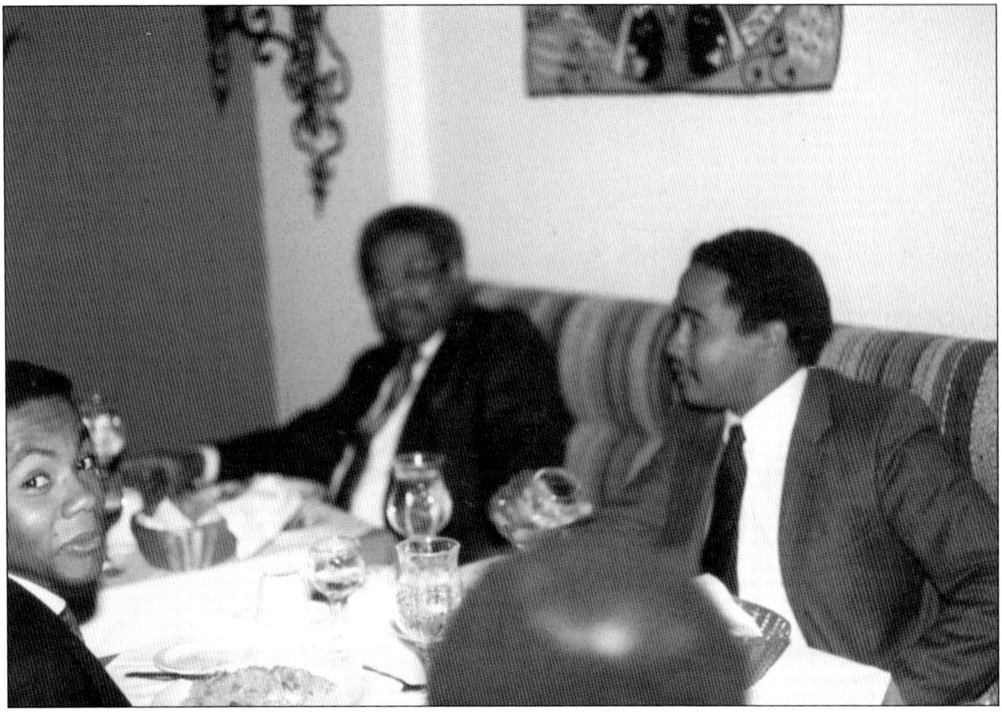

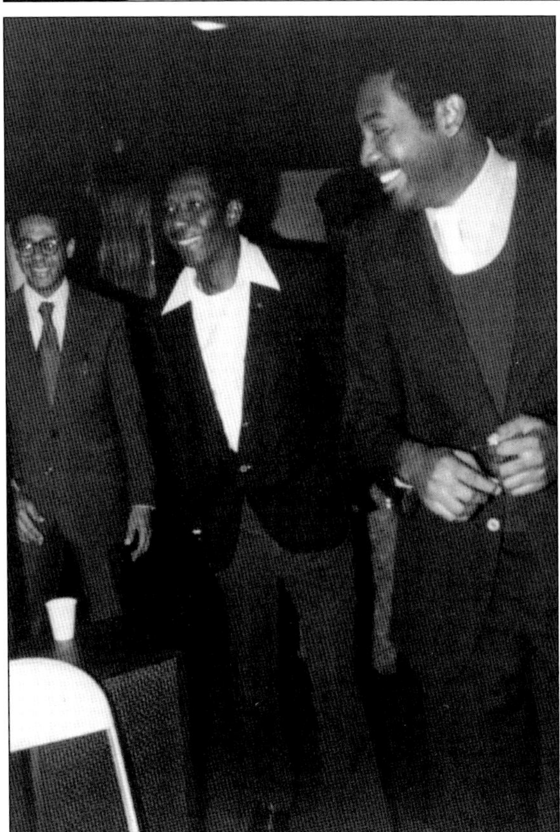

Another representation of a group of Haitian men bunched together, their camaraderie and shared experiences culminating in an alive and talking atmosphere of Haitian cultural heritage. This scene portrays lively discussion and interaction, putting forth the importance of community and connection to these individuals. Each individual makes up a special and unique part of this group, strengthening and unifying their friendship.

Most importantly, finding laughter and fun with other community leaders within one's new Chicago home just uplifts a person. People connect with and find a feeling of belonging; hence, they begin to feel at home when they are surrounded by similar values and goals. Such a relationship nurtures the people around and helps in creating a positive atmosphere where everyone is motivated to speak their mind. And all this might lead to friendships and a change that lasts.

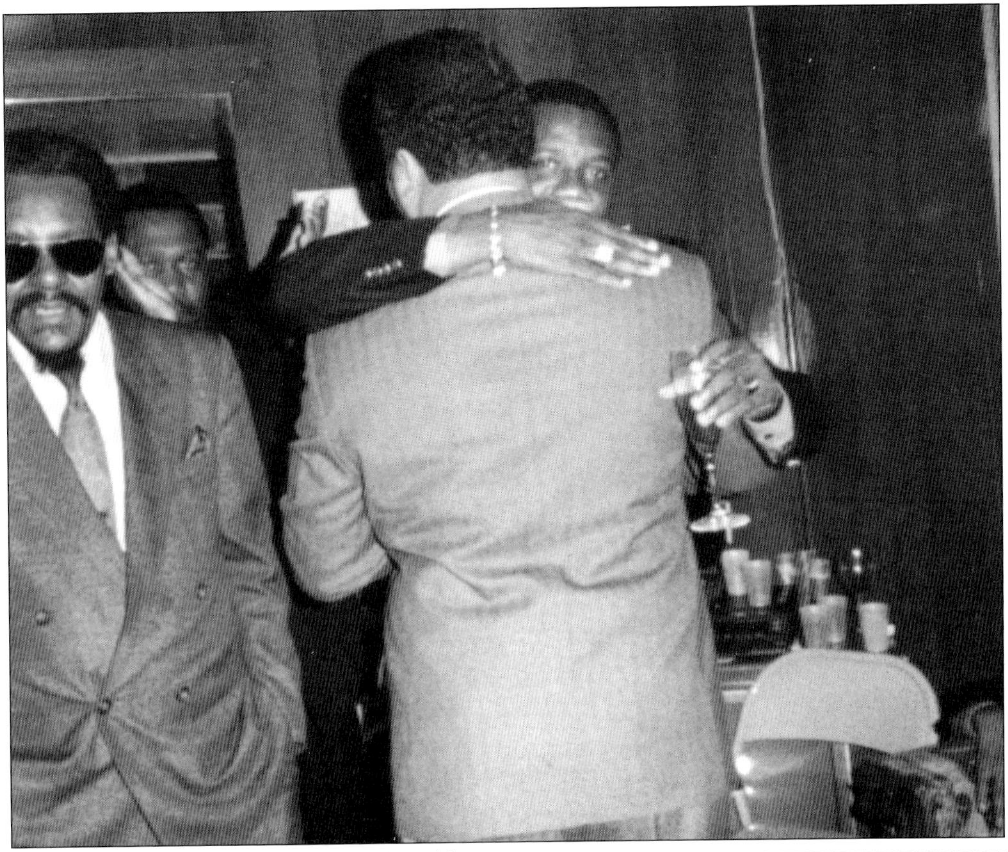

Love, friendship, and solidarity are shared by the Haitian men in the city of Chicago as they are reunited. The warm embraces and joyful laughter show how strong the bonding is that they have nurtured over time and space and their commitment to one another. This image acts as a potent reminder of how powerful connections are. The individuals are reunited and celebrate their shared experiences from their home country, where distance and time had separated them.

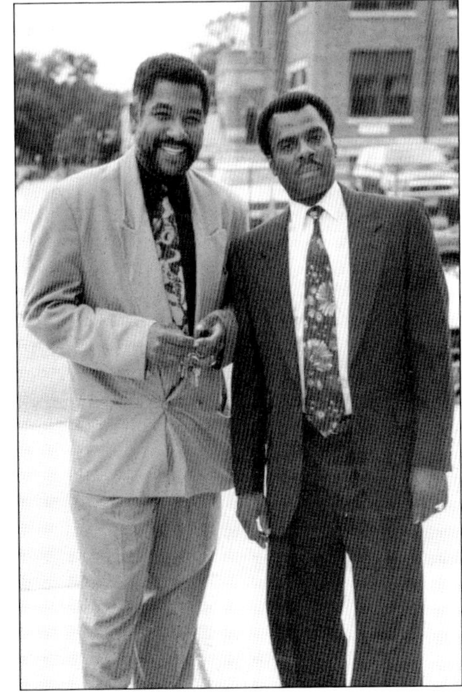

There was a contrast in emotion from the community leaders; one man was ever the life of the party and had a beaming, infectious grin, while the other was stern, serious, and thus, very much the dedicated leader who gets things done. Together, they form a balanced momentum of both energy and efficiency, neither more important than the other, vital parts of their community, inspiring others in their different ways.

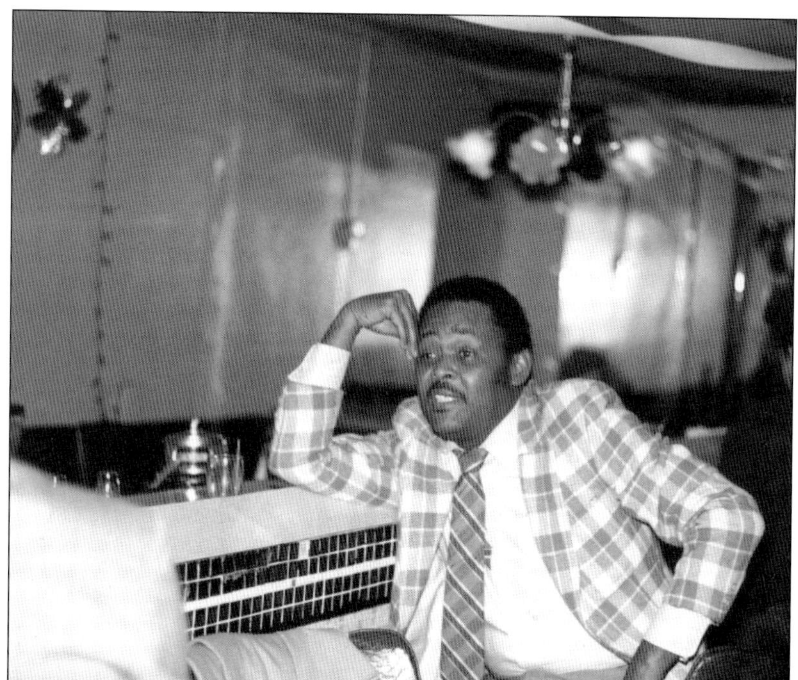

A Haitian man deeply cares for his country. His concern for Haiti shows how unstable its politics are and its weight in economic burdens. The weight in his heart keeps his hopes high as he longs to see his citizens at peace and enjoying prosperity, with a sense of stability in life.

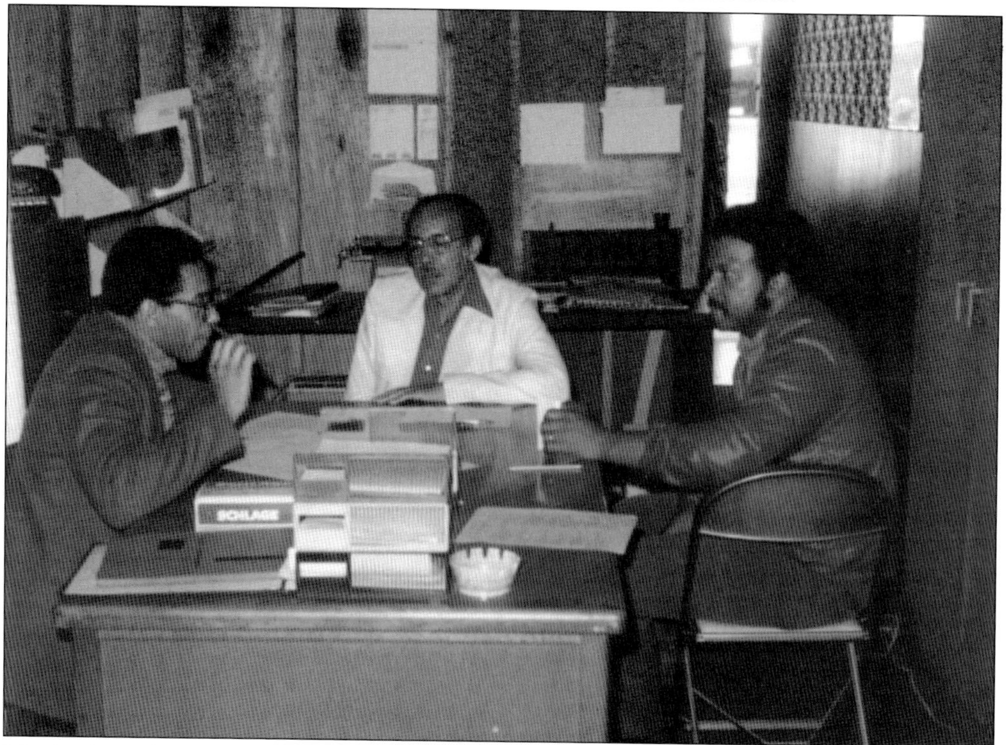

The leaders of Haiti are indeed showing a real interest in the business challenges of the local community. Their sensitive approach underlines the need to create an enabling environment for entrepreneurs, so that the concerns of the business sector are taken seriously in their quest for sustainable growth and development of Haiti.

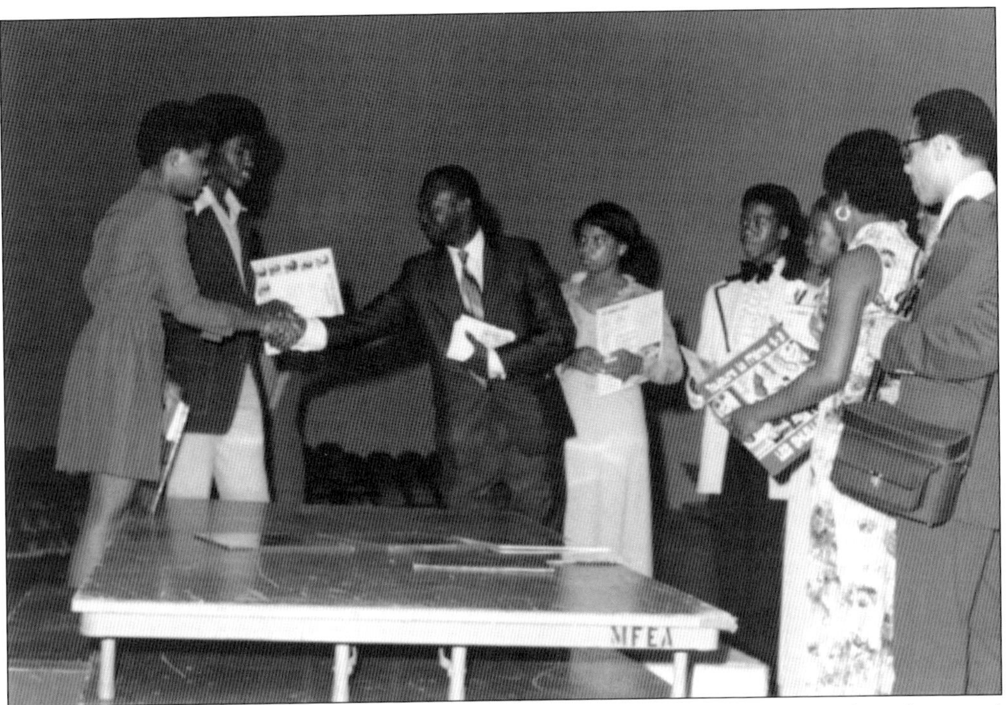

The main leader of Haitians in the 1970s led these young people into training for culture and thanksgiving. These leaders wanted young Haitians to be well-grounded in appreciation and thanksgiving so that these traits may become a habit that will provide a better foundation and way of responding to life in an optimistic manner.

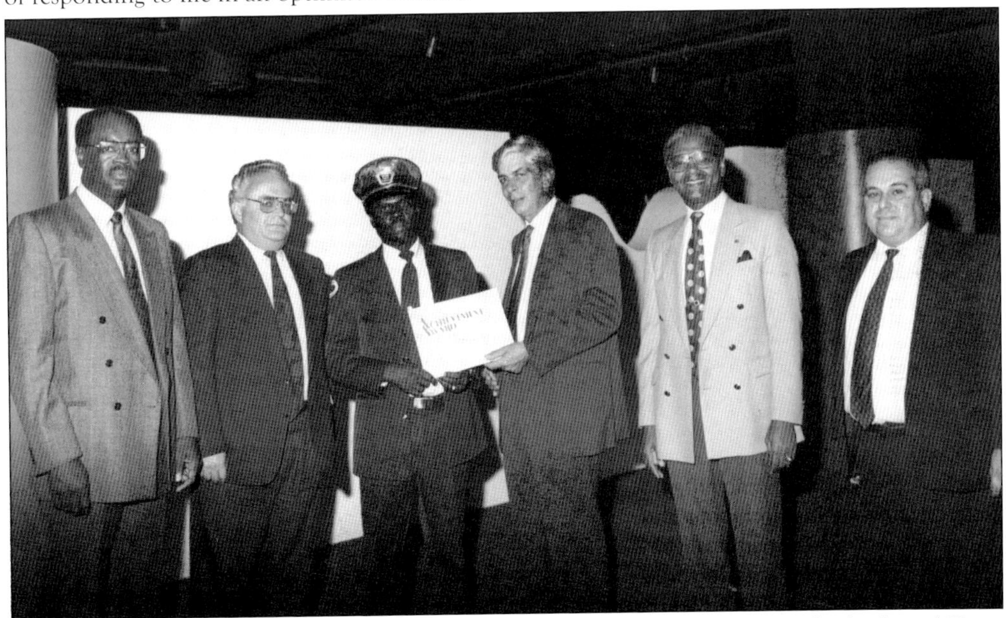

The heads of the Chicago Transit Authority are recognizing and honoring the leader of Haiti. This act demonstrates international relations that are being built and also points to community involvement. These endorsements increase the prestige of the leader while improving relations between different cultures and their organizations in terms of cooperation and mutual respect.

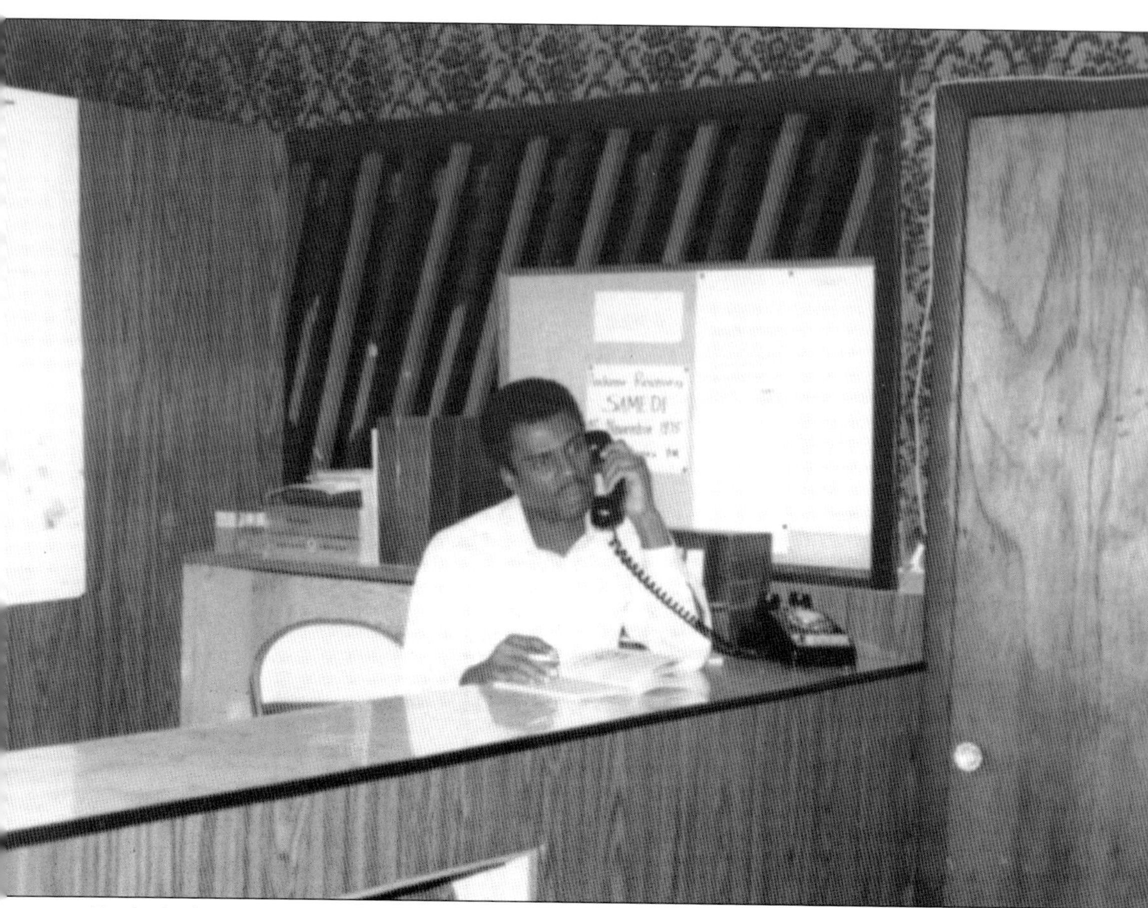

Emile Andre was an important figure in communications and radio, known primarily for his work hosting Radio Union at Loyola University. In 1975, he had become one of the leading figures in the Haitian community, dedicating himself to helping solve the problems of those who were suffering under the repressive political regime of Pres. François Duvalier. His leadership came during a time when most Haitians sought refuge away from the country's harsh conditions, now imposed by Duvalier's rule. Andre's commitment to advocacy and support of the Haitian diaspora helped raise their voices and needs during a tumultuous period. He was able to bring people together, fostering resilience and providing an avenue of support for those who suffered under the regime by offering a forum for discussion and a point of connection. His contribution to the media and leadership within the community continues to speak volumes about his dedication to human rights and social justice for the Haitian people.

Eight

New Generation and Future Contributions to Chicago

The new Haitian population is coming from many parts of the United States and abroad. Below is a personal story from Dr. Herrica Telus of the new generation and future contributions to Chicago:

> I remember moving to Chicago in the Summer of 2012 to complete the last two years of my undergraduate degree in fine arts. I came here knowing no one and was very eager to connect with all of the creative individuals living here.
>
> In 2014, while in my last semester in college, I saw that the Field Museum was opening an exhibition centered on Haitian Vodou that I knew I had to attend, mainly to see how this institution was positioning such a rich aspect of Haitian culture and to meet more of the Haitian community. Upon entering and reading the introduction, because as an art school student, reading the curator's words mattered to me, I noticed a plaque that read, "Haitian American Museum of Chicago," and up until that point, I had not known of this institution existing.
>
> After being in Chicago for 13 years, that amount of time still surprises me, as I planned on leaving right after completing my degree. But when asked, I always tell people it is the arts and community that keep me here. I can say confidently that the Haitian community here continues to grow stronger and more vibrant. I have watched as so many of my fellow Haitian peers go on to intentionally create vibrant creative spaces around the city, whether they are leading health and wellness events, delivering keynote speeches at annual events, exhibiting work in beautiful exhibitions, crafting the musical vibes of DJs at parties, or catering our well-known cultural dishes at events.

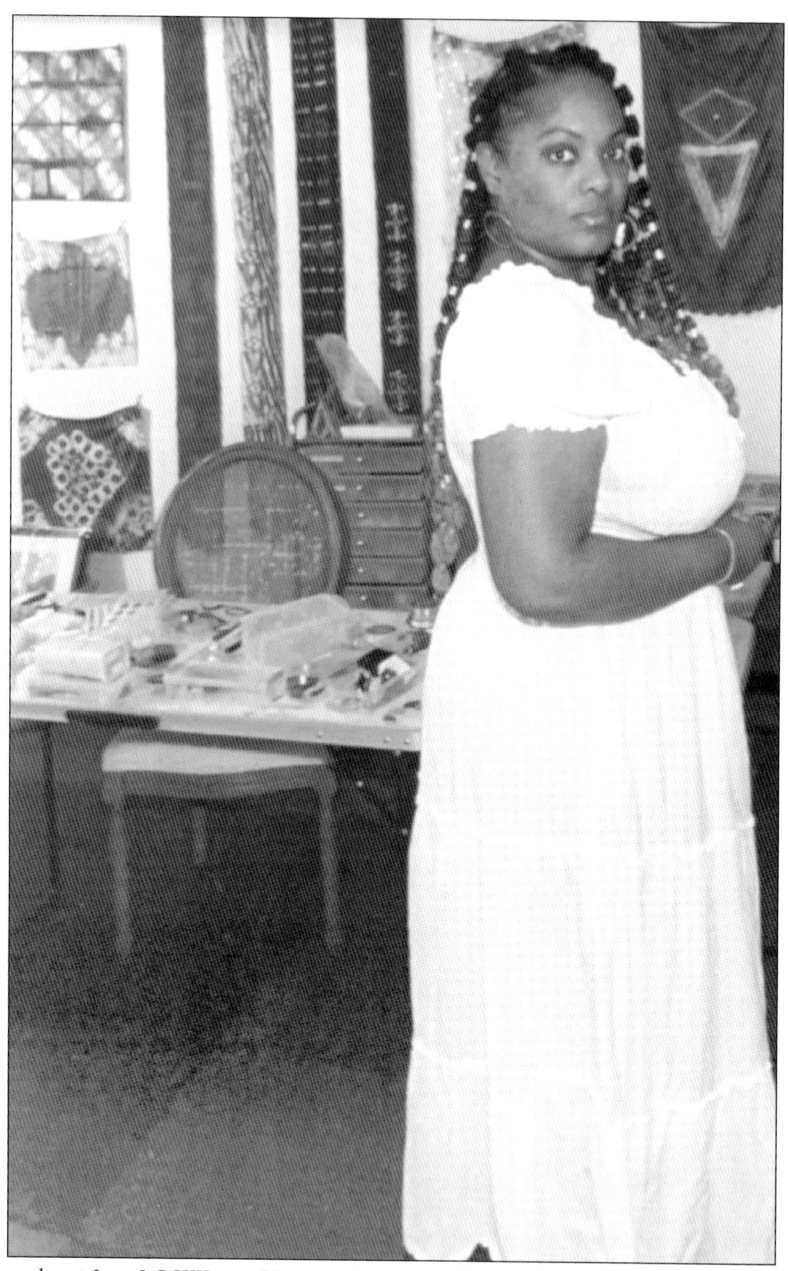

Ameera Pernebsati Lys, LCSW, is a Haitian American fiber and mixed media artist creating with textile design, indigo, Japanese shibori, collage, stamping, painting, ink, sculpture, quilting, jewelry design, photography, and graphic design. Lys was born and raised in Chicago and has her bachelor of arts degree from Carleton College and a masters of social work from Smith College School for Social Work. Lys is an initiate of Kemetic and Dogon philosophy, healing, and spirituality at The Earth Center. Lys's work is inspired by her Haitian heritage, traditional African culture and spirituality, and the injustices of racism. She has had solo exhibitions at the Haitian American Museum of Chicago, Riverside Arts Center, and Lys Art Gallery as well as multiple group exhibitions at the Hyde Park Art Center. Some of her original artwork is a part of and can be found in the permanent collection of the Haitian American Museum of Chicago.

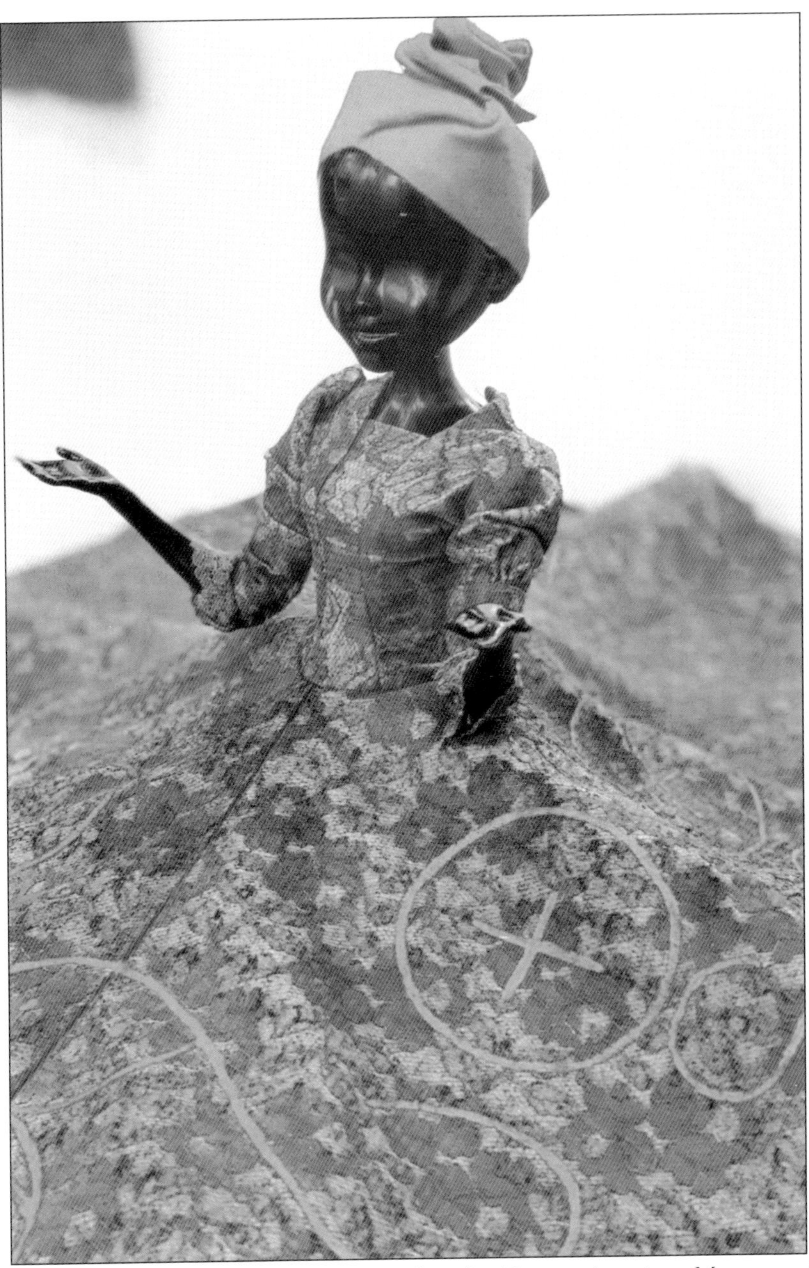

This artwork, titled *Open the Gate*, first appeared at the Haitian American Museum of Chicago in 2019 as part of Ameera Pernebsati Lys's solo exhibition, "Spiritual Marronage." The piece quickly drew attention and acclaim, later earning second place in the 2020 Black Creativity Juried Art Exhibition at the Griffin Museum of Science and Industry. That year's show was especially significant, marking the 50th anniversary of the Black Creativity Program, which honors the profound contributions of African Americans across science, technology, engineering, art, and medicine. With over 700 submissions and only around 200 chosen for display, being awarded second place was an extraordinary recognition. *Open the Gate* reflects Lys's Haitian heritage through the incorporation of Vodou symbolism and her distinctive use of textiles, embodying a dialogue between tradition, spirituality, and contemporary artistic expression.

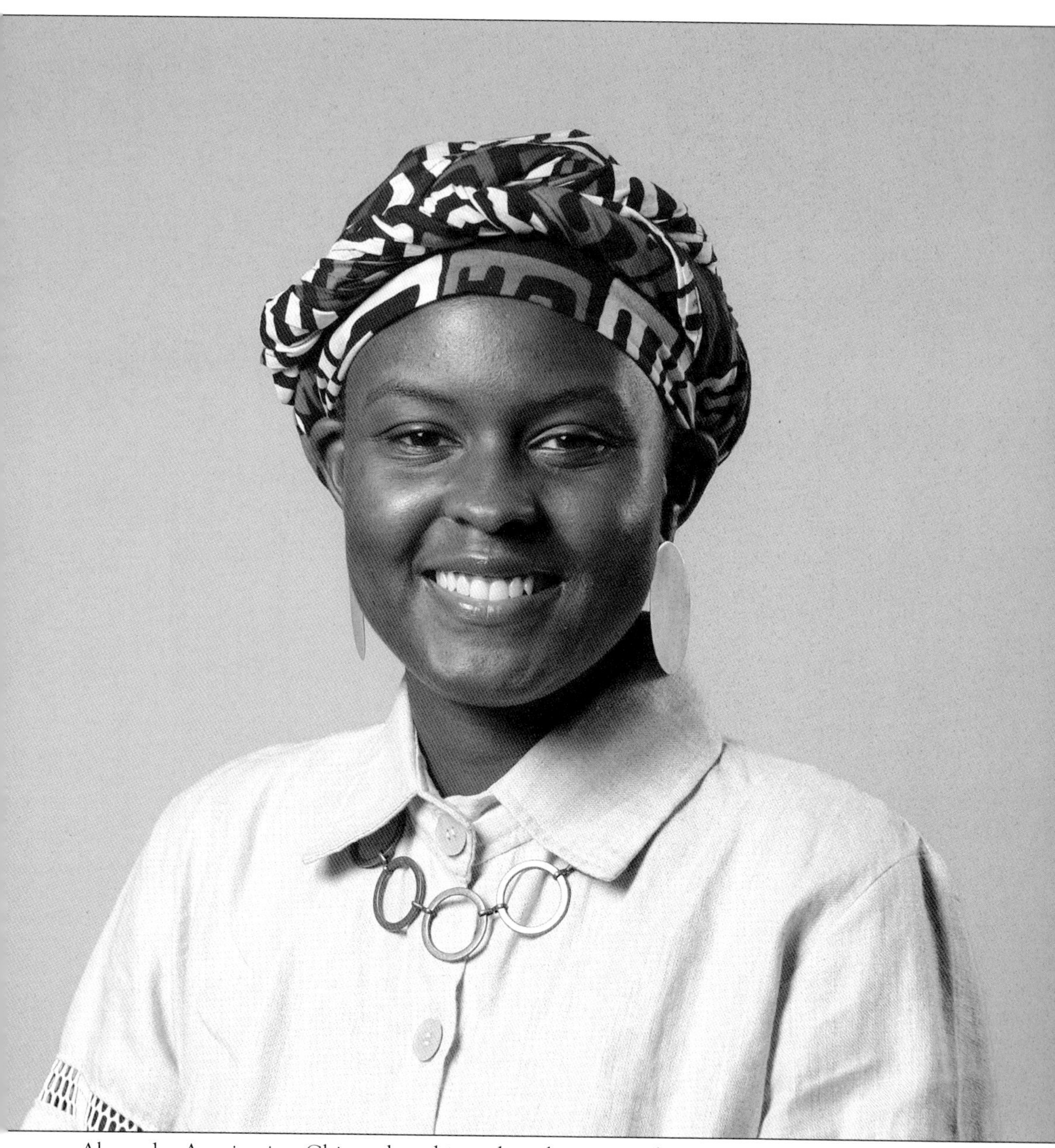

Alexandra Antoine is a Chicago-based interdisciplinary visual artist and cultural apprentice who was deeply influenced by her Haitian heritage. Creating work on portraiture, food, and farming, she connects with the physical work associated with traditional Afrikan artistic practices. She has grown food in community gardens, working in respect and remembrance of the stories, memories, and cultural ways of her ancestors and the land of Haiti.

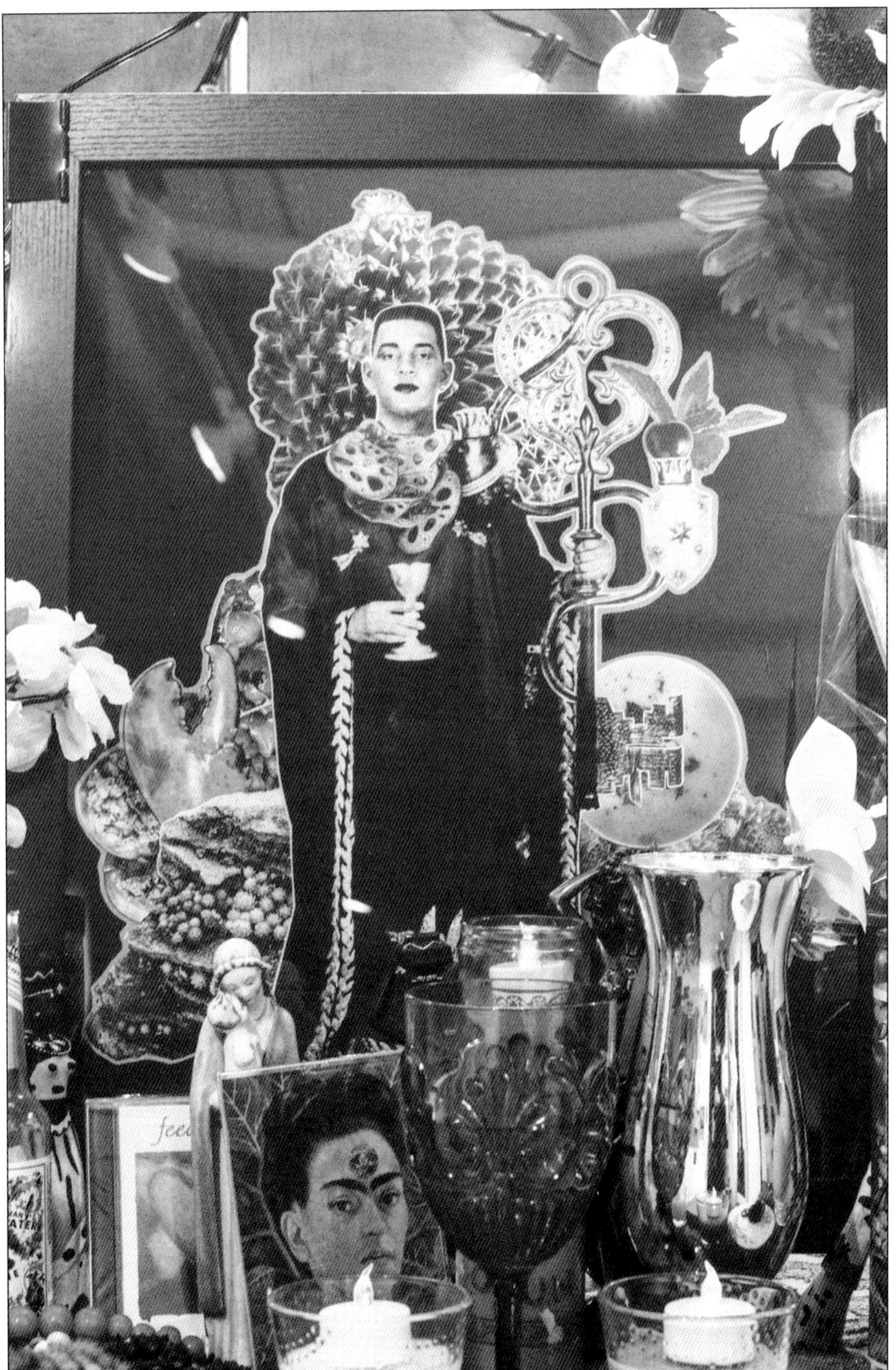

Alexandra Antoine received an undergraduate degree from a fancy art school and exhibited her work in many places, collaborating with folks and learning within the Afrikan diaspora is her life's work. Seen here is her collage image on an altar as part of the 2021 "Assoto's Child at the Altar" exhibition, in collaboration with Mario LaMothe, at HAMOC.

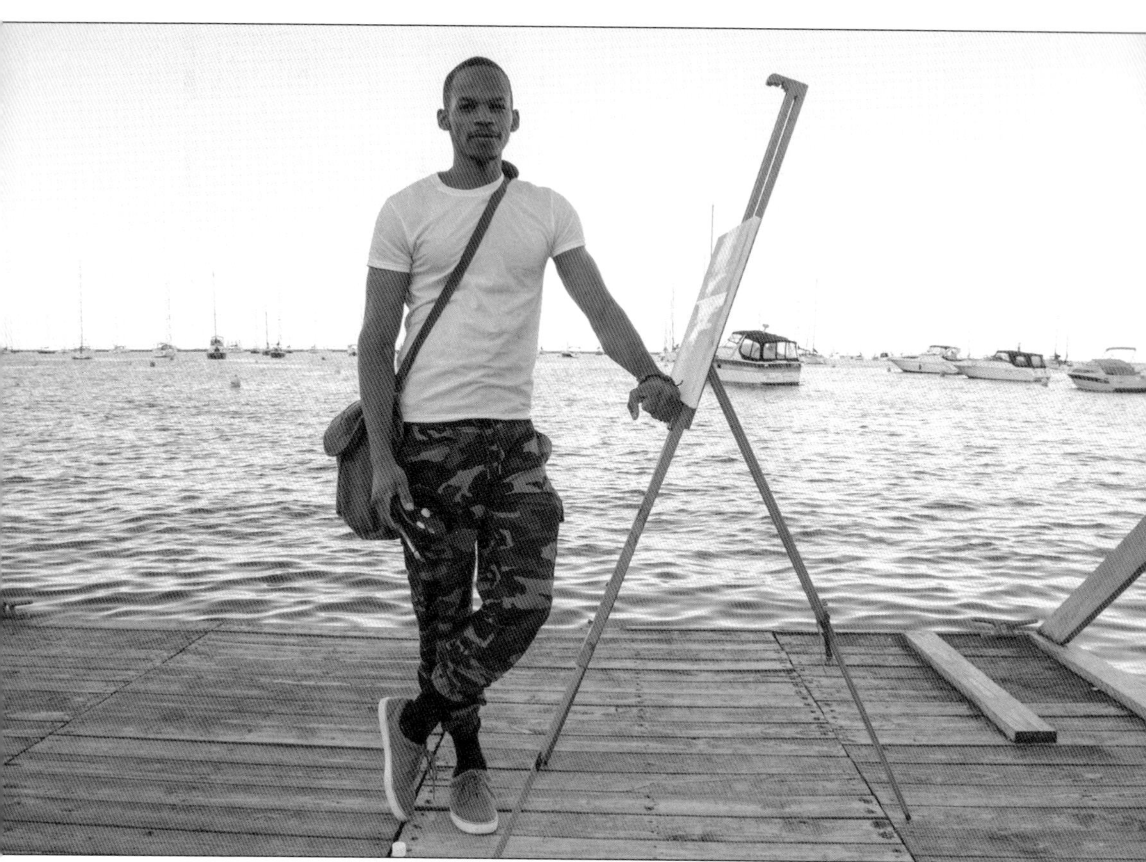

Jean Yves Héctor is a multidisciplinary artist whose multilevel vision has developed works in different areas such as painting, poetry, generative art, and animation. The spiritual reflection of his artwork deepens the dichotomy of existence, family, religion, identity, and social concerns. Since Héctor's first exhibition at the Haitian American Museum of Chicago in 2015, he has spoken about complexity within immigration and identity. He reflects, "It's so hard to leave your country, your friends, your family. Sometimes when people tell you to integrate, it's a sign of disrespect. Immigrants don't forget; they evolve. Chicago, with its well-developed artistic environment and its wonderful landscapes, has welcomed me. I value the exchanges with Haitian artists as much as those with American ones. I also hope that a stable space would create stability that may allow me to continue making artwork that reflects and resonates with my journey and identity with consistency."

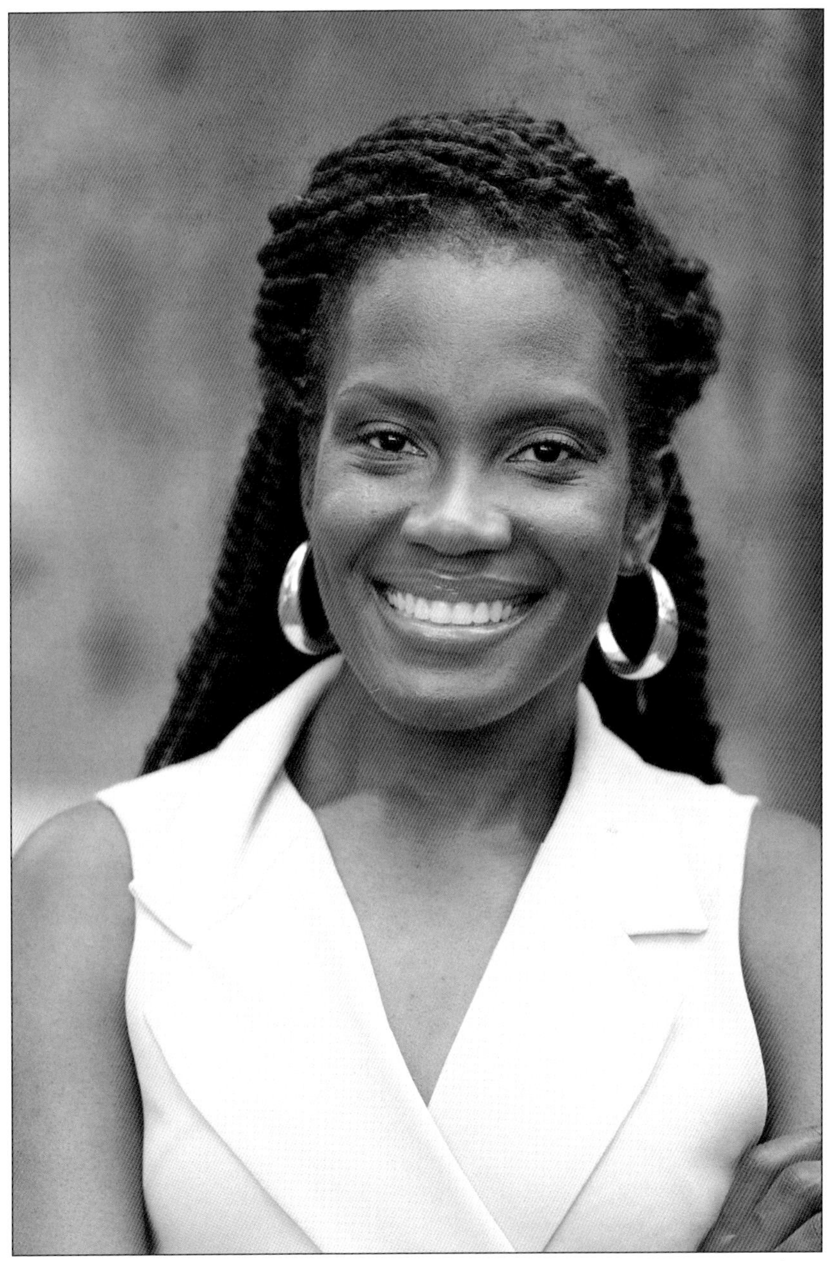

Growing up in South Florida, Dr. Herrica Telus was exposed to the rich Haitian culture through language, music, and activism. As a young adult, Telus was passionate about learning more about Haitian culture and advocating for immigrants. Most notably, for six years, she tutored Haitian immigrants enrolled in an ESL program looking to improve their language skills. In 2014, Telus moved to Chicago and found a home at the Haitian American Museum of Chicago, where she organized art exhibits and Haitian flag day events. Telus believes her experiences at the museum and other Haitian organizations helped deepen her understanding of Haitian culture and informed her dissertation work on "identity formation among Chicago Haitians." Since earning her doctorate in sociology from the University of Illinois at Chicago, Telus continues to conduct research as an analyst at a federal agency and volunteers her time promoting the Haitian culture in Chicago.

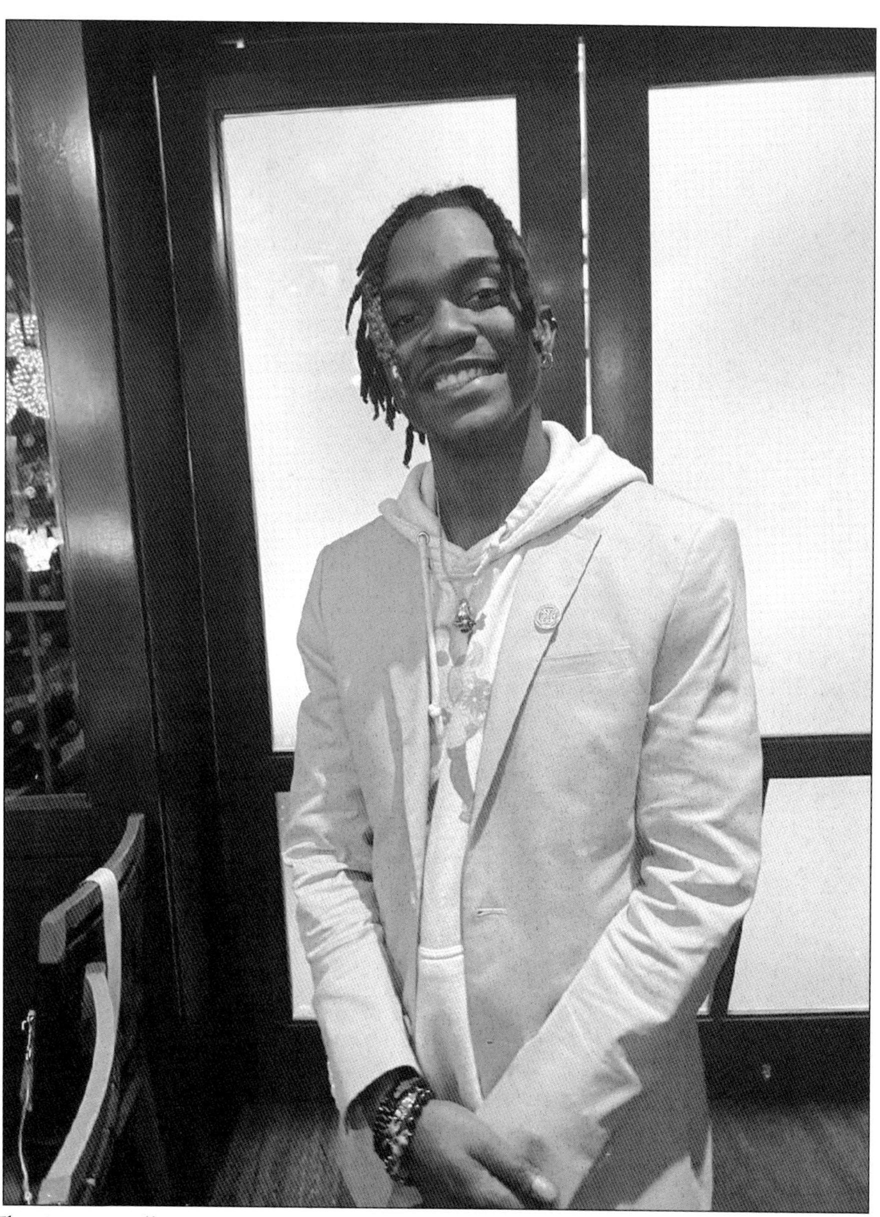

Alex Fleming is an illustrator, cartoonist, and graphic designer currently working in Chicago. He studied and graduated with a bachelor's degree in fine studio art at the prestigious School of the Art Institute of Chicago. He draws immense influence from the superhero comics and anime from his childhood, which inspires him to produce dynamic characters frozen in dramatic poses or during breathtaking action sequences. His artistic practice is richly flavored with the peculiar mixture of humor and richness of cultural heritage, reflecting his being African American and Haitian American. He has often taken to comedy by exploring his ideas and themes in his work, relating to a varied audience while rejoicing in celebrating his identity. Fleming's artwork is born of an enthusiasm for storytelling and a passion for illustration. Moreover, his work provokes the mind with deeper meanings that can be sought on either side of his rather surrealistic illustrations. His desire is to inspire others to appreciate the richness of diverse cultural backgrounds and the fun of imaginative storytelling.

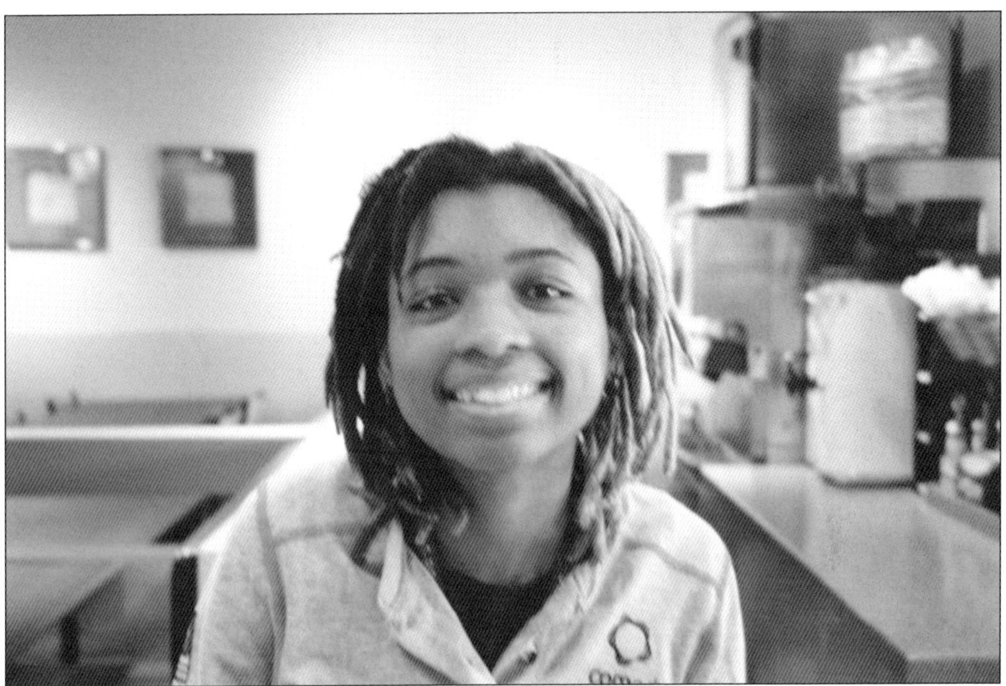

Swahdreeznya Rosier was born and raised in Chicago to immigrant parents who were from Haiti. She received her bachelor's in mechanical engineering from the University of Illinois at Chicago. She is a multimedia artist and a violinist who considers her Haitian heritage, learned through her grandmother, very important. Rosier expresses culture through food, art, and music; the celebrations include homemade pate and traditional dishes.

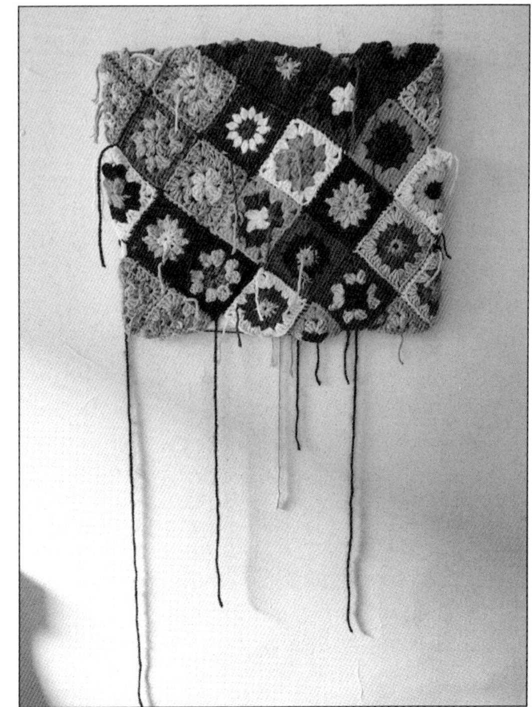

Rosier is a multimedia artist who enjoys the dynamic world of art fairs, showcasing her innovative works while networking with fellow artists and great people. Her passion for diverse artistic expressions motivates her to try new mediums and techniques, hence finding each event an exciting opportunity for growth, inspiration, and community engagement within the art world.

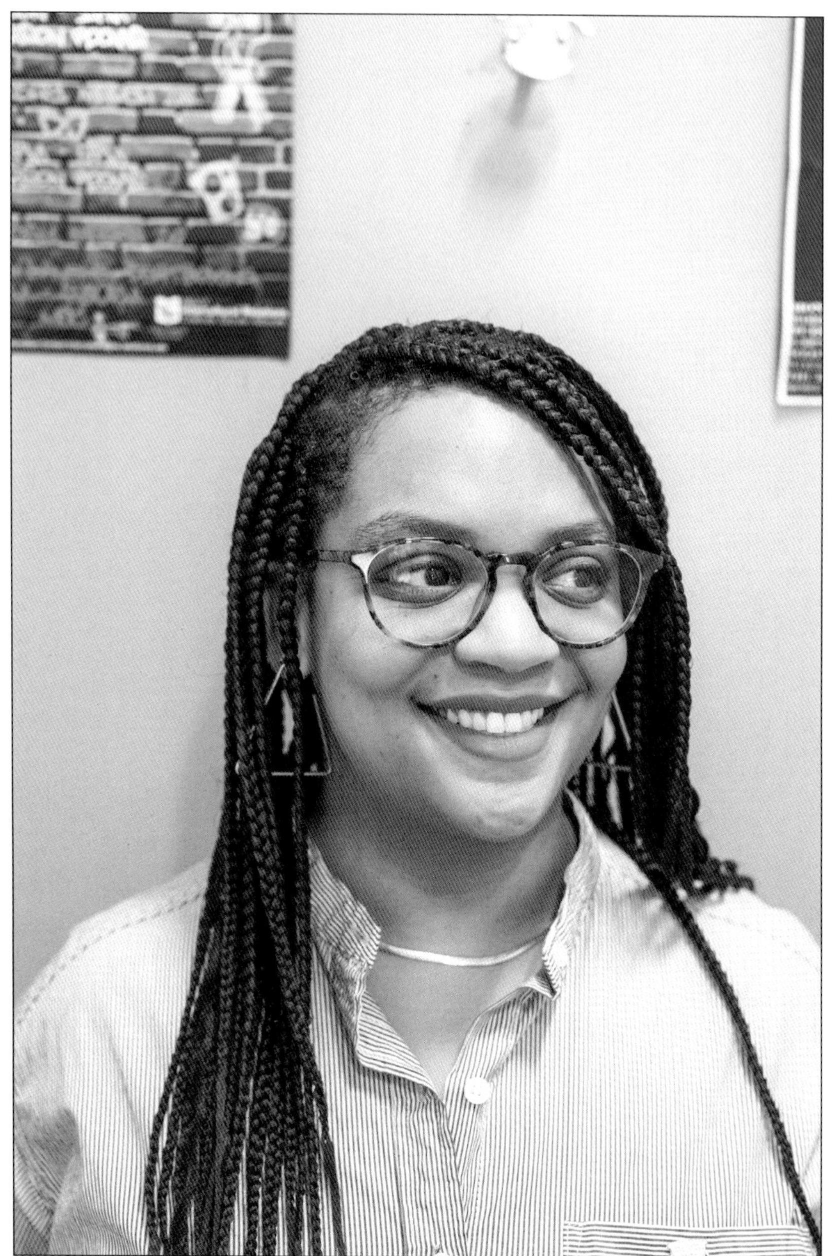

Courtney Pierre Joseph is an assistant professor of history and African American studies and the inaugural chair of the African American studies department at Lake Forest College. Her specializations are in African American history and culture, Haiti and its diaspora, women and gender studies, and hip-hop culture. Joseph earned her doctorate in history from the University of Illinois at Urbana-Champaign in 2017. She has spoken at numerous institutions and events, including the DuSable Museum of African American History, the Newberry Library, and the fall 2020 Chicago Humanities Festival. She is collaborating with the Haitian Museum of Chicago to create the first oral history archive dedicated to the Haitian diaspora in Chicago. Joseph is currently working on her first book, titled *DuSable's Diaspora, Haiti, Blackness, and Belonging in Chicago*, which will be published by the University of Texas Press.

Bibliography

dceo.illinois.gov
hamoc.libraryhost.com
images.chicagohistory.org
Rashid, Haroon. *The City of Chicago in the Spirit of DuSable*. The Pointe! Image Book Publishing, 2018.
Reed, Christopher Robert. *"All the World is Here!" The Black Presence at White City*. Indiana University Press, 2000.
Rosier, Marc O. *Chicago's Authentic Founder: Jean Baptiste Point DuSable or Haitian Secret Agent in the Old Northwest Outpost 1745–1818*. Trafford Publishing, 2016.
photoarchive.lib.uchicago.edu
Thompson, Lowell. *African Americans in Chicago*. Arcadia Publishing, 2012.
www.chipublib.org
www.loc.gov.
www.nps.gov.